The
Illusion of
the Epoch

H. B. Acton

The
Illusion of
the Epoch

Marxism-Leninism as
a Philosophical Creed

H. B. Acton

Liberty Fund

Indianapolis

Amagi books are published by Liberty Fund, Inc.,
a foundation established to encourage study of the
ideal of a society of free and responsible individuals.

The cuneiform inscription that appears in the logo and
serves as a design element in all Liberty Fund books is the
earliest-known written appearance of the word "freedom"
(*amagi*), or "liberty." It is taken from a clay document
written about 2300 B.C. in the Sumerian city-state of Lagash.

07   06   05   04   03   P   5   4   3   2   1

Library of Congress Cataloging-in-Publication Data
Acton, H. B. (Harry Burrows), 1908–
    The illusion of the epoch: Marxism-Leninism as a
philosophical creed / H. B. Acton.
        p.   cm.
    Originally published: London: Cohen & West, 1955.
    Includes bibliographical references and index.
    ISBN 0-86597-394-6 (pbk.: alk. paper)
    1. Philosophy, Marxist.   I. Title.
B809.8 .A32 2003
335.43 — dc21

                                        2003047473

LIBERTY FUND, INC.,
8335 Allison Pointe Trail, Suite 300, Indianapolis, Indiana 46250-1684

Contents

Preface

The following work arose from a Seminar which I gave in the University of Chicago in the summer of 1949. I am grateful to my wife for her help in removing obscurities, to Mr. R. N. Carew Hunt for generously putting his Marxist scholarship at my disposal and for reading and commenting on the major part of the manuscript, and to Professor E. E. Turner, F.R.S., for advice in connection with Part One, Chapter II, Section 7. The Aristotelian Society has been good enough to allow me to reproduce a passage that originally appeared in their 1951–52 *Proceedings*.

For this second impression I have corrected some misprints and expanded footnotes and references when new editions and translations of the books referred to have made this necessary.

 Mr. Emile Burns's remark in *The Marxist Quarterly* (October 1955) suggesting that Engels did not regard equality as the chief element of the morality of the future raises the question of the importance of equality of reward in Marxism-Leninism. Marx applauded the Paris Commune for paying a working-man's wage to all revolutionary functionaries no matter how important, but he also said that during the period of socialism (as distinct from the ultimate communism) payment would vary in accordance with output. Lenin regarded differential rewards as unwelcome and temporary necessities. Stalin, however, said it was un-Marxist to advocate equality of incomes during the period prior to communism (see S. Dobrin, "Lenin on Equality and the Webbs on Lenin," *Soviet Studies* 1956–57). The conclusion I draw is that on the Marxist-Leninist view equality of incomes is impracticable before the advent of communism and unnecessary afterward, when there will be enough to satisfy all needs. Marxist-Leninists who live in non-Marxist societies will, of course, as Engels says, advocate equality "as an agitational means in order to rouse the workers against the capitalists on the basis of the capitalists' own assertions" (*Anti-Dühring*).

Mr. John Plamenatz (*The British Journal of Sociology,* June 1956) makes two interesting criticisms of what I wrote. He says that Marxists are not necessarily committed to "total planning," but only claim to have knowledge which would enable the planners to decide what to control and what to leave alone. In practice this may be so (though even democratic governments find that their plans have to take in more and more of human life), but in principle I think the Marxist ideal requires nature to be wholly tamed and humanized. Mr. Plamenatz also criticizes my view that the Marxist distinction between basis and superstructure requires what are really inseparable factors to act causally upon one another. Social factors, he says, which may be distinguishable but incapable of existing in isolation, may be related to one another in such a way that some are more fundamental than others. There is not space for me to discuss this interesting point here. All I can say is that insofar as aspects are abstractions, they are fundamental or derivative in a *logical* sense, according to which what is not fundamental is what is logically derivative. Discussion of this topic, therefore, takes us into the realm of sociological concepts and their logical relationships.

Since the first impression of this book, the Foreign Languages Publishing House, Moscow, has published translations in English of *The Holy Family* (Moscow, 1956, Lawrence and Wishart, London, 1957), and of the *Economic and Philosophic Manuscripts* (Moscow, no date, Lawrence and Wishart, London, 1959). Reference should also be made to *Osnovy Marksistskoj Filosofii* (Moscow, 1958), the joint work of a number of Soviet philosophers. A summary and brief discussion of it may be read in J. M. Bochenski's *Die Dogmatischen Grundlagen der Sowjetischen Philosophie* (Reidel, Dordrecht, Holland, 1959). The Foreign Languages Publishing House, Moscow, has also published (no date given) *Fundamentals of Marxism-Leninism, Manual* (described as translated from the Russian and as edited by Clemens Dutt). This is also a joint work, but by a different set of Soviet authors. I do not think that either of these books renders necessary any alteration of my account of the Marxist-Leninist philosophy.

H. B. Acton

Bedford College, July, 1961

Introduction

Marxism is such an important influence in the contemporary world that there is no need to apologize for trying to understand and assess it. In Great Britain the tendency has been to consider it primarily as a body of economic and social doctrine, and to concentrate attention on such parts of it as the accounts of surplus value, historical materialism, the class struggle, the alleged decline of capitalism, the struggle for markets and imperialism. This is natural enough, since these are the elements of Marxism that are most obviously relevant to policies of action. Marxism, however, is much more than a system of social and economic doctrines. It is also, in a wide sense of the word, a philosophy. When we talk about a philosophy in this way we mean a system of thought and conduct comprising views about the most general and significant features of the universe, and about the principal purposes of human life. In the German language the word *Weltanschauung* is used for such a system, but the translations "world-outlook" or "world-view" do not seem to have established themselves in English, so that we had better continue to use the word "philosophy," which is, indeed, widely understood in this sense. It will be seen that a philosophy comprises views about the most general and significant features of the universe. Such views are often called metaphysical, and the study of them metaphysics. A philosophy, in the sense we are considering, also comprises an account of the principal purposes of human life, and this is its ethical part. Thus a philosophy consists of a metaphysics and an ethics that is generally supposed to depend on it. Some philosophies are fundamentally religious, and people may thus talk of the Christian or the Buddhist philosophy. Some philosophies, again, have been carefully reasoned out and defended by arguments, as were those of Plato, for example, or of Epicurus or Spinoza. Marxism is an anti-religious philosophy first formulated by Marx and Engels, who did not, however, attempt such a closely reasoned account of their view as a whole as

Plato or Epicurus or Spinoza did of theirs. The economic and social doctrines of surplus value, historical materialism and the rest are believed by Marxists to gain in depth and significance by belonging to such a system, and in countries where they can decide what is taught in schools and universities Marxists see to it that their philosophy informs the whole curriculum. It is this philosophy in its most general terms as metaphysics and as ethics that I wish to discuss in language that presupposes no technical training in philosophy.

Contemporary British philosophy is not at all sympathetic toward philosophical systems of any kind, and is especially opposed to those of them that provide reasons for policies of individual or social action. Metaphysical theories according to which, for example, the universe is all matter, or all mind, or both, or neither, are criticized on the ground that their propounders unwittingly misuse language and appear to be saying something important about the world when they are really talking nonsense, or recommending a peculiar vocabulary, or following a linguistic trail that ends up in the wilderness, or stressing an analogy that other people may not wish to stress. It is further argued that, even if metaphysical theories about the universe as a whole were not fundamentally misconceived, they could still provide no grounds for one sort of social policy rather than another. The philosophers who accept these views believe, therefore, that they have exposed the illegitimacy of *all* metaphysical theories about the universe as a whole, and of *all* practical policies in so far as they are supposed to be based on such theories. The result is that, though they are themselves called philosophers, many of them do not very often discuss philosophies in the sense in which I have been using the word. Even if they do, it is usually by the way and in very general terms, so that Marxism, as one of them, is thus left to be dealt with by economists, social theorists, or historians. I think it is possible that some economists, social theorists, and historians might welcome an attempt on the part of a philosopher to discuss the philosophy of Marxism in some detail instead of merely stigmatizing it as one disreputable member of a thoroughly disreputable class. In any case, the educated public are entitled to expect that some philosopher will try to interpret this philosophy on its merits, with a view to its consistency and suggestiveness, in case there are things of importance to be said about it apart from the criticisms that apply no more to it than they do to other metaphysico-ethical systems.

Now the writings of Karl Marx, and of his faithful supporter Friedrich Engels, form the basis of two socialist movements that are bitterly opposed to one another, the reformist Marxists on the one hand, who are often known today as Social Democrats, and the Communist Party Marxists on the other hand, who regard the government of the U.S.S.R. as the chief vehicle and director of Marxist policy. It is this latter form of Marxism that I shall discuss. There has been, so to say, an apostolical succession from Marx and Engels themselves, through Lenin to Stalin and the spokesmen who have succeeded him. The exponents of this form of Marxism call it "Marxism-Leninism." Indeed for a time, I believe, they contemplated calling it "Marxism-Leninism-Stalinism," but were happily deterred by the cumbrousness of the expression. But whatever we call it, its exponents are right, it seems to me, in regarding it as based on and continuous with the doctrines and directives that Marx and Engels handed on. Certainly both Lenin and Stalin were most assiduous in using the writings of Marx and Engels as their chief theoretical guide. It is not inappropriate, therefore, to give the name "Marxism" to the whole tradition that Marx and Engels inaugurated and which Lenin and Stalin have continued. Indeed it has on occasion an advantage over the term "Marxism-Leninism" in that it enables us to avoid the awkwardness of calling Marx and Engels "Marxist-Leninists" before Lenin had been born.

I have not dealt with the doctrines of the Marxist philosophy in the historical order in which they were published. What I have called the Marxist metaphysics, and what they themselves call Dialectical Materialism, is regarded by Marxists as fundamental, and I have therefore given over the first part of the book to a discussion of it, leaving the social theory and ethics, which they call Scientific Socialism, for the second part. Nor have I been concerned to keep a historical order within each part, but have chosen those statements of a view that seemed best designed to introduce it, whether they were by Marx, Engels, Lenin, or Stalin. I have frequently referred, however, to such early writings as the *Holy Family*, the *German Ideology*, and the *Paris Manuscripts*. These are the writings that philosophers are likely to find of most interest because in them Marx—and in the *Holy Family* and *German Ideology* Engels also—discusses philosophical issues raised by Hegel and Feuerbach. Marx's doctoral dissertation was on the philosophies of Democritus and Epicurus, and at one time he had hoped to become a professor of philosophy. In these early writings we can sometimes see fundamental features of Marx's thought more clearly than in the later ones. I agree, therefore, with those scholars who have used these works to throw light on the argument of *Capital*. Their influence on later Marxism was, of course, only via Marx and Engels themselves, since the *Paris Manuscripts* and the *German Ideology* were only published in their entirety in the nineteen-thirties, and the *Holy Family* was extremely rare until it was republished about the same time. These early writings, then, are valuable as aids to the interpretation of the general drift of the Marxist philosophy, and that, as well as their intrinsic interest, is what has led me to refer to them so often.

In a work of this sort it is essential to base one's interpretations on detailed references to the texts. When I know of English translations I have referred to them, and have generally, though not always, used them in quoting. I have had to make my own translations of passages from works that have not been translated into English. This documentation of the Marxist classics has led to so many footnotes that I have been very sparing with other references. I have not, for example, given references to those views of Fourier which, I believe, must have greatly influenced the Marxist ethics. Nor, again, have I discussed the views of other expositors and critics of Marxism at the length that they deserve, so that the number of my references to the writings of Hans Barth, Karl Popper, Hook, and Bober, to mention only a few—all of them writers on Marx himself rather than on Marxism in the sense in which I am using the word—is small in proportion to their importance and to the benefit to be derived from them. In brief, I should say that the chief aim of this book is to expound and interpret the philosophy of Marxism, that the next aim is to criticize it, and that a subsidiary aim is to show its kinship with some other philosophies.

The book commences, then, with an account of Dialectical Materialism. The word "materialist" is often used by preachers and others to stand for someone whose life is spent in the pursuit of material wealth for his own satisfaction. In this moral sense of the word a materialist is a selfish seeker after comfort and luxury. I need hardly say that it is not in this sense of the word that Marxists regard themselves as materialists. Nevertheless, there is an important connection between their moral beliefs and their materialist theory. For while they advocate the pursuit of objects more valuable than food and drink, they put great stress upon the ways in which higher values are rooted in such essential physical needs. Thus, while their opponents sometimes accuse Marxists of having low aims, Marxists, for their part, are apt to reply that the idealism of their critics is impracticable or even hypocritical. This, however, is a matter that must be left over for discussion in Part Two. In the meantime it is sufficient to say that "materialism" is not primarily understood in the moral or rhetorical sense just indicated.

Involved in their description of themselves as materialists there are, I think, three main contentions. In the first place, Marxists hold that material things exist independently of perception of, or thought about, them. This is the view which philosophers call Realism. In the second place, they hold that matter existed before minds existed, and that minds have developed out of matter. This is a view about the world that philosophers have sometimes called Naturalism. In the third place, they hold that matter is not adequately understood in mechanical terms, but needs to be understood in dialectical terms. This is the main respect in which Marxist materialism differs from other forms of that philosophy. In Part One I shall discuss each of these views in turn.

Part One

Dialectical Materialism

I

Marxist Realism

1. Idealism and Phenomenalism

"'Naïve realism,'" writes Lenin, is "the instinctive, unconscious materialist standpoint adopted by humanity, which regards the external world as existing independently of our minds."[1] He also says: "The 'naïve realism' of any healthy person who has not been an inmate of a lunatic asylum, or a pupil of the idealist philosophers, consists in the view that things, the environment, the world, exist independently of our sensation, of our consciousness, of our *self,* and of man in general. . . . Materialism deliberately makes the 'naïve' belief of mankind the foundation of its theory of knowledge."[2] From these sentences it is clear that Lenin believed it was important to say that a physical world exists independently of any single mind, and independently of all human minds.

To say these things, however, is to say what everyone (apart from a few Christian Scientists and perhaps some visionary philosophers) regards as obvious. Is it not quite certain that mountains, seas, and nebulae exist whether anyone is observing them or not? It is true, of course, that there are some material things, such as bridges and spoons, which owe many of their features to the men who made them. But surely they, no less than things which men have had no part in shaping, exist, once they are made, independently of their being perceived? Indeed, once this question is raised, the simple answer seems to be that what distinguishes perception from imagination or hallucination just is that what we perceive is something independent of our perceiving, whereas what

---

1. *Materialism and Empirio-Criticism.* English translation in *V. I. Lenin: Selected Works,* vol. 11, p. 127 (London, 1939).
2. Ibid., pp. 135–36.

we imagine or are deceived about somehow depends on some activity or defect within ourselves. We are thus inclined to say that unless the object perceived is something that exists independently of our perception, we are not really perceiving at all. Perceiving (which includes seeing, hearing, touching, tasting, smelling, or a combination of these) just *is* becoming aware of something independent of the perception.

This is taken for granted by the vast majority of people, but by Marxists and by other philosophers who hold a realist theory of perception it is proclaimed as an important truth. It is almost as though someone were to make a parade of enunciating some such platitude as that fishes live in water. It would only be worth while asserting this if someone had denied it, and the reason for asserting the realist platitude is that in modern times some men of obvious ability and seriousness have denied it, or have appeared to do so. The non-Marxist realists are mainly concerned to show that the denial of this platitude is an error. Marxists endeavor to show that its denial is not only mistaken as a matter of theory but is practically harmful too.

The circumstances in which the realist platitude came to be denied may be briefly described as follows. In the seventeenth century a number of writers, of whom Thomas Hobbes was the ablest and best known, inspired, in part, by the growth of mathematical physics, revived in a modified form the materialism which had been advocated in the ancient world by Democritus and the Epicureans. These ancient materialists had held that the physical things that to sight and touch appear solid and undivided are really composed of large numbers of ultimate, indivisible particles. In the heavier bodies the particles, which were called atoms, were closely packed together; in the lighter ones there was more empty space between them. They also held that souls were composed of similar but smaller atoms capable of slipping in between the larger atoms that composed living bodies. At death, both the atoms that formed the body and those that formed the soul became disarranged and at last dispersed, forming new bodies and new souls. These philosophers combined with their materialism a moral and psychological theory known as hedonism, according to which all living beings necessarily sought pleasure and avoided pain, the moral terms "good" and "bad" being therefore names for the pleasant and painful respectively. Thus, on their view morality consisted in the intelligent pursuit of pleasure and avoidance of pain. Materialists of the seventeenth century thought that this system of ideas, which in ancient times had been mainly a brilliant speculation, was supported by the mathematical physics of their own day. They believed that the behavior of things like rivers and billiard balls depended upon the nature and arrangement of the minute physical parts that composed them, so that an understanding of the larger scale things depended upon a knowledge of these material elements. As views such as these spread from scholars to the wider educated public, there were some who came to talk as though the sole realities were atoms and the space in which they moved, and everything else mere appearance or illusion. Heat was really a certain sort of agitation of particles, sound was really a movement of the air, and there was good authority for maintaining that even light was corpuscular in nature. Some of "the wits" of the time associated with this view about nature a cynical version of the morality of pleasure quite foreign to anything that Epicurus had taught, but nevertheless based on his views. Free-thinkers, atheists, and men of the world thus found a philosophy on which could be supported their denials of the existence of God, of the immortality of the soul, and of the freedom of the will.

It was in refutation of views of this sort, as well as in refutation of the skepticism that prepared the way for them, that Berkeley constructed his "idealist" philosophy. This may be seen in his *Philosophical Commentaries,* the notes and arguments he recorded in preparation for his first books. Entry number 824, for example, reads: "My Doctrine rightly understood all that Philosophy of Epicurus, Hobbs, Spinoza etc. wch has been a declared enemy of Religion Comes to ye Ground." The sub-title of his *Treatise concerning the Principles of Human Knowledge* runs: "Wherein the chief causes of error and difficulty in the Sciences, with the grounds of Scepticism, Atheism and Irreligion, are inquired into." That of the *Three Dialogues between Hylas and Philonous* begins: "The design of which is plainly to demonstrate the reality and perfection of human knowledge, the incorporeal nature of the soul, and the immediate providence of a Deity." His *Alciphron or the Minute Philosopher,* written later in life, enlarged the scope of the argument to take in the hedonism and egoism of Mandeville, the cynical author of the *Fable of the Bees.* Throughout Berkeley's life it was "the modern free-thinkers"

he had in mind, "the very same with those Cicero called minute philosophers;[3] which name admirably suits them, they being a sort of sect
which diminish all the most valuable things, the thoughts, views and
hopes of men; all the knowledge, notions, and theories of the mind
they reduce to sense; human nature they contract and degrade to the
narrow low standard of animal life, and assign us only a small pittance
of time instead of immortality. . . ."[4] The master strokes in Berkeley's
idealist arguments were his denial of "material substance" and his assertion that the existence of the objects of sense experience was not
distinct from their being perceived. The significance of this assertion
may be seen from entry number 799 of the *Philosophical Commentaries,*
which reads: "Opinion that existence was distinct from perception of
Horrible Consequence it is the foundation of Hobb's doctrine etc."
The arguments by which he hoped to establish idealism are complex
and subtle, but for the purposes of our discussion of Marxism it must
suffice to enumerate the following main contentions.

(i) It may well be, Berkeley argues, that whenever we feel something hot there is normally a rapid movement of material particles in
the hot thing. If, however, we attend to our experience of heat it will
be seen that it is quite a different sort of thing from the movement
of invisible particles. In order to attach any meaning to the view that
heat is a movement of invisible particles we must first have had experience both of visible things in motion and of sensible heat, i.e.,
of the heat we feel when we touch something hot. So also with the
movements of air which come to be called physical sound, and the
movements of corpuscles which Newton held to be the basis of our
experience of colors. Berkeley thus distinguished between the tem-
peratures, sounds, and colors which we directly experience, and any
entities, such as invisible particles, not directly experienced that may
be regarded as their basis. The former he called "sensible qualities"
(today they are generally called "sense data"), and the alleged unexperienced basis of them—not the atoms or particles themselves, but
the entities supposed to *have* the size, shape, and motion of the par-

3. Cicero uses *minutus* pejoratively to mean "petty," and applies the epithet
to philosophers who deny the immortality of the soul.

4. *Alciphron,* First Dialogue. 10.

ticles—he called "corporeal substance." His first contention is that, so far from the former being illusory or doubtful by comparison with the latter, any knowledge we may have of the latter can only be by means of the former.

(ii) From what has been said it is clear that sense experiences cannot be dismissed as mere illusions whose reality is to be found in a hidden world of ultimate material substances. Having established that the existence of sense data is certain, Berkeley's next task is to determine what sort of thing they are. On his view they depend on minds and are incapable of existing apart from them. His use of the word "idea" marks this dependence, although others before him had used the word in this way. His arguments for the view that ideas, i.e., sensible qualities or sense data, cannot exist, as he put it, "without the mind," are difficult to summarize, but considerations such as the following weighed with him. Things existing independently of perceivers would have characteristics that did not vary with the position and condition of the perceiver. At any given time a liquid would have to have some definite temperature, a building some definite size and shape. In fact, however, a liquid may feel warm if the hand we plunge into it is cold, and cold if the hand we plunge into it is warm. Again, when, as we say, we look at a tall round tower on a distant hill, what we directly see is something small and flat. The same liquid cannot simultaneously be hot and cold, neither can the same tower be simultaneously big and small, round and flat. Berkeley showed, by a detailed analysis of each of our senses, that the nature of our sense experience varies with changes in ourselves. Perspectival distortions, mirror images, microscopes and telescopes, drugs and intoxicants, were all adduced by him to support the view that there is something in the very nature of sensible qualities that unfits them for existing apart from minds. (In recent years this interpretation of Berkeley's meaning has been denied by eminent scholars, but there is no need for me to discuss this, since the interpretation I have given is that of most of Berkeley's readers, and is that of his realist and materialist critics.)

(iii) It might be suggested, however, that sense data are mental existences *caused* in us by independently existing physical objects. If this were so, sense data, as the mental effects of physical causes, would be incapable of existing outside minds and so could be rightly called "ideas," but would nevertheless presuppose non-mental existences that were not sense data. Berkeley considered that such a supposition was meaningless. He challenged his readers to make clear what such non-sensible things "without the mind" could be, and thus set them the task of describing something that had no color, hardness, shape, size, speed, etc., that is, he set them the task of describing the indescribable. A "corporeal substance" that had no sensible temperature, taste, color, hardness, or shape, could be neither large nor small, rapid nor slow. Any definite characteristics attributed to it could only be described in terms of one or more of the senses, and so in terms of something that cannot exist "without the mind." In order to avoid such attributions recourse must be had to *indefinite* characteristics, and it then becomes necessary to talk of something or other that has no color, no shape, no size. This, Berkeley held, was to talk to no purpose. To attribute wholly indefinite characteristics to matter was to imply that matter was nothing at all. To say that matter has characteristics that belong to sense data is to say that matter has characteristics that cannot exist "without the mind," and this is to deny that there is any matter at all.

(iv) Berkeley also argued that the notion of something existing independently of mind was a contradictory notion. For, in order to conceive of something existing independently of mind, we must conceive of it, and this, he considered, was the same thing as to conceive of something that is not conceived of, and that is contradictory.

(v) The four preceding contentions make up what is sometimes referred to as Berkeley's "immaterialism," i.e., his denial of the existence of matter. But although Berkeley denied the existence of matter, he was not so foolish as to deny that such concrete things existed as stars, stones, animals, and fruit. These, he held, were not inaccessible nothings behind the scenes, but were the very things we saw, touched, smelled, and tasted. A cherry, for example, was not some recondite whirl of featureless atoms, but something round and red that is seen and tasted. It is not, of course, revealed in any single view, or touch, or taste; we are only entitled to say there is a cherry when we know there is a whole series of such sense data to be expected. To say there is a cherry on the tree in the garden is to say that someone who goes into the garden will see certain colored shapes and will be able to enjoy certain tastes and smells. The cherry just *is* the whole group (Berkeley called it a "congeries") of sense data that we say belong to it. And in general terms the view is that material things are certain classes or series of sense data.

(vi) We have so far considered Berkeley's theory of "ideas," but minds we have only mentioned as those things on which "ideas" depend, as those things that "ideas" must be *in,* since they cannot exist "without" them. It was his view that each of us has direct knowledge of mind in the experience he has of himself. Such experience is quite different from the experience we have of "ideas," in that "ideas" are passive objects whereas mind is experienced as active subject. Apart from minds and their "ideas" there is nothing else, according to Berkeley, that we can conceive of.

(vii) Nevertheless we cannot possibly deny that a world exists independent of human minds, and that parts of it continue to exist when no human minds are conscious of it. There are, for example, things buried in the earth or carried in the stars which no human being has ever been aware of. Berkeley believed that once it has been established that nothing can conceivably exist except minds and "ideas," it follows that the parts of nature that are not "ideas" in the minds of human beings or of other finite creatures must be "ideas" in the mind of an Infinite Being. In this way, he held, the existence of God could be proved in a way not hitherto thought of. He held further that, since the only conception we have of activity is the conception we have of a mind's acts of will, and since there can be no cause without activity, "ideas," not being minds but merely depending on them, cannot be causes at all. What is not caused by the acts of will of finite minds can, therefore, only be caused by God's activity. Hence, the regularities of nature are the regularities of God's acts of will, so that as we extend our knowledge of nature we gain an indirect knowledge of the Divine decrees. According to Berkeley, therefore, just as we gain a knowledge of other men's minds from what we see of their behavior, so we gain a knowledge of God from our exploration of the natural world. Hence the experimental sciences do not undermine religion, but continually vindicate and enrich it.

We may now summarize this summary as follows. According to Berkeley, (i) there is a class of directly perceived passive entities which we may call sense data. (ii) Sense data would not exist unless minds existed, but (iii) cannot depend for their existence on non-sensible beings independent of minds since no conception of such "corporeal substances" can possibly be formed. (iv) The conception of "corporeal substance," indeed, is self-contradictory. (v) Nevertheless, such things as stars, stones, and cherries do exist, but are not "corporeal substances," but groups of sense data. (vi) Minds are known to exist by the direct knowledge we have of our own. (vii) The system of nature distinct from human minds is a system of "ideas" willed by God.

Now Berkeley developed these views in criticism of men who, priding themselves on accepting nothing as true which experience did not guarantee, regarded matter as the sole reality and mind and sense experience as somehow illusory. Berkeley agreed that the appeal should be to experience, but thought he could show that whereas the views of materialists went beyond what experience could justify, a resolute refusal to go beyond it leads to the conclusion that matter does not exist, and that minds, both human and divine, do. For matter, as distinct from what is seen, felt, heard, etc., is a meaningless conception, whereas we know our own minds directly, and gain a knowledge of God by analogy. Thus Berkeley held that a resolute attachment to experience leads, not to materialism and atheism, but to immaterialism and theism. He has thus been regarded as a founder of the philosophical movement known as idealism.

Many subsequent philosophers, however, have distinguished between Berkeley's policy of refusing to go beyond what experience can justify, and the idealistic and theistic conclusions he thought resulted from it. They have distinguished, that is, between his attempted justification of Christian theism, and his careful analysis of experience. The latter, they have said, was the cleverest attempt hitherto made to show precisely what we refer to in experience when we talk about "things," "perception of things," "illusions," "mere imaginations," "causes," "general ideas," and the like. The former, however, they think does not fit in very well with the latter, if indeed it is compatible with it at all. Thus they distinguish between the *empiricism* in Berkeley's philosophy, that is, the aspect of it that is an attempt to base all knowledge on experience, and the theism in it, and this latter they ignore or reject.

The essence of his empiricism is that no conceptions or principles of explanation are to be admitted which refer beyond experience to something that could not be experienced. In so far as matter is something distinct from any sense datum or group of sense data, and distinct also from the minds on which they depend, it is something that could not be experienced, and therefore, according to Berkeley, nothing at all. Nevertheless, things such as stars, stones, and trees certainly exist, but they are not distinct from sense data but are rather groups of them. Any meaning that words such as "atom," "force," and "infinitesimal" may have must be in terms of the sense data we experience rather than in terms of matter lying beyond them. According to Berkeley, therefore, the knowledge gained in the natural sciences is a knowledge of how sense data or groups of sense data accompany one another or are signs of one another. This view of the nature of science according to which there is no matter beyond sense data, and according to which natural science is a knowledge of the regular associations and sequences of sense data, is today called phenomenalism. We may say that phenomenalism is the working out of the implications of propositions (i), (iii), and (v) above, although some phenomenalists may accept propositions (ii) and (iv) as well. Most phenomenalists would reject proposition (vi), since they would hold that, just as physical things are groups of sense data, so minds are another sort of group of sense data with which are connected feelings, feelings being a different sort of experience from sense data. All phenomenalists would reject proposition (vii), since they would hold that "God" does not stand for anything that could be experienced. If "matter" is meaningless if understood to stand for some unexperienced basis of experience, then, for the same reasons, "God" is meaningless if used to stand for some different unexperienced basis of experience. Phenomenalists have sometimes said that their view is *consistent empiricism.*

Perhaps the best known statement of phenomenalism is that contained in J. S. Mill's *Examination of Sir William Hamilton's Philosophy,* where the existence of matter is not *denied* but where Berkeley's view is upheld by *defining* matter as "a Permanent Possibility of Sensation."[5] On this view, to say that a physical object, say a chair, exists even when no one is observing it, is to say that in such and such circumstances, for

5. Fifth edition (1878), p. 233.

example, by entering the room and turning on the light, it *can* be observed. So long as it remains possible to observe it, so long the physical thing may be said to exist. In effect, the phenomenalist *defines* matter as the "congeries of ideas" that Berkeley substituted for the materialists' "material substance." Phenomenalism is regarded as the necessary outcome of the intellectual policy of refusing to go beyond what experience guarantees. If phenomenalism is true, then the task of science is to explore the regularities of actual and possible experiences and feelings. We might say that when God and active mind are subtracted from Berkeley's philosophy the result is phenomenalism.

2. *Marxist Criticisms of Idealism and Phenomenalism*

A detailed discussion of these matters from a Marxist point of view is to be found in Lenin's *Materialism and Empirio-Criticism.* An account of how this book came to be written is contained in chapter 4 of the Soviet *History of the Communist Party of the Soviet Union,* as well as in Lenin's own preface to the first edition (1909), and Professor Deborin's preface to volume 13 of the 1927 edition of the English translation of Lenin's *Collected Works.* In brief, it appears that a number of members of the Russian Social Democratic Party had been reading books by Ernst Mach and Richard Avenarius in which, under the name of "empirio-criticism," a phenomenalist account of matter was advocated. These Russian socialists became convinced both that phenomenalism was true and that it was compatible with Marxist materialism. Lenin considered they were wrong on both counts, and thought it most important to convict them of error. Thus he says that he wrote *Materialism and Empirio-Criticism* "to seek for the stumbling block to people who under the guise of Marxism are offering something incredibly baffling, confused and reactionary."[6] Lenin worked on the material for this book in the British Museum in 1908.

---

6. *V. I. Lenin. Selected Works,* vol. 11, p. 90 (London, 1939). For the sake of brevity later quotations from this book will be given in the form: *M. and E-C,* p. . . ., the page reference being that of the *Selected Works.* The phrase "seek for the stumbling block" is obscure, and the rendering in the 1927 translation: "to find out what is the trouble with" is more comprehensible.

In *Materialism and Empirio-Criticism* Lenin touches on many topics in a highly controversial manner. It seems to me, however, that he argues for four main positions which may be summarized as follows:

(*a*) Phenomenalism cannot be detached from idealism. Since, therefore, the function of idealism is to provide philosophical support for religious faith (called by Lenin "fideism"), phenomenalism too is religious in its tendency, whatever its supporters may say about it.

(*b*) Phenomenalism is false. Lenin thinks he can show its falsity, in the first place by reference to practice or action, and in the second place by showing that if it were true, then well-attested scientific theories to the effect that the world existed for a long time before living beings inhabited it, would have to be denied.

(*c*) The denial of phenomenalism involves the assertion that matter exists, in the sense of a reality that is neither sense datum nor mind. Matter, according to Lenin, is "the objective reality which is given to man by his sensations, and which is copied, photographed and reflected by our sensations, while existing independently of them."[7] He also says: "To regard our sensations as images of the external world, to recognize objective truth, to hold the materialistic theory of knowledge—these are all one and the same thing."[8]

(*d*) At the end of the book Lenin argues that there is no foundation for the view that materialism is being rendered untenable by new discoveries in physics, and in particular by "the electrical theory of matter." In his view, new physical discoveries such as those that led to the abandonment of the "billiard ball" view of matter, can only lead us to the discovery of new characteristics of matter, not, as had been held by some, to its "disappearance."

In the following sections of this chapter I shall discuss the first three of these contentions.

3. Phenomenalism, Idealism, and the Religious Outlook

In effect, what Lenin (and subsequent Marxist writers) maintain is that the proposition that there can be no "material substance" (which

7. *M. and E-C,* p. 192.
8. Ibid., p. 193.

I labelled (iii) on page 7), and the proposition that inanimate things such as tables are groups of sense data (which I labelled (v) on page 8), and which together comprise the essentials of phenomenalism, are inseparable from the other parts of Berkeley's philosophy, so that once we accept them we open the way to theism and religion. Now this may be understood in two ways. In the first place it may be suggested that *in fact* phenomenalism is a step on the road to idealism and religion. On this view, what is being suggested is that whether or not idealism *follows from* phenomenalism and theism *follows from* idealism and religion *follows from* theism, those who accept the phenomenalist arguments either themselves pass on to idealism, theism, and religion, or at any rate encourage others to do so. In the second place it may be suggested that phenomenalism, idealism, theism, and religion are logically connected, so that were the first true, the second, third, and fourth would also have to be true. I think that Lenin held both of these views, and in this section I shall say something about each of them.

First, then, as to the view that phenomenalism is in fact connected with idealism, theism, and religion. Lenin, following Engels,[9] believed that idealism and materialism were the only two philosophies that counted, that idealism was a system of thought that constantly endeavored to put the best possible face on what Marx (following Feuerbach) had called the "mystifications" of priests and other agents of the ruling classes, and that the revolutionary working class must base their thought and action on materialism if they are to succeed in freeing themselves from the bonds which their masters have fastened on them. Idealism, Lenin wrote, "is merely a subtle, refined form of fideism, which stands fully armed, commands vast organizations and steadily continues to exercise an influence on the masses, turning the slightest vacillation in philosophical thought to its own advantage."[10] His objection to phenomenalism is a social one. The emergence of phenomenalism as a philosophical theory which criticizes both idealism and materialism confuses the clear-cut issue which Lenin is intent on establishing. Who is not for the working class movement is against it.

9. In *Ludwig Feuerbach and the Outcome of Classical German Philosophy.*
10. *M. and E-C*, p. 406.

Idealism, theism, and religion, Lenin thought, are obviously against it, and any other view that is not wholeheartedly materialistic, although it may not be openly and consciously against it, is so in tendency, and perhaps covertly also. Thus he concluded: "The objective, class rôle played by empirio-criticism entirely consists in rendering faithful service to the fideists in their struggle against materialism in general and against historical materialism in particular."[11] Stalin allows these thinkers even less credit than Lenin when, in chapter 4 of the *History of the Communist Party of the Soviet Union,* he writes: "In reality, they were hostile to Marxism, for they tried to undermine its theoretical foundations, although they hypocritically denied their hostility to Marxism and two-facedly continued to style themselves Marxists."[12]

I cannot hope to deal, at the present stage, with all the issues that would need attention if this view were to be discussed fully. In particular, it will be seen that Lenin thinks it relevant to criticize a philosophical theory about perception on the ground of its possible social and political repercussions. On the face of it, this may not seem defensible, since a true theory might conceivably have bad political results, and a theory which had good political results might conceivably be false. However that may be—it is a theme discussed on page 191 below— Lenin's generalization that phenomenalism is allied with idealism and religion is much too narrowly based. He refers to a few Russian Social Democrats who flirted with empirio-criticism and suggested that some form of religious organization was desirable in which God was equated with the social good, and also to some associates of Mach and Avenarius who were willing to be called philosophical idealists. In the history of European thought as a whole, however, the exponents of phenomenalism have generally been indifferent, if not hostile, to religion. We need only mention such thinkers as Protagoras, Hume, Bentham, James Mill, J. S. Mill, and Karl Pearson. It is worth noting that J. S. Mill, a few sentences after he has given his phenomenalistic definition of matter, writes: "But I affirm with confidence that this conception of Matter includes the whole meaning attached to it by the com-

11. Ibid., p. 406.

12. English translation, Moscow, Foreign Languages Publishing House, 1939, pp. 102–3.

mon world, apart from philosophical, and sometimes from *theological* theories."[13] It is difficult to resist the conclusion that Lenin's attitude to phenomenalism is that of the revolutionary administrator, for whom clear-cut decisions were essential. The revolutionary workers needed a this-worldly philosophy of matter to arm them against the enervating influence of religion, and Lenin felt that those who departed from the materialist simplicities were unreliable palterers.

We now pass to the contention that idealism, theism, and religious belief follow logically from the doctrine of phenomenalism. According to the phenomenalists, the only terms or expressions (apart from those of logic) that can have meaning are those which refer directly or indirectly to sense-experiences, among which, of course, are included experiences of pleasure and pain, of effort, resistance, and the like. Thus the term "matter," if it is not used to refer to actual or possible sense-experiences, is meaningless, and the term "mind" is meaningless also, unless it is used to refer to actual or possible feelings associated with actual or possible sense-experiences. Now the term "God" is generally held to refer to an infinite, active, non-sensible spirit who transcends the natural world. Most phenomenalists, I think, would argue that meaning cannot be attached to such a term, that they cannot conceive what it would be like to experience God, and that therefore what religious people call "the worship of God" cannot be what they take it to be. If phenomenalism is true, and if God is held to be a being that could not be directly or indirectly experienced by the senses, then the existence of God cannot be meaningfully asserted or denied. To argue thus that the notion of God is meaningless is, it seems to me, to oppose the religious view of things much more radically than even atheists do. The atheist has common ground with the theist in so far as he admits that the theist's belief has point, whereas the phenomenalist regards the dispute between them as insignificant, and when he says so both parties are disturbed.

We may conclude, therefore, that this part of Lenin's attack on phenomenalism is less effective as a social tactic than he himself supposed. For, whereas phenomenalism, by denying meaning to any conceptions except those based directly or indirectly on sense-experience, con-

---

13. *Examination of Sir William Hamilton's Philosophy*, p. 233 (my italics).

signs both God and material substances to a common and irrelevant grave, materialism, by asserting the reality of material substances beyond sense-experience, allows also the *possibility* of a God that transcends sense-experience too. Phenomenalism excludes God but appears committed to some sort of idealism. Materialism excludes phenomenalism but only at the expense of making God appear a possibility. The revolutionary tactician cannot afford to ignore this dilemma.

To be offset against the atheism of phenomenalism is, however, its alleged conflict with natural science. This made Lenin particularly suspicious of it, since he considered that the natural sciences provided the detailed content of materialism. Our next step, therefore, must be to consider his direct arguments against a phenomenalistic, and in favor of a realistic, theory of perception.

4. Lenin's Criticisms of Phenomenalism

Marxists hold that religion is used by the rich as a means of reconciling the poor to their poverty, and that idealism (with which, as has already been explained, they associate phenomenalism) is a deliberate attempt to reinforce this policy in the face of the religious unbelief that the natural sciences encourage. There is no doubt that they think that idealism is a dishonest view. They feel that, however subtle the arguments in its favor, it is fundamentally unbelievable. A man may deny the reality of matter with his lips, but his life and actions belie what his lips have uttered. For most men life has been a losing struggle against scarcity and disease, and for everyone the end is death. The few fortunate have material things at their command, the many unfortunate are the slaves of circumstance. Rich men and their clients, therefore, may affect to despise material things, and may even employ their leisure in demonstrating that there are none. But their ability to do these things depends upon there being food and shelter and leisure at their disposal. If they reflected on how the majority of men lived, they would realize that ingenious idealist speculations are frivolous insults to suffering mankind.

It is in the light of such considerations, I think, that Lenin's attack on phenomenalism is to be understood. In the first chapter of

Materialism and Empirio-Criticism he suggests that it is characteristic of contemporary (i.e., Marxist) materialism to hold that "arguments and syllogisms alone do not suffice to refute idealism, and that here it is not a question of theoretical argument."[14] Further on he writes: "The standpoint of life, of practice, should be first and fundamental in the theory of knowledge, and it inevitably leads to materialism, brushing aside the endless fabrications of professorial scholasticism."[15] Again, in his *Philosophical Notebooks* Lenin comments on a passage in Hegel's *History of Philosophy* in which the great idealist philosopher criticizes Epicurus for not having gone beyond "the common human understanding." Lenin's comment is: "*Slanders* against materialism. . . . Its [i.e., Idealism's] non-agreement with 'the common human understanding' is the lazy whim of the Idealists."[16] Lenin also quotes with approval Feuerbach's remark that before we can perceive we must be able to breathe and feel. He does not do so, but he might have quoted the following passage from Feuerbach's *Preliminary Theses towards the Reform of Philosophy* (1842) which had undoubtedly impressed Marx: "The denial in metaphysics of the reality of space and time in the very nature of things has the most injurious practical consequences. Only a man who everywhere bases himself on time and space can achieve tact in living and practical understanding. Space and time are the basic criteria of practice. A people which excludes time from its metaphysic, which bows down before eternal existence, that is, abstract existence cut off from time, excludes time also from its politics and bows down before an anti-historical principle of stability that is contrary to right and reason."[17] In section 33 of his *Foundations of the Philosophy of the Future* (1843) Feuerbach had also written: ". . . Love is the true ontological proof of the existence of an object outside our heads, and there is no other proof of existence except love, and sensation in general."

From Lenin's statements, and from those of Feuerbach from which they derive, we may extract the following main positions. (i) Even though an individual could not, from mere *observation* of his own sense-

---

14. *M. and E-C,* p. 104.

15. Ibid., p. 205.

16. *Aus dem Philosophischen Nachlass, Exzerpte und Randglossen,* ed. V. Adoratski, pp. 228–29 (Wien-Berlin, 1932).

17. *Werke,* ed. Bolin and Jodl (Stuttgart, 1903–11), II, p. 233.

experiences, prove the existence of a material world existing independently of him, all his actions, as distinct from his theorizing, demonstrate in a practical way the truth of the realist platitude. (ii) Even though we were unable to find satisfactory counter-arguments to the arguments of the idealists, it would be right for us to prefer to the most brilliant of such arguments the naïve realism which we presuppose when we eat our meals and associate with our fellows. (iii) To accept the conclusions of elaborate philosophical arguments rather than what is presupposed in our dealings with the world and other men is socially disastrous and unjust.

Before we consider these arguments, it should be mentioned that they are not new. In the ancient world the Stoic philosophers, seeking to uphold the practical moral certainties against the subtle arguments of the Skeptics, argued in somewhat similar terms. Zeno of Citium, the founder of the School, had spoken of the "grasp" by which real things were certainly known. Cicero, in reproducing Zeno's view, writes: "Therefore those who assert that nothing can be grasped deprive us of these things that are the very tools and equipment of life. . . ."[18] The following passage from the *Moral Discourses* of Epictetus stresses the superiority of practice to speculation. "Let the followers of Pyrrho or of the Academy [i.e., the Skeptics] come and oppose us. Indeed I, for my part, have no leisure for such matters, nor can I act as advocate to the commonly received opinion. If I had a petty suit about a mere bit of land, I should have called in someone else as my advocate. With what evidence, then, am I satisfied? With that which belongs to the matter in hand. To the question how perception arises, whether through the whole body, or from some particular part, perhaps I do not know how to give a reasonable answer, and both views perplex me. But that you and I are not the same persons, I know very certainly. Whence do I get this knowledge? When I want to swallow something, I never take the morsel to that place but to this;[19] when I wish to take bread, I never take sweepings, but I always go after the bread as to a mark. And do you yourselves, who take away the evidence of the

18. *Academica,* II. x. 31 (Loeb edition, translated by H. Rackham).

19. We must suppose that at this point Epictetus gestured, first toward another part of his body, and then toward his mouth.

senses, do anything else? Who among you when he wishes to go to a bath goes to a mill instead? Ought we not to the best of our ability to hold fast also to this—maintain, that is, the commonly received opinion, and be on our guard against the arguments that seek to overthrow it?"[20] In this passage we may particularly note (*a*) the scorn with which Epictetus says he has "no leisure for such matters," thus suggesting that Skepticism is the fruit of irresponsible idleness; (*b*) the claim that practical certainty rightly overrides theoretical perplexity; and (*c*) the weight given to "the commonly received opinion." In chapter 5 of the same book Epictetus had discussed the skeptical argument that there is no certain means of distinguishing between dreaming and waking, and had asserted that a man who persists in maintaining this argument is devoid of shame and modesty, and is like a drunk man who says whatever comes into his head. It would be tempting for the Marxist to say that it was because he was a slave that Epictetus came to express, eighteen hundred years ago, a view so very like the Marxist one. This temptation, however, should not be yielded to, since Epictetus was re-stating views which had been expressed long before his time by Stoic philosophers who were not slaves.

In the eighteenth century, Thomas Reid, the philosopher of Common Sense, maintained a similar point of view. In his *Inquiry into the Human Mind* (1764) he wrote: "The belief of a material world is older, and of more authority, than any principles of philosophy. It declines the tribunal of reason, and laughs at all the artillery of the logician." In his *Essays on the Intellectual Powers of Man* (1785) he included among his Principles of Common Sense the proposition: "That those things do really exist which we distinctly perceive by our senses, and are what we perceive them to be." He also argued that, although Berkeley did not intend it, his philosophy would lead each individual, if he were to be consistent, to believe that he could be certain only of his own existence and must be doubtful of that of others. "It stifles every generous and social principle."[21] In our own day, Professor G. E. Moore has said

---

20. *Arrian's Discourses of Epictetus,* I, xxvii, 15–20 (Loeb edition, translated by W. A. Oldfather).

21. The quotations from Reid are from *Works,* ed. Sir William Hamilton, vol. 1, pp. 127, 445, 446.

that, in order to prove that there are at least two external objects, it is sufficient for a man to hold up both his hands to his own view and that of other people. In the face of the arguments of idealist philosophers, it is appropriate, he holds, to restate the realist platitude with a number of supporting explanations.[22]

It will be seen that Epictetus, Reid, Feuerbach, and Lenin are all, in their different ways, concerned lest certain subtle philosophical arguments should turn men from their social duties by raising doubts about the existence of matter and of other people. Epictetus had in mind those Skeptics who argued that the result of admitting their skeptical conclusions should be a holding back from human affairs, a refusal to commit oneself in the uncertainties of social life. What effects, however, could the acceptance of the skeptical or idealist arguments have on anyone's attitude to what they had previously taken to be material things and other people? Could anyone ever seriously say: "I have been reading Hume, and have been convinced by him that there are no satisfactory grounds for believing in the independent existence of material things or of people other than myself. I shall therefore cease to eat and drink, and I shall take no further interest in such doubtfully existing beings as other people." Hume's own conclusion was very much less dramatic. "I dine," he wrote, "I play a game of backgammon, I converse, and make merry with my friends; and when after three or four hours' amusement, I wou'd return to these speculations, they appear so cold, and strain'd, and ridiculous, that I cannot find in my heart to enter into them any farther." Arguments to show that the existence of a material world and of other people is doubtful, carry conviction, if at all, only while they are being propounded and attended to, and are overwhelmed by the ordinary affairs of living. We may compare someone in doubt whether the substance he sees before him is cheese or soap, with someone else in doubt whether cheese or soap or any material thing really exists at all. The doubt of the first man can be set at rest by smelling or tasting or in some other obvious way. It is the sort of doubt that can be fairly readily removed after a few tests have been made. The doubt of the second man is rather different, since no

22. *Proof of an External World,* British Academy, Annual Philosophical Lecture, 1939.

amount of looking or tasting will get rid of it. One reason for this is that he considers that *it is always possible* that some new experience will arise to conflict with what the previous tests have established. These tests, he reflects, have only been applied *up to now*, so that we cannot be *quite sure* what they will reveal when next they are made. But *such* a doubt, surely, is never relevant in the sphere of action, since if it were, action could never take place, but would remain ever poised on the brink of an ever receding penultimate test. If we are to act at all, we must be willing to use tests which establish reality in a finite number of moves. The skeptic's doubts, therefore, are not of practical relevance in a world where, as we know, doubts have to be, and frequently are, brought to a settlement. Furthermore, were a skeptic to use *his* sort of doubt as reasons for not troubling about the material needs of other people—"if there is no matter and if there are no other people with material needs, then I need not trouble about them"—and were he to continue attending to his own material needs we should say that he was dishonest as well as irrelevant. I cannot suppose that anyone ever has argued in quite this way, but Marxist thinkers may well have believed that something of the sort was the philosophical counterpart to the wealthy Christian's advice to the poor man to seek for heavenly rather than for earthly treasures. We can now see that there is some point in Lenin's favorable view of the common human understanding. Skeptics and idealists must act as if they were fully assured of the existence of matter and of embodied mankind.

These considerations, however, have not disposed of phenomenalism. For phenomenalism is not the view that there is *no* material world, nor the view that the existence of the material world is problematical, but the view that the material world is nothing but actual and possible sense data. It will be remembered that Berkeley was careful to say that he did not deny the existence of cherries; his view was that cherries are what can be seen, touched, and tasted when, say, someone goes into the garden. On his view, a cherry is the whole group of sense data that we say "belong" to it. Now arguments about practice can be used to overthrow the view that the existence of matter may be doubted or denied, but they do not succeed, as Lenin thought they did, in disposing of the view that matter *just is* actual and possible sense data. The sort of practical activity that Feuerbach and Lenin cited in refutation of phenomenalism were such things as loving, eating, and breathing, but these, and other practical activities, can be accounted for by the phenomenalist within his scheme. According to the phenomenalist, the activity of eating would consist of certain feelings of effort and of pressure, along with the visual, tactile, and taste sensations which link the eating with the thing that is being eaten. Similarly, in terms of what is being experienced, breathing consists of certain visual sensations of movement (e.g., the observed movements of the chest), certain auditory sensations which we describe as the sound of breathing, and, in the breather, the feelings he has when he attends to his breathing or when something interferes with it. What especially seems to be involved in action is sensations of effort meeting with some resistance. The phenomenalist will say, however, that both the effort and the resistance to it are only describable in terms of sensation. If phenomenalists were to confine their descriptions to the data of the so-called five senses, then, of course, practice would be a notion that could not be comprised in their theory. Once, however, the notion of sense-experience is extended to include pleasure and pain and the bodily feelings called "organic sensations," practice presents the phenomenalist with no insuperable theoretical difficulties. He would claim to be giving a different account of what material things are and of what practice is from that assumed by the realist, and he would also claim that his account is superior to that of the realist, since the realist believes in things-in-themselves which are never directly experienced and transcend all possible experience, whereas the phenomenalist brings into his theory only such entities as are or could be directly experienced and cannot therefore be questioned. It does not seem to me, therefore, that the Marxist can, by appealing to practice, refute the phenomenalist who sets out to give an account of matter in purely empirical terms.

We may briefly restate the argument as follows. The phenomenalist says that a material object, say a cherry, is "a permanent possibility of sensation." The Marxist replies that we know of the existence of cherries, not by merely experiencing sense data, but by picking and eating and other such *deeds*. It is absurd, he may continue, to suggest that we can pick and eat permanent possibilities of sensation, and therefore practice shows that it is cherries—material things, not sense data—

that are the objects of our perception. It seems to me, however, that the phenomenalist has a thoroughly satisfactory answer to this. The absurdity of talking about picking and eating permanent possibilities of sensation, he will say, depends upon giving the analysis of cherries in terms of sense data and at the same time refraining from giving the analysis of picking and eating in similar terms. If matter is reducible to actual and possible sense data, then action is reducible to actual and possible feelings and sense data. The argument from practice, therefore, has force against the doubter and denier of matter, but not against the phenomenalist, who is not really doubting or denying matter but claiming to say what it is.

Let us then see whether Lenin's other main line of criticism succeeds in refuting phenomenalism. This other line of criticism has already been briefly indicated as the view that if phenomenalism were true, then well-attested scientific theories according to which the world existed for a long time before there were living beings would have to be denied. Lenin argues[23] that if the material world consists of sense data, and if, as seems to be scientifically established, sense data depend upon the existence of suitably equipped living organisms, then the material world could not have existed before there were living organisms. (Lenin writes in terms of "sensations" rather than of sense data, but this makes no difference to the argument, since sense data, like sensations, are supposed to be inseparable from percipients.) Yet the combined evidence of geology, physics, chemistry, and biology is to the effect that living organisms could not have existed in the earliest stages of the world's history, but have evolved as favorable physical conditions developed. Avenarius had tried to avoid this difficulty by introducing the notion of an imaginary spectator, and phenomenalists in general have argued that to say there was a material world prior to the existence of beings that could be conscious of it is to say that *had* there been such beings they *would* have had such and such sensations. Lenin abusively asserts that this view is only a particularly unplausible form of idealism. His exposition is aided by quotations from philosophers who had tried to bolster up the phenomenalist position by referring to the experiences of ichthyosauruses and even of worms. "The phi-

23. *M. and E-C,* pp. 140–51.

losophy of Mach the scientist," he writes in another part of the book, "is to science what the kiss of the Christian Judas was to Christ."[24]

Sir John Percival, a friend of Berkeley, wrote to Berkeley on 26 August 1710, just after the publication of the *Principles of Human Knowledge*, as follows: "My wife, who has all the good esteem and opinion of you that is possible from your just notions of marriage-happiness, desires to know if there be nothing but spirit and ideas, what you make of that part of the six days' creation which preceded man." Lady Percival, like Lenin, felt that there must be some incongruity in holding that ideas depend on spirits, that seas and mountains are groups of ideas, and yet that seas and mountains exist before the spirits do. But Berkeley had an answer that the modern atheistic phenomenalist cannot utilize. ". . . I do not deny," he said, "the existence of any of the sensible things which Moses says were created by God. They existed from all eternity in the Divine intellect, and then became perceptible (i.e. were created) in the same manner and order as is described in Genesis. For I take creation to belong to things only as they respect finite spirits, there being nothing new to God. Hence it follows that the act of creation consists in God's willing that things should be perceptible to other spirits, which before were known only to Himself. . . ."[25] The ichthyosauruses and worms mentioned by Lenin were ludicrous substitutes for God, and Berkeley's polite comments on Lady Percival's argument (". . . she is the only person of those you mentioned my book to, who opposed it with reason and argument") may, with due allowances, be transferred to Lenin's analogous objections.

Lenin, I think, saw certain essential weaknesses of phenomenalism, although he did not have the patience to probe them fully and unexcitedly. Present-day phenomenalists, however, sometimes reply that their account of matter is not and is not intended to be a scientific theory at all; that as philosophers they are not concerned to make scientific statements, but rather to clear up the *meaning* of such notions as cause, thing, and matter, which are accepted uncritically by common sense and science alike; and that therefore, since it is not a scientific

24. Ibid., p. 397.

25. *Berkeley and Percival,* by Benjamin Rand, p. 81 and pp. 83–84 (Cambridge, 1914).

theory, it cannot conflict with any scientific theory, and hence no scientific theory can be adduced to refute it. In my opinion this argument will not do at all. For phenomenalism is a philosophical theory which has been developed in modern times largely in order to give a consistent account of that attention to experience which is held to be the fundamental feature of modern science. Phenomenalism is advocated as consistent empiricism, as the ultimate codification of the natural scientist's instinctive procedures. The phenomenalist's rejection of any conception of matter that goes beyond actual or possible sensations, is the philosophical counterpart of the natural scientist's distrust of untestable hypotheses. Of all philosophical theories, therefore, modern phenomenalism, which is openly parasitic on natural science, must guard against giving an account of matter that fails to square with any important class of propositions belonging to natural science. It is not only scientific statements that can clash with other scientific statements; it is possible for a suggested analysis of the notion of matter that is held to be in accord with common sense and natural science, not in fact to be so. Therefore the objection that phenomenalism is inconsistent with certain scientific theories cannot be initially ruled out of court.

The point that was worrying Lenin was this. If phenomenalism were true, then talk about the world as it was prior to the emergence of consciousness would be talk about what a potential observer would have observed had he been there to observe, although in fact he was not there at all, and could not have been there in any case since the conditions for life were not yet in existence. This view evokes immediate dissatisfaction for the following reasons. In the first place, the notion of a possible observer is not very helpful. The first difficulty concerns the term "observer." To say that the world prior to living creatures is what living creatures would have observed had they existed before they did exist, seems to be a quite useless tautology. For to observe involves both an observer and *what* he observes, and if this is so, then to say that the world prior to life is what would have been observed if there had been living creatures is merely to say that if there had been observers they would have observed whatever was there to be observed. The whole question of independent existence is wrapped up in that of an observer, so that the introduction of observers, whether actual or possible, does nothing to clarify the issue. In the second place, we cannot think of a *possible* something without thinking of the *something*. If, therefore, in order to say what matter is we have to say something about *possible* observers, we have to say or imply something about observers. Thus, when matter is defined in terms of possible observers or possible sensations, the notion of "observer" or the notion of "sensation" is contained in the definition. Now if "father" is defined as "a male parent," it is self-contradictory to say that someone is a father but not male. And similarly if matter *is* a permanent possibility of sensation, or what would be observed if an observer were in a position to observe it, it is self-contradictory to say that matter could exist apart from all possibility of sensation or observation. It might be said that even the most fervent realist would hardly wish to maintain the existence of matter that could not *possibly* be observed, and this is true if we interpret "possibly" widely enough. But it does not follow from this that "possibly observed," i.e., "would be observed if . . .," is part of the definition of "matter," any more than it follows from the fact that it is possible for some men to jump seven feet in the air, i.e., "would jump seven feet in the air if . . .," that that is part of the definition of "man." By bringing observers or sensations into their definition, even if indirectly, phenomenalists are giving to observation or sensation an importance by relation to "matter" that ordinary users of the term are unwilling to confirm. This is the point at which phenomenalism is in conflict with the "ordinary human understanding," and thus fails to do what it sets out to do, viz., to show what people *mean* when they speak or think about material things.

However, these are matters that I cannot claim to settle in a paragraph. It must be clear, from what has already been said, that further discussion of it would require us to consider the nature of the hypothetical or if-then connection involved in saying that a material thing is what would be, or would have been, observed if an observer were to be, or had been, in a position to observe. In our own day, the problem of phenomenalism, like so many other philosophical problems, has been discussed in terms of language, in this case in terms of the merits and defects of the "physical object language" on the one hand, and the "sense datum language" (the one preferred by phenomenalists) on the other. An advantage of this approach is that it calls attention to the possibility that philosophers, in talking of sense data, are not referring to recondite entities the existence of which is unsuspected by non-philosophers just as the existence of viruses was unsuspected by everyone in the seventeenth century and by ignorant people today, but are introducing a terminology in order to make their discussion of perspectives and illusions more precise. Whether those who hold this sort of view are right in their contention that phenomenalism, in this sense, does not imply idealism is a problem I do not propose to discuss here as it would take us too far from our main subject. For the present it is sufficient to say that the sort of phenomenalism or consistent empiricism that Lenin was criticizing appears on the one hand to render meaningless the notion of a God who transcends experience, and yet appears also to require there to be some Observer (not necessarily God, but perhaps merely a Sensitive Gas) to make sense of the conception of the world that existed before the coming of animal or human life.

There are other objections to phenomenalism that, with a certain amount of good will, can be extracted from Lenin's *Materialism and Empirio-Criticism,* but I think that enough has been said to show that he was on pretty strong ground when he concluded it was not true.

5. *The Marxist Account of Perception*

According to Marxists, then, matter can be known to exist, and is not reducible to actual and possible sense data. We have now to consider their positive view of it, in so far as this concerns their theory of perception. Lenin wrote that matter is "the objective reality which is . . . copied, photographed and reflected by our sensations, while existing independently of them,"[26] and he considered that this was also the view of Marx and Engels. Engels had written: "The influences of the external world upon man express themselves in his brain, are reflected therein as feelings, thoughts, instincts, volitions. . . ."[27] That present-day Marxists have adopted this view of sensations as "reflecting" external realities can be seen from Professor V. Adoratsky's *Dialec-*

26. *M. and E-C,* p. 192.
27. In *Ludwig Feuerbach,* pp. 40–41 (London, 1935).

tical Materialism, where he writes: "Our knowledge contains an absolute (unconditional and unquestionable) truth, viz. that it reflects the external world."[28] In his next sentence Professor Adoratsky writes: "The truth of our knowledge is tested and confirmed by practice." This last also was the view of Engels and Lenin. Engels emphasized the importance of practice in perception, notably in the introduction to *Socialism, Utopian and Scientific,* and Lenin followed suit when he wrote: ". . . things exist outside of us. Our perceptions and ideas are their images. Verification of these images, differentiation between true and false images, is given by practice."[29] In the course of a long footnote in which he compares William James's Pragmatism with Mach's Phenomenalism, Lenin obviously holds it against James that he had denied that science provides an "absolute copy of reality."[30] The suggestion, therefore, is that being a reflection or copy and being verified by practice are both of them conditions of perceiving correctly. Lenin also quotes with approval the second of Marx's *Theses on Feuerbach* (1845) in which Marx had written: "The question whether objective truth is an attribute of human thought is not a theoretical but a *practical* question. Man must prove the truth, i.e. reality and power, the 'this-sidedness' of his thinking, in practice."[31] In the Soviet Russian *Handbook of Philosophy* by Rosenthal and Yudin we read, in the article "Sensation": "As against mechanical materialism, which tended to conceive sensation as a passive reflection in the mind of things outside, Marxism insists on sensation as an active process arising through the efforts of the organism to satisfy its needs."[32]

It will be noticed that some of these quotations refer to perception or sensation, and that others appear to be concerned with the *truth of theories.* Now these are very different things, since theories are, at the very least, very much less *elementary* than perceptions or sensations are. We very much more often describe statements or theo-

28. International Publishers, pp. 66–67 (New York, 1934). He refers to "knowledge," but the view applies to sensation.

29. *M. and E-C,* p. 173.

30. Ibid., pp. 391–92.

31. Printed in *The German Ideology,* vol. 17 of the Marxist-Leninist Library (London, 1942), p. 197.

32. Edited and adapted by Howard Selsam, New York, 1949.

ries as true than we do perceptions or sensations. It is Marxists themselves, however, who group these things together and maintain that
copying and practice are involved in both, so that the expositor and
critic must commence by following suit. The Marxist view of sensation,
therefore, appears to be that there are material things, that among
these material things there are organisms with brains, that the material
things that surround the organisms with brains act on them, thus producing reflections, impressions, copies, or images, and that the reflections, impressions, copies, or images are verified or rejected as a result
of practical activity. Now this view seems at first sight to be liable to
an obvious objection that has very often been made against so-called
"copy" theories of perception. If the percipient *never* has direct access
to the material realities that exist outside him, but only to the copies
that they produce in him, then he can never know which copies are
true copies and which ones false, which are like and which are unlike
their originals. He is like a Martian who has never seen a human being
and is asked to pronounce on whether Gainsborough painted good
likenesses.

Now clearly if the Marxist theory is to escape this difficulty it
must be by means of the conception of practice, and this, it seems to
me, must be the importance of Lenin's dictum: "Verification of these
images, differentiation between true and false images, is given by practice." The attempt appears to be made in two rather different ways.

The first and most obvious way may be developed by means of an
example. While I am very weary and thirsty, I see, as I think, the water
of a mountain stream. On the Marxist view this amounts to my having
an image, reflection, copy, or impression. Is it a mirage, or is it real
water? I approach, dip my hand in the stream, and *feel* the water running through my fingers. The visual sensation is corroborated by sensations of touch, and I drink and am satisfied. I have not only touched
but I have made use of the water. The copy, therefore, was a true one
and my deed has proved it. There is the initial sensation, there are expectations, and there is the active putting oneself in a position to obtain sensations that corroborate or disappoint the expectations. Someone who is good at this sort of thing survives and gets pleasure from
his life. Those who too often fail are miserable or die. But is there any
stage in the process at which I can be said by practice to have bro-

ken through the screen of images, reflections, copies, or impressions? It may be answered that I do this when I move toward what I hope is the water. Certainly, when I move to investigate I am not passively receiving sensations, but am deliberately seeking for them. But this deliberate seeking is, on the view we are considering, something that must be terminated in more sensations, not something that enables me to reach beyond them to some material object that is not a sensation. Once Marxists accept the view that perception is by means of images, then there is nothing to distinguish their view from phenomenalism except the wish that it were not.

The other way in which the notion of practice may be thought to function in the Marxist theory of perception can be seen if we suppose the theory to be that there are no *mere* reflections or *mere* copies at all, but that each separate sensation is itself active as well as passive. This view, which seems to be suggested in the passage I have quoted from Rosenthal and Yudin, might be recommended for its "dialectical" character. Activity, however, is not necessarily the same thing as practice. The opposite of activity is passivity, the merely being affected by something else, and it is possible to be active without being *practically* active. A being that is practically active makes changes in the world outside him by means of his practical acts. But it is possible to be theoretically active *without* making changes in the world by means of the theoretical acts. It is obvious that thinking is something that we *do*, but it seems equally obvious that, although it may *lead* to the sort of doing that changes things besides the doer, it is not, in itself, that sort of doing. Now seeing, hearing, and perceiving are activities of living creatures, but they are more like thinking than they are like practical activity, in that they do not consist in *changing* what is seen, heard, or perceived. No doubt when a creature perceives, changes go on in its body, but these are not activities and therefore not practical activities.

It may be objected at this point that, having accepted the Stoic and Marxist view that skeptical doubts about perception have no practical relevance, I ought also to accept the Marxist view that perception involves practice. The two positions, however, are quite distinct. It is one thing to say that no one in fact doubts the existence of the material world in any way that is relevant to practical action, and quite another thing to say that practical action is involved in perception itself. In the Marxist theory of perception there is a notion that is altogether repugnant to common sense, viz., the notion that we directly perceive the images or copies of things rather than the things themselves. The notion of practice is then introduced in an attempt to overcome the difficulties in this philosophical theory. If it were not being argued that in perception we directly apprehend the images or copies of things, there would be no need to say that it is in practice that we know whether the copies are true ones. The same word "practice" may be used for (*a*) the difference between a purely theoretical argument and an argument that carries the sort of conviction that emerges in practical action, and (*b*) an alleged passage from mere awareness of sense data (images, photographs, copies, reflections, etc.) to the perception of independently existing physical things, and it is with (*b*) that the philosophical difficulties arise.

Some contemporary Marxist writers appear desirous of abandoning the "copy" element in the Engels-Lenin theory of perception while retaining the emphasis on practice. Thus, Mr. Cornforth, in his *Science versus Idealism*,[33] writes that "the *objects* of sense-perception, the objects *known* through the senses, are material objects, objects of the objective external world," and goes on to suggest that we should not suppose "a set of special non-material sense-objects, private to the sentient mind—whether these are called 'sense-impressions,' 'ideas,' 'sensations,' 'elements,' or whatever they are called by the philosophers who invented them." It should be mentioned, however, that in *Materialism and Empirio-Criticism* Lenin went out of his way to insist on this "copy" relationship. The physicist Helmholtz had suggested that the sensations that physical objects cause in the percipients of them need not be copies of their causes but only non-resembling natural signs or symbols. Lenin, however, would not accept this view (which he called "hieroglyphic materialism"[34]) and wrote: "If sensations are not images of things, but only signs or symbols, which do not resemble them, then Helmholtz's initial materialist premise is undermined; the existence of external objects becomes subject to doubt; for signs or symbols may quite possibly indicate imaginary objects, and everybody is familiar

33. London, 1946, pp. 87–88.
34. *M. and E-C,* p. 290.

with instances of *such* signs or symbols."[35] In support of this, Lenin cites the authority of Engels: "Engels speaks neither of symbols nor hieroglyphs, but of copies, photographs, images, mirror-reflections of things."[36] This would seem to suggest that Lenin believed that the sensations by means of which we perceive material objects are exactly like them, but he goes on to say: "It is beyond doubt that an image cannot wholly resemble the model, but an image is one thing, a symbol, a *conventional sign,* another. The image inevitably and of necessity implies the objective reality of that which it images. 'Conventional sign,' symbol, hieroglyph are concepts which introduce an entirely unnecessary element of agnosticism."[37] This passage shows that Lenin realized that there are different sorts of copy, and different degrees of likeness, and the question therefore arises of the sort and degree of likeness that he thought there must be between a sensation and a physical object. Soviet philosophers generally answer this by referring to the following passage in *Materialism and Empirio-Criticism:* "This is how science views it. The sensation of red reflects ether vibrations of a frequency of approximately 450 trillions per second. The sensation of blue reflects ether vibrations of a frequency of approximately 620 trillions per second. The vibrations of the ether exist independently of our sensations of light. Our sensations depend on the action of the vibrations of ether on the human organ of vision. Our sensations reflect objective reality, i.e. something that exists independently of humanity and of human sensations."[38] On the face of it, ether vibrations and sensations of color are very different from one another, so that it seems odd to suggest that sensed colors are copies, photographs, or mirror-images of vibrations. Soviet philosophers have given some attention to this problem; they reject the "naïve realism" according to which there would exist in the physical world colors and sounds exactly like the colors we see and the sounds we hear, but they have nothing clear to say about what sort of copy or what degree of likeness is involved.[39]

35. Ibid., p. 292.
36. Ibid., p. 290.
37. Ibid., p. 293.
38. Ibid., p. 355.
39. See Gustav A. Wetter, *Der Dialektische Materialismus: Seine Geschichte und sein*

Lenin was more concerned to proclaim the *independent* existence of the physical world than to explain how sensations can copy it, and has bequeathed to his followers some pretty intractable material. However that may be, both Lenin and the Soviet philosophers who follow him distinguish between physical occurrences on the one hand and sensations that copy or reflect them on the other, so that Mr. Cornforth must have been expounding his own opinion rather than the accepted Marxist view in the passages I have just quoted.

It is no great reproach to Lenin that he should have failed to put forward a coherent view about a problem that still puzzles scientists and philosophers. I suspect that his difficulties arise from his agreeing so far with his idealist and phenomenalist opponents that in perceiving we must become aware of entities (images, copies, sense contents, sense data) which are not the physical things themselves. Now we all begin by taking it for granted that it is physical things that we directly perceive—that we see and touch and hear such things as mountains, rocks, and thunderstorms. But as the result of two main lines of argument some people come to believe that what we directly perceive are entities the very existence of which we had not hitherto suspected. The first line of argument arises from considering the things that go on in and about our bodies when we perceive. Living beings, or at any rate animals, perceive, but metals, crystals, and machines do not. For in order to perceive, a suitable bodily equipment is necessary (eye, nerves, brain, etc.), and perception takes place when this bodily equipment is acted upon by some external object. It is possible, however, for something that is at any rate very like perception to take place even though there is no external object that affects the perceptive organs. For example, as Descartes pointed out, a man who has no foot may feel as though he still has a foot. This is thought to be because what finally and directly causes a perception is the nerves and brain, and these may be brought into the condition that causes perception either by an external object or by some condition within the body. Thus the perception of a tree normally arises from an organism's being acted on by a tree, but it may on occasion arise from some in-

---

System in der Sowjetunion, pp. 515–24 (Freiburg, 1952). *Dialectical Materialism,* translated by Peter Heath (London, 1958).

jury to the brain causing a perception *as if* it had been caused by a tree. It is thought that what finally counts in bringing about a perception is the last link in a chain of causation running normally from a stimulus outside the body, but sometimes commencing in some other way. It is therefore concluded that what is *directly* perceived is never a thing like a tree, nor even a set of wave-frequencies, but something quite different, viz., a sense datum that has for its immediate cause a state of the percipient's body. This is one line of argument to show that what we directly perceive is sense data. The second line of argument—called by philosophers "the Argument from Illusion"—briefly is that the direct objects of perception must be something other than material things, since the former frequently have properties which do not belong to the latter. For example, as I look at a penny I see, from most angles, various sorts of colored ellipse. The penny, however, is circular, and as what is elliptical cannot be at the same time circular, what I see cannot be a circular penny, but must be an elliptical sense datum. Philosophers who argue in this way then go on to consider how sense data can be related to material things. It will be seen that the common conclusion that the immediate objects of perception are sense data is reached by two different arguments, but this should not lead us to overlook their common preoccupation with illusions. A very important difference, however, is that the word "sense datum" is, in the first argument, defined in terms of physical causes, animal organisms, and their interactions, whereas in the second argument it is, as it is said, *ostensively* defined as what you see, hear, smell, touch, etc., quite apart from any theories about sense organs and the rest. That is to say, in the second argument "sense datum" is alleged to be defined in such a way that there could not possibly be any doubt that there are such things, since there cannot possibly be any doubt that colored shapes are seen, sounds are heard, and so on.

Some form of the first argument seems to have been accepted by Engels and Lenin, so let us see where it is likely to lead us. As I have just said, in order to say, for the purposes of this argument, what a sense datum is, reference has to be made to material objects, animal organisms, and sense organs. Sense data are entities that arise when certain physical conditions are fulfilled. It would therefore be contradictory to say within the framework of that argument that, while sense data certainly existed, material things were doubtful or non-existent—just as it would be contradictory to say, in ordinary discourse, that gifts certainly existed but that the existence of donors and recipients was a matter for doubt or denial. This is not a play on the derivation of the word "datum," but a plain statement of how the expression "sense datum" is introduced into the sort of argument we are considering. Marxists, therefore, may be regarded as making the valid point that "sense data" or "sensations" are, in this context, terms that bear their meaning by relation to other terms such as physical stimuli, animal organisms, etc., and so could not, without contradiction, be regarded as sole denizens of the world. Another feature of the argument is that *perception* of physical things must be indirect because it takes place after a series of causes has come into play commencing with the external object and ending with some supposed physical modification of the brain. But why *should* perception be regarded as indirect just because the brain's connection with the external stimulus is indirect? It seems to me that there may well have been confusion between the indirect connection that holds between the first and last members of a chain of physical causes on the one hand, and some allegedly indirect perception on the other. It makes sense to apply the word "indirect" to some sorts of knowledge. I may be said to know a man indirectly when I know someone who knows him but have never met the man myself, and knowledge gained by inference, hearsay, or reading may be called indirect by comparison with perceptual knowledge or with acquaintance generally. But in all these cases I might possibly have had direct knowledge; I might have met the man myself, or have gained the knowledge without inference or hearsay. But direct perception is apparently quite impossible, and this suggests, although it does not prove, that the notion of indirect perception is not a clear one. Such difficulties arise, I think, because we think of a chain of causes that runs as follows: external (physical) object—sense organ—nerves—brain—change in brain cell—sense datum—perception of sense datum. The first five members of this series are physical, and then there is a jump to entities of a different status, to sense data and perceptions. And it is hard to resist the conclusion that there *is* a jump of this sort, since becoming conscious of something seems to be quite different from any series of merely physical changes. Sir

Charles Sherrington is surely right when he says: "It is a far cry from an electrical reaction in the brain to suddenly seeing the world around me . . .,"[40] but this is no reason for concluding that we see sense data rather than physical objects. Consciousness is not made any less mysterious by introducing objects of a special, half-way type for it to be directly concerned with.

The second line of argument, the Argument from Illusion, raises rather different problems, and were I to dwell on them I should stretch this already long chapter beyond reasonable bounds. There is one aspect of it, however, on which I should like to comment briefly. The crux of the Argument from Illusion is that it must be sense data, objects distinct from physical objects, that are directly apprehended, since what is directly apprehended usually has features—shapes, sizes, colors, etc.—which are not features of the physical object being perceived. The elliptical shape I see cannot, according to this argument, be the circular penny; the yellow color I see when sick with jaundice cannot be the color of the white walls of my bedroom; the image of it in the mirror is not the penny in my hand; there is no stream the other side of the sandhill—what we saw was a mirage; the mad miser scratching for coins on the pavement was obviously seeing something, but it could not have been real pennies. But perhaps it is a mistake to treat all these cases in the same way. In the first place, mirages and hallucinations appear to involve illusions in a more intensive degree than do perspectival distortions, mirror images, or even jaundice. Indeed, the extension of the term "illusion" to perspectival distortions is probably due to philosophers anxious to discredit sense experience in favor of something else. So far is the word "illusion" from being apt to describe the case of the elliptical appearance of the circular penny, that we may well ask whether we could form any conception of what it would be to perceive a penny or any other physical object *without* perspectival distortion. How *could* anything look exactly the same from all sides and distances? What would it be like to see all things the same size no matter how far off they were? Again, it is very difficult to form any notion of what it could be to perceive all the surfaces of something at once, especially if the shape of each surface is always to remain the

40. *The Physical Basis of Mind*, ed. Peter Laslett, p. 4 (London, 1950).

same. It would seem that physical things are *essentially* things that reveal themselves differently from different distances and points of view.
In the second place, it is misleading in the extreme to regard mirror
images as analogies for the perspectives or appearances of physical
things. For whereas we can, and frequently do, see at the same time
both the object itself and its reflection in a mirror, we can never at
the same time see both the penny's elliptical appearance and its circular shape. Furthermore, perspectival distortions are seen in the mirror, and are for this reason too a different type of thing. Mirrors add
to the ways in which physical objects may appear, but there could be
physical objects without mirrors, although physical things could not
conceivably appear without appearing in different ways from different
places. The mirror's power of multiplying has fascinated the tellers of
stories from Ovid to Carroll and Cocteau, and philosophers too have
fallen under its spell when they allow it to dominate their account of
perception. I suggest, in the third place, that hallucinations should be
linked with mental images and with dreams rather than with the sort of
case already mentioned—unless, indeed, some mirages are collective
hallucinations. For the miser seeing imaginary pennies is like a man
dreaming with his eyes open rather than like a man seeing things in
a mirror. Nor is he like the man with jaundice, for unlike him he sees
what is not there rather than what is there wrongly. When we close our
eyes and remember or call up things that we have seen, some *representative* of it is, as we say, before our minds, and sometimes this representative is a sort of copy like those we experience in dreams. Thus
Turner, when a boy, trained himself to form visual images of the prints
he saw in shop windows so that he could draw them when he got home.
Such images are, so to say, disconnected from their sources in a way
in which perspectives and mirror images are not. It is one thing for
an object to seem or to appear in a certain way, or even to seem what
it is not, and quite another thing for a representative or image to be
observed instead of its original. Those who hold that sense data are
involved in all perception, and still more those who talk of "copies" or
"images," have been influenced by the spell of the enchanted mirror,
and seek to describe waking life in terms of dreams and the dreamlike.
I do not think it is out of place to quote, in illustration of this, the following remarks made by d'Alembert about Berkeley's *Three Dialogues*

between Hylas and Philonous: "At the beginning of the French translation there has been placed an allegorical engraving that is both clever and unusual. A child sees its face in a mirror, and runs to catch hold of it, thinking he sees a real being. A philosopher standing behind the child seems to be laughing at its mistake; and below the engraving we read these words addressed to the philosopher: *Quid rides? Fabula de te narratur.* (Why are you laughing? The story is being told about *you*.)"[41]

That Engels and Lenin held that there were sense data, and that sense data were a sort of reflection, copy, or image of physical things, cannot in the light of the texts be doubted, and I very much doubt whether Marxists today really wish to deny this. However that may be, the view that the immediate objects of perception are sense data is difficult, if not impossible, to reconcile with a realist account of perception. Thus I do not think that Engels and Lenin succeeded in putting forward an adequate account of the sort of view they wished to establish. They saw that a realist account of perception was a first step in establishing a materialist philosophy, but in stating it they did not get much beyond assertions and wishes. There is little point in repetition of the realist platitude by people who are not really interested in the arguments that have led to its denial. We can easily turn away from philosophical problems, but we can only clarify or solve them by philosophical argument.

There are two historical observations I must make before concluding this chapter.

(1) In the *Theses on Feuerbach* (which were not written for publication), and in the *German Ideology* (which was not published until long after Marx and Engels were dead), there are some remarks about perception of the physical world which appear to give the outlines of a theory. In the first of his *Theses on Feuerbach* Marx says that in all materialism up to his time, including that of Feuerbach, the object apprehended by the senses is understood "only in the form of the object or of perception (*Anschauung*); but not as sensuous human (*sinnlich-menschlich*) activity, as practice (*Praxis*), not subjectively." And he goes on to say that in his *Essence of Christianity* Feuerbach had considered only man's "theoretical behavior" as truly human, and had dealt with

41. *Oeuvres,* II, p. 133 (Paris, An XIII–1805).

practice "only in its 'dirty Jewish' manifestation." Again in the fifth of the *Theses* he wrote: "Feuerbach, not satisfied with *abstract thought,* wants perception (*Anschauung*): but he does not grasp our faculty of perception (*Sinnlichkeit*) as practical, human-sensuous activity." This, I suggest, may be read along with passages in the *German Ideology* (written about the same time) in which Marx and Engels criticize Feuerbach for not seeing how the "sensible world around him is not a thing given from all eternity, ever the same, but the product of industry and of the state of society," and go on to say that "unceasing sensuous labor and production" have made nature into something very different from what it was before man came into it. These passages are obscure, and the last one not a little foolish, but the following appear to be the points that are of importance for our present purpose. Feuerbach, whose *Essence of Christianity* (1841) greatly influenced Marx and Engels, had criticized Hegel for depreciating the knowledge we gain through our senses and for preferring philosophical thought to it. Furthermore, in his *Essence of Christianity* Feuerbach maintained that the characteristics that men attribute to God are really human characteristics in an idealized form. In particular he had said the Jewish notion of God as *creative will* indicated a lower stage of human development than the Christian notion of God as *contemplative mind.* (The phrase "dirty Jewish" does not occur in the book.) Marx appears to be saying, in his discussion of all this, that Feuerbach was right to see that perception could not be superseded by mere thought but that he should have gone further and concluded that practical activity cannot be superseded by mere theoretical contemplation. A thoroughgoing materialist, he is suggesting, should not admit the existence of any *purely* theoretical activity in human beings, since this would presuppose some disembodied spiritual force that in fact could not exist. At first sight it seems ridiculous to criticize anyone for not considering how human practical activity has changed the natural world, for it is so very obvious that it has, and we naturally suppose that work on the one hand and awareness or consciousness on the other are very different things. But Marx, in these passages, appears to assert that awareness or consciousness is somehow (he does not say how) inseparable from physical manipulation of the material world. Some Soviet Marxists in the late twenties interpreted Marx as meaning that consciousness just *is* behavior, but this view has not remained in favor. Nevertheless, Marx does seem to be saying that whatever consciousness may be, it is inseparable from the manipulative activities of organisms. Views of this sort are not, of course, confined to Marxists, and in recent years interesting theories have been developed in which perception is regarded as a sort of practical achievement. Marx, however, did not elaborate his suggestions, and Marxists have been faced with the necessity of making the most of the "copy" theory that they have inherited from Engels and Lenin.[42]

(2) In chapter 7 of the *Holy Family* Marx gave a brief account of the growth of modern materialism, and particularly of the French materialism of the Eighteenth Century.[43] He considered Bacon[44] to be the founder of the movement and went on to show how Locke's *Essay concerning Human Understanding* was a decisive influence in the minds of the men who created and led the French Enlightenment, a movement which Marx described as both an attack on the Church and its doctrines and a criticism of the metaphysical thinking that had been so prominent in the preceding century. It was within this movement that the materialist views of Diderot, Helvétius, and d'Holbach were developed. Marx, in this chapter, is concerned primarily with the social bearings of French materialism, and so has no occasion to refer to views about the perception of the material world. I think, however,

---

42. The *Theses on Feuerbach* are printed at the end of Professor Pascal's translation of the *German Ideology* (London, 1942 reprint), but the translations given above are mine. The passage from the latter about the influence of men on the natural world is from pp. 34–36, but in the first phrase I have rendered *sinnlich* by "sensible" as the sense seems to require. The above very brief account of the first *Thesis* is indebted to Professor N. Rotenstreich's invaluable *Marx' Thesen über Feuerbach* (Archiv für Rechts- und Sozialphilosophie, Bern und München, 1951), XXXIX/3 and XXXIX/4. An account of the behaviorist developments of Marx's views in Soviet Russia in the twenties is given in chapter 5 of R. A. Bauer's *The New Man in Soviet Psychology* (Harvard University Press, 1952). Since then, behaviorist theories of mind have been given up there (chap. 6 of the same book).

43. *Marx-Engels Gesamtausgabe* (in future to be abbreviated as M.E.G.A.), I, 3, p. 301.

44. He did not but could have quoted with effect Bacon's statement in *Cogitata et Visa* (1607): ". . . Truth is shown and proved by the evidence of works rather than by argument, or even sense."

that a very brief account of what was said about this by the leading French thinkers of the period will throw some light on the Marxist theory. Marx, like Feuerbach, thought that the leading thinkers of the French Enlightenment had "seen through" metaphysics, and it is reasonable to suppose that they took much the same attitude to idealist accounts of perception. Now Locke had said that all our knowledge is based on "ideas." Ideas became naturalized in France as "sensations." But it soon became apparent that simple-minded theories about sensations and their "external causes" were liable to the criticisms that Berkeley had brought against Locke. Diderot, in his *Letter on the Blind for Those Who Can See* (1749), wrote: "Idealism is a system which, to the shame of the human mind and philosophy, is the most difficult to overcome, though the most absurd of all." He therefore urged Condillac to undertake the refutation of idealism on the basis of the current empiricism, and Condillac's *Treatise on the Sensations* (1754) contained the most notable attempt to do this. In effect, Condillac argued that it is by means of *touch* that we become aware of an external world, and he tried to show how this happens by reference to the double sensation we have when we touch some part of our own body and the single sensations we have when we touch something external to our body. "Touch," he wrote, "teaches the other senses to judge about external objects." This, of course, is no answer to Berkeley's idealism, and Condillac, not very happy about it, later thought that the sensation of a resisting obstacle provided a better defense of realism. D'Alembert, too, was puzzled by the apparent conflict between empiricism and realism, and, distinguishing the question *how* we get knowledge of external objects from the question *whether* such knowledge is demonstrative, answered the first question much as Condillac had done, and the second in the negative. The existence of matter, he said, should be regarded as known to us "by a sort of instinct to which we should abandon ourselves without resistance . . . sensations were given us in order to satisfy our needs rather than our curiosity; in order to make us aware of the relation of external beings to our own being, and not to give us knowledge of those beings in themselves." Turgot, who in 1750 thought he could refute Berkeley, subsequently gave, in the article in the *Encyclopédie* entitled "Existence," a brilliant account of the phenomenalist view. In general, the empiricism of these thinkers led them to phenomenalist conclusions which they mitigated by off-hand references to instinct and practice. The little I have been able to find in the writings of Helvétius and d'Holbach that bears on this matter does not distinguish them from their more eminent contemporaries. All this suggests to me that when Marx and Engels regarded idealism as refuted by practice they meant by "practice" touching and manipulating and the survival value of discriminative sensations, much as their eighteenth century forerunners had done.

II

Marxist Naturalism

1. Basic Ideas of Marxist Naturalism

Just as Marxist realism is the denial of the idealist *theory of knowledge* put forward by Berkeley, and of its phenomenalist offshoots, so Marxist naturalism arises from criticism of Hegel's *speculative* idealism. Hegel believed that it could be shown, by the dialectical method, that the universe as a whole is a rational mind within which matter and mere vegetative and animal life are dependent abstractions. On this view, someone who said that the world is material would be neglecting most of its most significant features, someone who said that it was alive would be neglecting many, but not quite so many of its most significant features, and someone who said, with understanding of what was implied in it, that the world is a mind, would be saying what is true and would not be denying that it had material and animal features too. Hegel claimed that his speculative idealism was the most *complete* philosophy that had hitherto been put forward, that it did justice to what there was of truth in previous philosophies, and that it was superior to Berkeley's in that it put *sense* knowledge in its proper, rather subordinate place. The arguments are elaborate, and difficult to summarize, but their principle is that all views other than the view that the world is Absolute Spirit can be shown to involve contradiction, whereas the theory of Absolute Spirit retains all that is true in each of the more limited views without being itself limited in any important way. Hegel thus thought he had established a sort of philosophical religion, for he held that the Hegelian philosophy was the definitive rational expression of the truths which in Christianity, the highest form of religion, were expressed in imaginative terms only. The element of this view that is most important for our present purposes is the claim to establish by philosophical argument, that is to say by *speculation,* that all conceptions short of the Absolute Idea involved contradictions, and that nature is not an independent being but a moment or aspect of Spirit. "Nature," Hegel wrote in the *Encyclopedia* (§ 248), "in itself, in its concept, is divine, but exists in such a way that its mode of being does not correspond to its concept; on the contrary, nature is the unresolved contradiction. . . . Nature appears as the primary, as immediate being, only to that consciousness which is itself external and immediate, that is, only to the *sensuous* consciousness."

Now in opposition to all this Marxists argue that nature not only *appears* to be primary, as Hegel had said, but that it really *is* primary, and that there is nothing fundamentally misleading in our sense perceptions of it. In his *Ludwig Feuerbach,* Engels argued that there are at bottom only two main philosophies, idealism and materialism. According to the idealists, mind in some form or another is the primary being from which everything else has sprung, while according to the materialists matter is the primary being from which mind has taken its origin. Engels goes on to say that the group of philosophers known as the Young Hegelians turned "back to Anglo-French materialism" in order to develop their criticisms of the Hegelian system, and that the appearance of Feuerbach's *Essence of Christianity* (1841) was decisive in giving form to the materialist outlook of Marx and himself. "Enthusiasm was general; we all became at once Feuerbachians."[1] Now in this book Feuerbach had upheld the two theses mentioned above, viz., that sense experience is trustworthy and reveals nature to us, and that nature is the source of mind and consciousness and stands in no need of a supernatural Creator. More particularly he argued that speculative philosophy is the form that theology takes in an age when natural science has discredited it, and that the explanation of theological doctrines is to be found in the needs and desires of men. "Man," wrote Feuerbach, "—this is the mystery of religion—projects his being into objectivity, and then again makes himself an object to this projected image of himself thus converted into a subject; he thinks of himself, is an object to himself, but as the object of an object, of another being than himself. . . . Thus, in and through God, man has in view himself alone. It is true that man places the aim of his action in God, but God

---

1. *Ludwig Feuerbach*, pp. 27–28 (English translation, London, 1935).

has no other aim of action than the moral and eternal salvation of man; thus man has in fact no other aim than himself. The divine activity is not distinct from the human."[2] From all this a number of closely related topics emerge: (*a*) It is held that sense perception is reliable, and reveals an independently existing material world. (*b*) It is held that nature stands in need of no supernatural Creator, but is itself the source of men and minds. (*c*) It is held that we can improve our knowledge of nature by employing the methods of the natural sciences, but that the methods of theology and speculative philosophy do not lead to knowledge of anything supernatural. (*d*) It is held that a natural account can be given of the religious beliefs of men, and that, in particular, God is an imaginative projection of human needs and desires.

We need spend no longer on (*a*), since we have treated this topic fairly fully in the preceding chapter. But it is important to see how (*b*), (*c*), and (*d*) are connected. Clearly (*b*) is considered to follow from our scientific knowledge, so that the fundamental questions are whether scientific knowledge is to be preferred to theology and speculative philosophy, and whether these latter give any knowledge of the world at all. Thus (*c*) is logically prior to (*b*). (*c*), however, is also logically prior to (*d*). For (*d*) purports to be a psychological (or, as Feuerbach put it, an "anthropological") account of belief in God, and could only be regarded as not "explaining away" such belief if God's existence could be proved by theology or speculative philosophy or (contrary to (*b*) above) by some scientific procedure other than that of psychology or "anthropology." Thus, if the theological and speculative methods are valueless, and if the only way of getting knowledge of the world is by means of the methods of the natural sciences, then belief in God is unfounded unless scientific methods establish it—and the assertion of (*b*) is that they do not—and religious beliefs and practices have to be accounted for in psychological or sociological terms. Let us, then, first discuss (*c*), the Marxist view that the scientific methods are supreme.

2. *The Essence of Christianity,* translated by Marian Evans (George Eliot) (London, 1854), p. 29. This book, which is very important for the understanding of Marxism, will be discussed in Part Two, Chapter I, below.

2. *Science, Philosophy, and Practice*

Marx's opposition to speculative philosophy is particularly apparent in his early writings, such as the *Holy Family* and the *German Ideology*. In the former of these writings (chap. 5, sect. 2, "The Mystery of Speculative Construction") there is a vigorous passage, quite in the vein of Feuerbach, in which the speculative philosopher is depicted as arguing that the substance or reality of apples, pears, strawberries, and almonds is *fruit itself,* an organic identity in difference which develops itself in the forms of the different species of fruit. "While the Christian religion recognizes only one unique incarnation of God, for speculative philosophy there are as many incarnations as there are things; in this way it sees in each sort of fruit an incarnation of the substance, of the absolute fruit. The main interest of the speculative philosopher consists, therefore, in producing the existence of real fruit, and in saying, in a mysterious manner, that there are apples, pears, etc. But the apples, the pears, etc., that we discover in the world of speculation, are only the appearances of apples, of pears, etc., for they are the manifestations of fruit, of the rational abstract entity, and are thus themselves rational, abstract entities. Thus the pleasing thing in speculation is finding in it all the real fruits, but as fruits with a higher mystic value, as fruits sprung from the aether of your brain and not from the natural world, incarnations of fruit, of the absolute subject."[3] Anything of value that there is in the Hegelian philosophy—and Marx thought that there was a good deal—was thus the result, not of Hegel's speculative arguments, but of his great knowledge of history, politics, and art. Speculative philosophers, according to Marx, give the appearance of adding to our knowledge by importing into their systems facts and principles derived from elsewhere. Generalities and abstractions are based on experienced particulars, but the speculative philosopher

---

3. M.E.G.A., I, 3, p. 230. Hegel (*Encyclopedia* § 13) had made the very same point, viz., that there is no "fruitness" except in the various fruits. The source of Marx's view may be seen in the following passage from Feuerbach's *Vorläufige Thesen zur Reform der Philosophie* (1842): "That which is expressed *as* it is, the true stated truly, appears superficial; that which is expressed as it is *not*, the true stated falsely, in reverse, appears profound."

thinks he can reach to a knowledge of real things by manipulating abstractions whose basis he has forgotten. Marx's objection to speculative philosophy is, therefore, that it falsely claims to obtain important knowledge of the world by reasoning that is not openly assisted by observation and experiment. He and Engels go even further than this, however, and pronounce the ineffectiveness of any form of philosophy that claims an independent status. "When reality is depicted," they write in the *German Ideology*, "philosophy as an independent branch of activity loses its medium of existence."[4] Developing an epigram of Feuerbach, they write in another part of the same work: "Philosophy and the study of the real world are related to one another as are onanism and love between the sexes."[5] The position is made clearer by Engels in the *Anti-Dühring* when he writes: "As soon as each separate science is required to get clarity as to its position in the great totality of things and of our knowledge of things, a special science dealing with this totality is superfluous. What still independently survives of all former philosophy is the science of thought and its laws—formal logic and dialectics. Everything else is merged in the positive science of nature and history."[6] In brief, then, Marxists maintain that the growth of the empirical sciences demonstrates the fruitlessness of the speculative method, that the validity of scientific thinking is tested by sense experience, and that the sole task of philosophy is to indicate the nature of scientific thinking ("formal logic and dialectics"). As to scientific thinking itself, the first and fundamental character is its practical nature. According to Engels, it is in practice that our views about the world are confirmed or refuted. Referring to those who raise skeptical doubts about human knowledge, he writes: "The most telling refutation of this as of all other philosophical fancies is practice, viz., experiment and industry. If we are able to prove the correctness of our conception of a natural process by making it ourselves, bringing it into being out of its conditions and using it for our own purposes

---

4. English translation, p. 15.

5. M.E.G.A., I, 5, p. 216. (This is not in the English translation.)

6. *Herr Eugen Dühring's Revolution in Science* (English translation, London, 1934), p. 31.

into the bargain, then there is an end of the Kantian incomprehensible 'thing-in-itself.'"[7] In the paragraph from which these words are quoted, Engels gives two examples of how practice can assure us that we have genuine knowledge of the real world. We really understand the chemistry of a coloring-matter hitherto only found ready-made in nature when we know how to manufacture it by artificial means. Again, the truth of the Copernican system was proved when, the position of a hitherto unknown planet having been calculated in terms of the Copernican theory, the planet was actually found to be there.

The reader with some knowledge of the main trends of modern philosophy will be inclined to say that the view so far expounded is pretty much what in England, France, and the United States is known as positivism. Positivism it certainly is, in its depreciation of theology, its linking of metaphysics with theology, its acceptance of the methods of the natural sciences as the sole means of acquiring genuine knowledge, and in its belief that the scientific method is the method of practice and industry. The substance of Comte's Law of the Three Stages is repeated by Marx, Engels, and Feuerbach, inasmuch as they all believed that in the modern era theological ideas were being dressed up in speculative terms and would be superseded by the positive scientific mode of thinking. Engels' phrase "positive science of nature and history" shows even a verbal similarity. The emphasis on practice is also common to positivism and Marxism, for Bacon's dictum "knowledge is power" is accepted in each. The following passage from Comte's *Course of Positive Philosophy* sets out his position on this matter: ". . . While the common reason was satisfied to grasp, in the course of judicious observation of diverse occurrences, certain natural relations capable of guiding the most indispensable practical predictions, philosophical ambition, disdaining such successes, was hoping to obtain the solution of the most impenetrable mysteries by means of a supernatural light. But, on the contrary, a healthy philosophy, substituting everywhere the search after effective laws for the search after essential causes, intimately combines its highest speculations with the most simple popular notions, so as finally to build up—apart from the

7. *Ludwig Feuerbach* (English translation, London, 1935), pp. 32–33.

difference of degree—a profound mental identity, which no longer allows the contemplative class to remain in its habitual proud isolation from the active mass [*de la masse active*—the *acting* masses]."[8] But Marx himself would not admit any value in the work of Comte. Writing to Engels on 7 July 1866 he says: "I am also studying Comte now, as a sideline, because the English and French make such a fuss about the fellow. What takes their fancy is the encyclopedic touch, the synthesis. But this is miserable compared to Hegel. (Although Comte, as a professional mathematician and physicist, was superior to him, i.e., superior in matters of detail, even here Hegel is infinitely greater as a whole.) And this positivist rot appeared in 1832."[9] And in a letter to Professor Beesly of University College, London, dated June 1871, he writes: "I as a Party man have a thoroughly hostile attitude towards Comte's philosophy, while as a scientific man I have a very poor opinion of it."[10] One would hardly suppose, from these attacks, that Marx and Comte were fully agreed in rejecting speculative philosophy, and that Hegel was the leading speculative philosopher of modern times. Marx, of course, differed from Comte on important matters, notably on politics and dialectics—though even here, as we shall see, the differences between Comte and the Marxists are not as great as the latter maintain— but it is worth considering for a moment why it is that Marxists so vehemently deny this manifest kinship. The Marxist writings are largely polemical, but the objects of attack are not, for the most part, representatives of the orders of society that the Marxists wish to destroy, but rival radicals whose competition they fear. Thus the *Holy Family* is directed against Bruno Bauer and other radical Hegelians; the *German Ideology* is critical of Feuerbach, Max Stirner, and certain socialists of the eighteen forties; the *Poverty of Philosophy* is an attack on Proudhon, whose socialist views had been held up to admiration in the *Holy Family;* Eugen Dühring, who because of his criticisms of the Hegelian elements in Marxism, was so fiercely attacked by the kindly Engels, was a determined opponent of speculative philosophy and of the cur-

8. *Cours de Philosophie Positive,* vol. 6, p. 650 (Paris, 1842).
9. *Selected Correspondence, 1846–1895. Karl Marx and Friedrich Engels* (London, 1943).
10. Ibid.

rent orthodoxies; Lenin's *Materialism and Empirio-Criticism* was directed against members of his own party who considered they were supporting a scientific view of the world; and in our own day Marxists are busy criticizing Logical Positivism and kindred views with which they clearly have much in common. I have already pointed out that Lenin's attitude toward the philosophy of Mach is in part that of the party administrator who wishes to be disencumbered of what he regards as distracting subtleties. It is important to bear in mind, however, that it is a Marxist view—which will be considered in Part Two—that philosophical theories are the expression of class interests. It is therefore never safe to welcome a set of philosophical views on the ground that they fit in with those that one has independently come to regard as true. For they may be linked with other views which reflect different class interests, so that approval of them may weaken the Marxist philosopher's exclusive devotion to the working class and its Party. Marx's opposition to a philosophy with which he had so much in common was thus mainly due to his dislike of Comte's political and social doctrines, which made it inopportune to admit the kinship. In the Soviet Union today, the procedure thus followed by Marx, Engels, and Lenin is vigorously advocated in leading circles. Thus the late Mr. Zhdanov, in his speech to the philosophers about Professor Aleksandrov's *History of Philosophy* (which had been awarded the Stalin prize) referred to "the passive, meditative, academic character" of the book, and criticized it for its "absence of party spirit," rhetorically asking ". . . did not Lenin teach us that 'materialism carries with it, so to speak, party spirit, compelling one, in any evaluation of events, to take up directly and openly the viewpoint of a definite social group'?"[11] Incidentally, Mr. Zhdanov defined philosophy, much as a positivist would, as "the science of thought and its laws, including epistemology."

The efficacy of the scientific method of hypothesis, observation, and experiment is no longer a matter of controversy, although much remains to be said about how its various features are related to one another. There still is controversy, however, concerning the applicability of the method to human affairs, and this question will have to

---

11. "Andrei Zhdanov's Speech to the Philosophers: An Essay in Interpretation," by J. and M. Miller, *Soviet Studies*, vol. 1, no. 1.

be touched on in Part Two. Must it also be admitted that there is no longer any place for speculative philosophy, or as it is more often called today, metaphysics? Hegel himself made the *obvious* reply to the opponents of metaphysics when, in § 38 of the *Encyclopedia,* a section devoted to empiricism, he wrote: "The fundamental mistake of scientific empiricism is always this, that it makes use of the metaphysical categories of matter, force, one, many, universality, of the infinite, etc., and furthermore draws conclusions under the guidance of these categories, at the same time presupposing and applying the forms of inference, yet with all this it does not recognize that it contains and pursues a metaphysics of its own and is making unconscious use of those categories in a thoroughly uncritical manner." Present-day "scientific empiricists" would not admit that they use such categories uncritically; on the contrary, they would claim that they are able to give an account of them that accords well with their point of view. This raises one of the major questions of modern philosophy, and we cannot here do more than indicate some very general grounds for not accepting the empiricist-positivist point of view as a presupposition of philosophical good faith as some of its exponents seem to require. In the first place, it seems to me that insufficient attention has been given to the question what sort of theory positivism, or any other philosophical view, must be. Clearly philosophical theories are not confined to particular aspects or areas of the world as scientific theories are, but are in some way *about* science and common sense. This is what the idealist philosophers of the nineteenth century meant when they said that philosophy is *reflective,* and it has been recognized, in one way or another, ever since Plato. Furthermore, there are bodies of thought such as history and law that have reached a high level of elaboration without being regarded as parts of science or as mere common sense, and these too need to be embraced in philosophical theory if it is not to remain one-sided or incomplete. Law, of course, is practical, and in many ways akin to morals, and we thus see that philosophical thinking must enquire into the connections of theoretical rational activities with practical rational activities. We may say that philosophy must be thinking in its most *self-conscious* form, and that such thinking must necessarily be very different from the thinking that is directly immersed in *particular* enquiries. We should not assume that it must be like the thought of mathematicians or physicists. As one or another special science becomes prominent, however, philosophers will tend to be influenced by their understanding—which may not always be adequate—of the notions current in it, and there will be mathematicizing periods, psycho-analyzing periods, and so on. In our day, many philosophers have been influenced by the conceptions of symbolic logic, and have sought to make use of them in dealing with the traditional problems of philosophy. There is much to be gained by trying out such specialized notions in the philosophical sphere, but it must always be done tentatively, with no more zeal than is necessary to carry such trains of thought effectively forward, since anything beyond this is an example of the very dogmatism or unselfconsciousness that philosophy is meant to correct. In the second place, then, I think that many people expect or claim an unreasonable degree of confidence for philosophical views. There are two main reasons why philosophy should not be considered an exact science. One is that the rules to be followed in thinking about thought (or talking about talk) are not—apart from the rules of formal logic—as obvious or as settled as are the rules of the primary thought activities. We are hardly entitled to have, for example, the degree of confidence in a theory about the nature of deductive inference as we may have in the validity of a particular deduction. The second reason is that, in so far as philosophy is concerned with matters more fundamental than those of any single science or range of activity, an element of what may be called *judgment* must enter in, as, say, the moral or historical point of view is related to the biological or physical in such a problem as that of free-will or of the nature of mind. Something akin to tact or taste is bound to be required, and it is this, I believe, that Hegel had in mind when he criticized the rigid categories of the Understanding by contrast with the more flexible ones of the Reason. (Hume seems sometimes to think of the Imagination in similar terms.) It is proper that many philosophers should be reluctant to say such things, since they rightly feel that, if dwelt upon, they could lead to a renewal of the uncontrolled speculation, the quasi-intellectual whims, of German "romantic" philosophy. It is right that rigor should be sought, but not right to impose it on unsuitable material. A third point to bear in mind is that we live at a time when scientific activity is more influential than ever before, so that philosophers, if they are to avoid deception by what Marx called "the illusion of the epoch," must take special care to distinguish between the power of science to discover and its power to impress. The age being as it is, our ideas of what is reasonable in these highly abstract regions of thought are likely to be influenced more than they should be by the might rather than by the rationality of science. It is useful, therefore, on occasion, to correct the bias somewhat, and to regard with perhaps exaggerated skepticism the arguments of those numerous thinkers who are positivists by inclination or as a practical principle. It is all the more important to do this if, as I have suggested above, the grounds for deciding between possible views at the highest level of philosophical abstraction are rational in a sense that has affinity with taste or tact as well as with formal logic. In such matters the barrier between reason and prejudice must be very thin.

Earlier in this section I mentioned Engels' view that scientific theories are established by "practice, viz., experiment and industry," along with his suggestion that we have full knowledge of something only when we make it. Now it is quite clear that both positivists and Marxists oppose practice to speculation. Speculation is the "arm-chair" activity of *mere* thinking. Speculative thought consists of such activities as imagining, considering, defining, and concluding. The man who engages in this sort of thinking does not test his conjectures or conclusions by reference to what goes on out of sight of his arm-chair. His line of argument rather is: "That is how things *must* be really, however they may *appear* to be." With him is to be contrasted the man who, perhaps also from an arm-chair, puts forward a view about how things work, but who, having done this, gets up from his chair and traverses ground to look or touch or listen, so as to ascertain whether the things work as he has said they do. He, or his agents, must walk, climb, lift up stones or make holes in the ground, pull things to pieces or mix them together, take measurements, look through microscopes or telescopes, whereas the speculator, like the mathematician, does not need to do these things. The things that the *mere* thinker does not do and that the other man does do may quite appropriately be called "practice." This is the sort of practice involved in the second of Engels' examples. Someone who accepts the Copernican hypothesis calculates on its basis the existence of a planet, but this remains *mere* calculation, unpractical paperwork, until the existence of the planet has been verified by someone who sees it through a telescope. "Practice" here means the verifying of hypotheses, that is to say, of suggested theories, emphasis being placed on the need for someone to bestir himself physically, to move or arrange things, or to use instruments of observation. Thus Engels' second example illustrates the "union of theory and practice" by reference to the generally accepted methods of the empirical sciences. There is nothing in all this that would not be accepted by any educated person—though there is room for a good deal of discussion about *the precise rôle* of the observation or experiment—and the critic of phenomenalism will be glad to point out that verifying is something that involves moving and manipulating and the use of physical means, so that it would be circular to use the notion of verifiability, as some phenomenalists have done, in analyzing the notion of a physical object. "Verifying," when used in the phenomenalist theory, is a philosophical, not a common sense, word, and requires us to give a clear meaning to the term "sense datum," which is far from easy.

Engels' first example, however, may be taken to suggest that a theory is not fully established until the things it is about can actually be made by human beings. Thus the practice necessary to complete mere theory would be manufacture as well as verification. From this it would follow, for good or ill, that theories about planets could never be as adequate as theories about dyes (Comte thought this, though for a rather different reason), since the latter can be made whereas it is unlikely that planets will ever be produced by human beings. It would hardly be maintained, I imagine, that ability to manufacture is in itself a proof of adequate knowledge, for if it were, then an intuitive cook or peasant distiller would know more than a physiologist or chemist. Can it, then, be reasonably held that physical things and processes are only incompletely understood until they have been or could be manufactured? In a perfectly trivial sense this may be admitted, since until the knowledge of how to make a thing has been acquired knowledge of it is, to that extent, defective. In the same way, knowledge of carrots is defective until the weight is known of all the carrots in the world, though it has to be admitted that knowledge of how to make something is generally more closely linked with a scientific understanding of it than such knowledge of carrots is linked with a scientific understanding of them.

Scientific understanding often, but not always, shows the way toward manufacture. The knowledge of how to make them is extremely useful knowledge to have of things that we want to have, and therefore great efforts are made to discover how to make them. In this way, human desires have led to mechanical inventions and the setting up of industrial plants. Scientific knowledge is then used to improve these industrial plants, and the plants can often be used to produce instruments which help the advance of scientific knowledge. Thus there is set up a process in which industry serves science and science serves industry. But this is far from demonstrating that science is an offshoot or sub-species of industry. Science has been developed by men whose aim was to understand rather than to make, and their activity is more like that of the consumers of industrial products than that of their makers. The plant used by the scientist supplements his sense organs, whereas that of the industrialist supplements his muscles. A scientist is not a practical man in the same sense that an industrialist is, for, if the scientist makes, it is in order to know, whereas the industrialist uses his knowledge in order to make.

In our discussion of the Marxist theory we have now distinguished four meanings of "practice." The first was that in which it stood for the common sense which cannot be shaken by fine-spun skeptical argumentation. The second meaning of the word was an alleged passage, in perception, from an "image" or "copy" to a real grasp of an independently existing physical object. In its third sense the word meant the process of verifying hypotheses by means of observation and experiment. Fourthly, the word was used to stand for that mode of manufacture which, by completing the process of verification, linked science with industry. To conflate these together in the slogan "union of theory and practice" is to invite and spread confusion. To distinguish them is to enable the true to be separated from the false. We have seen that it makes good sense to say that practice refutes skepticism about material things, and that empirical science is a practical activity by comparison with mathematics and mere speculation. The "practice," however, that is supposed to take us from "image" to material thing, is an expedient required to patch up an incoherent theory of perception, and the attempt to identify science and industry is only a plausible sophism.

3. *Science and the Supernatural*

We must now briefly consider the Marxist view that nature stands in need of no supernatural Creator, but is itself the source of everything, including men and minds. According to Marxists, theism is a form of idealism, since idealism is the view that matter depends on spirit, and theism is the view that matter and created minds depend on a divine spirit that gave them being. Now although Marxists have not, as far as I am aware, examined the arguments for the existence of God in any detail, I think it is fairly clear that when they hold that nature is not a creation of spirit but its source, they base their view on the assumption that the empirical sciences reveal nothing of the existence and operations of God but show that mind is dependent on certain types of physical organism which have arisen comparatively late in the evolution of the world. Thus they hold (i) that the only way of finding out about what exists is by experience and the methods of the empirical sciences, and (ii) that the empirical sciences do not reveal a supernatural cause of nature. In addition, however, they hold (iii) that the scientific study of man and his situation shows how the illusory belief in God's existence has arisen. Engels in *Ludwig Feuerbach* argues as if Feuerbach's account of the origin of belief in God, and Tylor's animistic theory of religion, were sufficient to show that belief in God is untenable. But in themselves "anthropological" and psychological accounts of how men come to believe in God do not disprove the existence of God. For such accounts may be regarded as descriptions of the natural origins of belief in God which supplement but do not disturb the metaphysical proofs of natural theology. It might be argued *both* that man "projects" his conception of an ideal man, *and* that the traditional arguments for the existence of God are singly or collectively successful. Engels, however, like Marx and Feuerbach, regarded the traditional arguments for the existence of God as *speculative* thinking, so that their rejection of speculative philosophy—today generally called metaphysics—was *a fortiori* a rejection of natural theology. On their view, that is, the methods of the empirical sciences are the only effective ones for exploring the world. Thus Marxist atheism is a consequence of Marxist positivism, and the central and decisive thesis of the Marxist philosophy is the denial of all forms of speculative philosophy in favor of the methods of the empirical sciences. This is a feature of Marxism which, in a world where the natural sciences are so obviously influential, has emphasized its accord with the spirit of the time. Positivism is the orthodoxy of a technological age, and the positivistic component of Marxism is sufficient to recommend it to a very wide public.

Must we then accept the view that the empirical sciences do not reveal a supernatural cause of nature? Such a cause would have to be either one of the objects studied in those sciences or else a hypothesis which they rendered more or less probable. It would be agreed by all parties that no such being is among the observed objects of the empirical sciences, as are trees, rocks, and stars. These are objects of the common sense world, and stand in need of no scientific argumentation in order to be accepted as parts of the real world. Objects such as genes and electrons do not appear in the common sense world of trees, rocks, and stars, and are only believed to exist as the result of complex though convincing argumentation. A supernatural first cause, however, does not figure among such objects either, for it would be more recondite than they, and their source no less than the source of the things in the world of everyday common sense. If, therefore, a supernatural cause of nature were to enter into the considerations of men of science, it could only be as a rather desperate hypothesis reluctantly employed to account for some very general feature of the world. It is idle, I suggest, to speculate further on this aspect of the matter, since it is only within the context of detailed scientific enquiry that such a hypothesis could take on definite shape. On the face of it, however, it appears less improbable that some form of theistic hypothesis involving creation might be called for in the cosmological enquiries of astronomers than elsewhere. To call such a hypothesis "theistic" is, perhaps, going too far, since it is most unlikely that a hypothesis framed in such circumstances would point to a being with the personal and moral characteristics usually attributed to God. Indeed, the more the hypothesis was bound up with specifically scientific conceptions (e.g., electrons or nebulae), the less connection it would have with such conceptions as benevolence or forgiveness.

It is very important to notice that being empirical is not necessarily the same thing as being scientific. An argument or notion may be based on experience, and have all the authority that such a basis can lend, and yet not form part of any recognized empirical science. This is the case with most of the notions and arguments of everyday life. A large part of our empirical knowledge is in terms of the common objects we live among, the objects of human concern, whether natural, such as trees and hills, or artificial, such as houses and roads. Now whereas some of the arguments of natural theology are highly technical, and employ unusual terms such as "necessary" and "contingent," others are empirical, i.e., based on experience, but do not fall within the ambit of any empirical science. The Argument from Design and the various Arguments from Moral Experience are of this nature. In the former the argument is from alleged similarities between the results of human workmanship on the one hand, and the structure of the physical world, or of parts of it not fashioned by human beings, on the other. In the latter, the moral beliefs of men are taken as data. In neither case is there any need, in formulating the argument, to refer to objects or conceptions that are specifically "scientific," although some people have thought that the Argument from Design can be *strengthened* by so doing. Thus, the general, positivistic rejection of speculative philosophy or metaphysics on the ground that it is an attempt to conjure conclusions about matters of fact from baseless premises, does nothing, in itself, to shake the strength of such empirically based arguments. The arguments in question may not be satisfactory, but they are not idle or senseless, and can claim to be empirical in spite of not forming part of any of the empirical sciences.

Granted that astronomy or some other natural science might conceivably need to make use of the hypothesis of an extra-natural cause of nature, and granted also that empirical arguments that do not form part of any special science might conceivably lead to theistic conclusions, we may still ask the further question: "Could there conceivably be a science of the supernatural comparable with the natural sciences in its objectivity and predictive power?" It is certainly the lack of such a science that leads many people to consider that theological enquiry is not worth the trouble of attention. They think that if anything could be found out about such matters, agreed findings would already have been reached and methods found of making predictions. The prophet would be believed if he correctly foretold the results of horse races, and when he protests that God is not interested in horse races, the doubters feel that a winning sequence would nevertheless increase their faith. The whole topic is rendered particularly obscure because of the implications of our vocabulary. Very largely as a result of the growth of science and the spread of the positivistic outlook, the expressions "science" and "the supernatural" tend to be regarded as mutually exclusive, so that the phrase "science of the supernatural" comes very near to being self-contradictory. This is because we tend to regard as part of nature whatever is discovered by the methods of the natural sciences. Thus we tend to regard "psychical research" as the attempt to bring to light hitherto insufficiently confirmed natural occurrences rather than as the search for the supernatural. This may be an effect of using playing-cards and statistical techniques in the study of telepathy and precognition. If the occurrence of such things were established by these methods, and if the conditions of their occurrence could be ascertained, we should be inclined to say that our knowledge of *nature* had thereby been extended. It would be as if a magician's formula were after all found to work, not only once and for some specific occasion, but always under given conditions. Magic verified would become science, in accordance with Frazer's dictum: "Magic is a false system of natural law as well as a fallacious guide of conduct; it is a false science as well as an abortive art."

If this were all, however, we should have to say that a science of the supernatural could only be understood as a science of what is unusual and particularly difficult to verify. But clearly we should not say this, for it is only *certain sorts* of unusual or latent things that would be regarded as supernatural. Positrons, for example, were difficult to discover, and manatees are rare, but neither is a class of supernatural being. To be classed as supernatural a being would have to be some sort of mind, not embodied in a normal manner, and capable of effecting changes in the natural world by means not available to humans or animals. Thus a supernatural being would be a disembodied or abnormally embodied personal being whose modes of operation in the physical world were not confined to the human or animal ones. If it were to be established that human beings can foresee the future, know telepathically, and move distant objects by merely willing to do so, then manifestations of these powers would only be called supernatural if they were the work of disembodied spirits, or of unnaturally embodied ones, such as talking trees. If a man were to dream of his dead father, to feel himself impelled to write an automatic script, and to find that this script, in his father's characteristic style, enabled him to discover some matter that only his father could have known, it would be evidence, though not conclusive evidence, that his father's mind had survived bodily death. If all the inhabitants of the British Isles woke up one morning recollecting an identical dream, and if the dream were to the effect that, unless they all refrained from drinking water until midday, Mount Snowdon would be split in half at midday precisely; and if some people were widely known to have drunk water before midday, and if Mount Snowdon was observed to split in half at midday precisely, this would be pretty strong evidence for the existence of a powerful being capable of communicating a threat or warning and of carrying out a spectacular task without the normal means. If such striking things happened from time to time, so as to render improbable any suggestion of coincidence, then we should feel there were strong grounds for believing in the existence of a powerful supernatural being. In a society where a great deal is known of the normal operations of nature, the type of event that would be taken as evidence for the supernatural would have to be extremely peculiar. It would weaken the force of the "miracle," for example, if Mount Snowdon split in two in the course of a severe earthquake, for then, in mid-twentieth-century England, *natural* causes would be widely presumed. Further, the prophecies or warnings would have to be in unmistakable terms. A disembodied superhuman being would have to adopt different methods to manifest itself in Detroit from those that would suffice in Calcutta or Killarney. Again, inasmuch as supernatural beings would be *minds,* our knowledge of them would have to be of the same general nature as our knowledge of human minds, for unless there were some analogy from the behavior of human minds, we should have no ground whatever for belief in disembodied minds. Thus, if there were to be a science of the supernatural, it would have to be analogous to the sciences of mind rather than to the natural sciences. The contrast between the social sciences and the natural sciences is not, of course, the same contrast as that between the supernatural and the natural, but it would be a complete misconception of what is possible to condemn theology for not being like the natural sciences. Furthermore, as it is obvious that it is the more mechanical and habitual aspects of human behavior that are amenable to experimental-scientific treatment, so a science of the supernatural would be more readily built up as a science of any *sub-human* supernatural there might be than of superhuman beings with high moral or aesthetic capabilities. If psychical researchers ever came to investigate spirit messages of a high intellectual, moral, or aesthetic value, psychical research would be becoming experimental theology.

We are now in a position to deal briefly with Lenin's view, already mentioned in Chapter I, Section 2, that "the electrical theory of matter" is perfectly compatible with materialism and does nothing to render it unacceptable. Lenin had in mind philosophers and physicists who, when it had been shown that the basis of the physical world is not atoms moving in space but something describable rather in terms of waves and energy, concluded that "matter" has disappeared and that materialism is therefore false. According to Lenin, all this is beside the point. For on his view, "the *sole* 'property' of matter—with whose recognition philosophical materialism is bound up—is the property of being *an objective reality*, of existing outside our mind."[12] Indeed, Lenin considers that the electro-magnetic theory of matter gives greater support to *dialectical* materialism than does the atomic theory.[13] Lenin's phrasing here is loose and unguarded, for it would imply that whatever was discovered by use of the scientific methods must be material, that "matter" just means "whatever has objective reality—whatever can be established as really existing." It would follow that if ghosts were verified by fully satisfactory tests, then they would be material things, and that human minds are necessarily material because we have unassailable evidence that they exist. I think that there is a certain impetus in our language toward using the word "matter" in this very wide sense, so as to regard as material anything that common sense and the natural sciences accept as real. This impetus is due to the fundamental character of physics in the hierarchy of the natural sciences,

---

12. *M. and E-C*, p. 317.

13. "Modern physics is in travail; it is giving birth to dialectical materialism." Ibid., p. 365.

and to the constant success that has resulted from extending physical and chemical conceptions into the biological realm. The tendency may be seen in the following remark of Engels: "The real unity of the world consists in its materiality, and this is proved not by a few juggling phrases, but by a long and protracted development of philosophy and natural science."[14] To use the word "material" as equivalent to "real" or "objective," however, is to invite all sorts of confusion. In particular, it tends to blind us to the extraordinary difference there is between intelligent and purely mechanical or inanimate behavior. The main reason why the electro-magnetic theory of matter does not disprove materialism is that the behavior of electrons, protons, neutrons, etc., while not reducible to that of solid atoms in empty space, is still not, as far as can be judged, the manifestation of mind or soul. Scientific research could only lead to the "dissolution of matter" in any non-tautological and interesting sense of the word, by showing some form of intelligence at work in things. Natural science could only reveal the supernatural by becoming a moral science too. And as the very notions involved in accurate discussion of the sub-atomic world are so very remote from such conceptions as "person," "will," "purpose," etc., it is not very likely that signs of intelligence and purpose will be found in that quarter. For our notions of mind and spirit are, as I have already indicated, framed in terms of the common-sense world of people, trees, and mountains, not in terms of recondite physical conceptions.

4. Marxist Dialectics

It is a remarkable feature of the Marxist philosophy that, although it discards Hegel's speculative idealism, it retains at least some of the terminology of his dialectical method. Marxists must therefore think that the dialectical method is compatible with the methods of the empirical sciences, even if not actually identical with them. Yet it is perfectly clear that Hegel does not use the methods of the empirical sciences in his major discussions of nature, man, and society. Fortunately, how-

14. *Anti-Dühring*, p. 53.

ever, Stalin, in the fourth chapter of the *History of the Communist Party of the Soviet Union*,[15] has given a general account of the Marxist theory of dialectics which goes some way toward solving the puzzle. According to Stalin, "dialectics is the direct opposite of metaphysics." Now the word "metaphysics" is today most often used to mean the same as "speculative philosophy," so that it would be natural to suppose that Stalin, in this sentence, is opposing dialectics to speculative philosophy as practiced by Hegel or Leibniz. If this were so, then dialectics would be linked with the scientific method in opposition to what is regarded as idle thinking that evades control by experience. I have no doubt that this association helps to recommend dialectics in some "progressive" circles, but in fact Stalin's usage is taken from Engels' *Anti-Dühring*, in which the following passage occurs: "To the metaphysician, things and their mental images, ideas, are isolated, to be considered one after the other apart from each other, rigid, fixed objects of investigation given once for all. He thinks in absolutely discontinuous antitheses. His communication is 'Yea, yea, Nay, nay, for whatsoever is more than these cometh of evil.' For him a thing either exists, or it does not exist; it is equally impossible for a thing to be itself and at the same time something else. Positive and negative absolutely exclude one another; cause and effect stand in an equally rigid antithesis one to the other. At first sight this mode of thought seems to us extremely plausible, because it is the mode of thought of so-called sound common sense. But sound common sense, respectable fellow as he is within the homely precincts of his own four walls, has most wonderful adventures as soon as he ventures out into the wide world of scientific research. Here the metaphysical mode of outlook, justifiable and even necessary as it is in domains whose extent varies according to the nature of the object under investigation, nevertheless sooner or later always reaches a limit beyond which it becomes one-sided, limited, abstract, and loses its way in insoluble contradictions. And this is so because in considering individual things it loses sight of their connections; in contemplating their

15. Pp. 106–9. As the quotations that follow come from these pages, there is no need for us to give references to each one. This chapter is reprinted in *Dialectical and Historical Materialism*, Little Stalin Library, No. 4 (London, 1941).

existence it forgets their coming into being and passing away; in looking at them at rest it leaves their motion out of account; because it
cannot see the wood for the trees."[16] Taking this use of the word "metaphysics" for granted, Stalin, in the work just cited, mentions four ways
in which the Marxist dialectic is opposed to metaphysics. In the first
place, whereas in metaphysics things are regarded as joined in "accidental agglomeration" and as "unconnected with, isolated from, and
independent of each other," according to the Marxist dialectic things
are "organically connected with, dependent on, and determined by
each other," and can only be properly understood as such. In the second place, according to the Marxist dialectic nature is in "continuous
movement and change," so that a proper understanding of things requires them to be grasped "from the standpoint of their movement,
their change, their development, their coming into being and going
out of being." The implication is that according to metaphysics nature
is in a state of "rest and immobility, stagnation and immutability." The
third proposition of Marxist dialectics mentioned by Stalin is that "the
process of development" is one in which there is passage "from insignificant and imperceptible quantitative changes to open, fundamental changes, to qualitative changes; a development in which the qualitative changes occur not gradually, but rapidly and abruptly, taking
the form of a leap from one state to another; they occur not acciden-
tally, but as the natural result of an accumulation of imperceptible and
gradual quantitative changes." The implication is drawn this time that
according to metaphysics processes of development take place "as a
movement in a circle," as "a simple repetition of what has already occurred" (see page 69 below). Finally, Marxist dialecticians hold that
"internal contradictions are inherent in all things and phenomena of
nature," and that "the struggle between these opposites, the struggle
between the old and the new, between that which is dying away and
that which is being born, between that which is disappearing and that
which is developing, constitutes the internal content of the process of

---

16. *Anti-Dühring*, pp. 27–28. It will be noticed that, now that Engels is talking about dialectics, common sense, so important in establishing realism and
materialism, is put down somewhat. There is a difficulty here for Marxism.

development, the internal content of the transformation of quantitative changes into qualitative changes." By implication, therefore, the view of metaphysics is that struggle and contradiction are not inherent in everything.

Summarizing, we may say that according to metaphysics, as expounded by Marxists, things are independent of one another, both static and gradual, and non-contradictory, whereas according to Marxist dialectics they are organically interconnected, dynamic, sudden, and contradictory.

It is, of course, obvious that these contentions are of special importance in the *social* sphere. Marxists, however, believe that they are basic principles that apply to inanimate nature as well as to human societies. In the next following sections I shall be concerned with their general bearing on nature as a whole rather than with their bearing on the merely human part of it.

5. *"Metaphysics"*

As I have already indicated, the word "metaphysics" is generally used to mean (*a*) philosophy itself, as the study of first principles, and (*b*) speculative philosophy, i.e., the philosophy which claims to reach conclusions about the world by *a priori* argument. But the use of the word which Stalin takes over from Engels differs from both of these, and I will now make some suggestions about its sources.

Both Marx and Engels learned philosophy from men who had studied in the Hegelian school, and we should therefore first turn to Hegel for the origin of this piece of nomenclature. Engels makes this clear when in his *Ludwig Feuerbach* he refers to "the old method of investigation and thought which Hegel calls 'metaphysical,' which preferred to investigate *things* as given, as fixed and stable." Now Hegel used the word "metaphysics" in the two ordinary senses already mentioned, and maintained that those philosophers who disclaim belief in any first principles or in any unverifiable truths must nevertheless presuppose a metaphysic into which they do not enquire. Thus in § 98 of the *Encyclopedia* he says that in modern times a good many political philosophers presuppose an atomistic metaphysics: and in the notes to this section he remarks that, since everyone who thinks must have some metaphysics, the important thing is to have the right one. In fact Hegel believed that in his system logic and metaphysics were shown to be one. In his *Science of Logic,* however, and in the logical part of the *Encyclopedia,* he writes about "the former metaphysics" (*die vormalige Metaphysik*). By this he meant such pre-Kantian metaphysical systems as that of Christian Wolff, in which the attempt had been made to establish definite conclusions as to the nature of being in general (Ontology), the soul (Pneumatology), the world (Cosmology), and God (Natural Theology), by means of rigorous deductions from propositions the terms of which had been clearly defined. This form of metaphysics, Hegel thought, was an attempt to apply mathematical or quasi-mathematical methods of reasoning to subjects they were not fitted for. This procedure, he agreed with Kant, was improperly dogmatical, and, again in agreement with Kant, he held that it was characteristic of the Understanding as distinct from the Reason. The categories of the Understanding are rigidly distinguished from one another and are accepted, in this sort of reasoning, pretty much at their face value from "popular conceptions." A critical examination of them shows, however, that they are not disconnected but can only be adequately grasped in their connection with one another. Thus, for example, according to the Understanding the world is either finite or infinite; but according to the Reason the notions of finite and infinite are not exclusive of one another. On Hegel's view, accordingly, the dialectical method of speculative philosophy "carried out the principle of totality." In § 80 of the *Encyclopedia* he writes: "Thought, as Understanding, remains with the firm and definite distinctions of things one against the other; it treats this form of limited abstract as having real existence." In § 81 he writes: "The Dialectical stage is that in which these finite characters are superseded and pass into their opposites." In § 82 he writes: "The Speculative stage, or stage of Positive Reason, apprehends the unity of properties in their opposition, the affirmation that is contained in their dissolution and transition." That Engels used the word "metaphysics" to mean something like Hegel's "former metaphysics" may readily be seen by referring back to the passage from the *Anti-Dühring* quoted in the previous section.

But of course Engels does not, as Hegel did, condemn abstract metaphysics in terms of a more satisfactory speculative philosophy. The

more satisfactory thing with which Engels compares it is a dialectics of
nature that is at the same time empirical and materialistic. Here, I suggest, he may well have been influenced from other quarters. As early as
the seventeenth century, the adjective "metaphysical" had been used
(by Bossuet among others) in a pejorative sense to mean "too abstract,"
and analogously the noun "metaphysics" had been used to mean the
misuse of abstract terms. In the nineteenth century this use of the
term was taken over by Comte and turned into a technical term of his
philosophy. According to Comte, human thought had passed through
two preparatory phases, and was about to enter upon a third and final
one. The preparatory phases were the theological, in which explanations of natural events were in terms of gods, and the transitional metaphysical phase, in which gods were replaced by abstract principles. At
the positive stage—Hegel, it will be recalled, had used the word "positive" for the highest stage of *speculative* thinking—explanations were in
terms of laws based on the facts themselves, and not in terms of causes,
whether gods or hypothetical principles. Positive, i.e., genuinely scientific, knowledge, is, furthermore, always regarded as relative, i.e., as
provisional. Whereas at the metaphysical stage of knowledge the claim
is made to know some things absolutely, anyone who has advanced to
the positive stage is aware that any single scientific proposition is modi-
fiable in the light of further discoveries. Thus, where positive knowledge is relative, metaphysical pseudo-knowledge is abstract and absolute. Comte gave as examples of metaphysical theories the theory of
natural rights, and the individualistic *laissez-faire* economic science of
the early nineteenth century. The exponents of these theories, he held,
not being concerned with real individuals but with abstractions invented by themselves, falsely believed that individuals could be understood in abstraction from their society and the stage of civilization it
had reached, and that the laws of economics were independent of the
more complex laws of society as a whole. Central to Comte's use of the
word "metaphysics," therefore, is the notion of thought which errs by
isolating what is in fact joined and by fixing what is in fact fluid. The
likeness to Hegel's "the former metaphysics" is apparent, but whereas
Hegel's contrast was between abstract metaphysical thinking and concrete metaphysical thinking, Comte's was between abstract metaphysical thinking and positive thinking that was not metaphysical in any

sense at all. The Marxist view is that genuinely empirical and scientific thinking is dialectical, so that it is possible to think dialectically without falling into the quicksands of speculation. We may see in the Marxist view, indeed, an exaltation of the methods of the empirical sciences by applying to them epithets which had previously added distinction to the higher flights of Hegelian speculation.

A further point to be observed in the Marxist notion of "metaphysics" is that it is not a consistent view. For the implication of the second characteristic of dialectics is that according to metaphysics nature is in a state of "rest and immobility, stagnation and immutability," whereas the third characteristic of dialectics implies that according to metaphysics things develop "as a movement in a circle," as "a simple repetition of what has already occurred." But clearly if nature is immobile and immutable, it does not move at all, whether in circles or by repetition, and if it moves in circles or repeats itself then it is not immobile or immutable. No one with any intelligence, therefore, who reads Stalin's account of it could possibly consider "metaphysics" worth subscribing to.

6. Nature's Changefulness

In order to bring out the logical structure of the Marxist dialectics of nature, I will start my discussion of it with the principle that Stalin mentions second, namely with the principle that "nature is not a state of rest and immobility, stagnation and immutability, but a state of continuous movement and change," etc. Anyone unfamiliar with philosophical literature will be surprised, perhaps, that it should be necessary to deny that nature is at rest and immutable, for it seems to be as plain as anything could be that changes are constantly going on. At the present moment, for example, the reader is running his eye down the page and thus losing sight of part of it and bringing another part of it into view, and this is surely a sort of change. Speculative philosophers, however, have written poems and books in which they have argued that change is impossible and that whatever is real is eternal, that is to say, outside time altogether. I think we may take it, therefore, that, when Marxists assert that nature changes, one of the things they are doing is denying this form of speculative metaphysics, just as they are denying idealism when they repeat the realist platitude. And just as the realist platitude has point only as a counter to idealism, so the assertion of change has point only as a counter to such metaphysicians as Parmenides and Bradley. Now whatever these metaphysicians say, things *seem* to change. Rivers seem to flow and fires seem to flicker. But according to the metaphysicians we have mentioned rivers do not *really* flow, fires do not *really* flicker, and it is only seemings or appearances that really flow and flicker. Thus it would appear that on their view appearances change but realities do not. *Are* there then appearances? If there are, then appearances are real and realities can change. If there are not, then rivers do not even seem to flow, and fires do not even seem to flicker. If the metaphysician accepts the first alternative, he abandons his assertion that there is no change; if he accepts the second, either he flies in the face of all experience, or he means something very different by "rivers," "fires," "flows," and "flickers" from what is ordinarily meant by these words. For ordinarily we mean by these words the flowing rivers and flickering fires that appear to us, not some recondite reality that only philosophers talk about. Unless the metaphysician is prepared to argue that it is always false to say such things as that rivers flow and fires flicker, his assertion that reality is changeless is not quite what at first sight it seems to be, and is compatible with the changefulness that is so obvious. In so far as Marxists mean to say something like this, it seems to me that they are correct to assert the reality of change.

A second point that Marxists may have in mind when they assert the reality of change is that the physical basis of the world we live in is the changeful, sub-microscopic world of electro-magnetism, of quanta and positrons, in which speeds and movements occur which are enormously greater and smaller than anything we meet with at the macroscopic level. That is, the Marxist accepts the scientific view of the physical world according to which what is behind the ordinary appearances of things is something much more labile than the appearances themselves. The Platonists had held that behind the appearances there were changeless forms. Contemporary physics holds that behind the appearances there is something even more changeful than they. Marxists claim to accept the view of modern physics. (It is interesting to note here another parallel between Marxism and ancient Stoicism. "The Stoics," writes M. Bréhier in his book on Chrysippus, "transformed the whole of logic into dialectic." In particular, they argued against the Platonic view that all movement is degrading, and refused to reduce activities, such as "walking," to states of the agent.)

In the third place, however, Marxists appear to hold the view, first put forward in Ancient Greece by Heraclitus, that only change is real and that rest is a mere appearance. Perhaps we may go so far as to say that the notion of absolute permanence or immutability does not refer to anything we could experience, but is rather an ideal limit. Lightning flashes are impermanent by comparison with houses, but houses are impermanent by comparison with mountain ranges. We always assess changes by reference to backgrounds of permanence, but we find that these backgrounds are themselves subject to change by reference to some further background. We can find no changeless physical thing. The everlasting hills are everlasting only by comparison with the generations of men. We may say with the Marxists, therefore, that the attempt to discover the laws of natural processes is the attempt to understand things "from the standpoint of their movement, their change, their development, their coming into being and going out of being." It does not follow from this, however, that *nothing* endures, that *all* things flow, unless we are using the word "endure" to mean "*absolute* permanence," and the word "flow" in a sense in which stagnant pools and mountains flow. It is one thing to say that absolute permanence is not found in nature, and quite another thing to suggest that all nature is equally changeful. It would be absurd to call a man who is a hundred years old a young man just because a range of mountains has existed for hundreds of thousands of years. When, therefore, someone says that nature is changeful, we may agree that this is true, and that it is a useful thing to say to someone else who had said that nature is changeless. But if what is meant is that there is no rest or permanence in nature in the ordinary meanings of "rest" or "permanence," then the statement is misleading in a way that has something in common with the misleadingness of the statement that change is not real. For it is obvious that, even though everything changes, some things change more than others. Just as, therefore, to say that nothing changes is to deny the manifest differences among things, so to say that everything changes may at any rate draw the mind away from these manifest differences. There is an absurdity in the suggestion that nothing changes because the very attempt to suppose it necessarily *appears* to involve change—as we strain our attention and reflect—and therefore *does* involve change in the ordinary sense of the word. There is not *this* absurdity in the suggestion that nothing moves, since the immobility of the things concerning which it makes sense to say that they move is quite consistent with changes in our thought about them, and quite consistent with changes in intensity, as with the intensities of heard sounds or seen colors. But there is no absurdity in the supposition that everything changes, and that what seems to be permanence is really very slow change. Nor is there any absurdity in the notion that everything about which it makes sense to say that it moves does really move, and that what seems to be immobility is really very slow movement. The reason for this difference is that whereas changelessness and immobility are *absolute* notions that admit of no degree—not changing is just not changing, and *any* departure from that must be a change, must be something opposed to changelessness—change and movement are *relative* notions that admit of degree, and therefore allow a place for changelessness and immobility as *very small degrees* of change or of movement. If this is so, it follows that metaphysical systems like that of Leibniz which make use of fundamental notions such as activity that admit of degree are superior to systems like those of Parmenides, Spinoza, or Bradley, in which the emphasis is on an absolute unchanging being. That is to say, metaphysical systems cannot be all rejected out of hand for defects that exist only in one class of them. I do not think, therefore, that the Marxist metaphysics is, as metaphysics, as objectionable as the metaphysics of changelessness to which it is opposed.

7. The Law of the Transformation of Quantity into Quality

Granted that nature is changeful, what forms do its changes take? The Marxists hold that they have discovered the law in accordance with which the changes of nature occur. They call this law "the Law of the Transformation of Quantity into Quality and *vice versa.*"[17] In what follows we shall discuss the transformation of quantity into quality and neglect the reverse operation, since this is not a matter that Marxists give much attention to. According to this law, as we have already seen, "the process of development" is (*a*) one in which a number of insignificant and gradual changes in the quantity of something are abruptly succeeded by a marked change in its quality, and (*b*) one in which these abrupt changes are not accidental but are "the natural result" of the preceding quantitative changes. In the passage from which I have already quoted, Stalin also says (*c*) that these changes of quality are "an onward and upward movement," (*d*) that they are a "development from the simple to the complex," and (*e*) that they are "from the lower to the higher." With this sort of change is contrasted the sort of change that nature is held *not* to undergo, namely gradual changes, "movement in a circle," "simple repetition of what has already occurred." Stalin quotes Engels to the effect that Darwin had helped to prove this law by showing that the organic world had evolved from the inorganic, and refers to the following illustrations of it given by Engels: the sudden change of water into steam when the temperature is raised, and to ice when the temperature is lowered; the melting points of metals; the critical points of temperature and pressure at which gases are converted into liquids, etc. Engels had also cited, as examples of the law, the fact that chemical combination takes place only when the combining substances are in the proper proportions—"Chemistry can be termed the science of the qualitative changes of bodies as a result of changed quantitative composition"[18]—and Marx's statement that to become capital a sum of money must be more than a certain minimum. Incidentally, in this passage Marx says: "Here, just as in the natural sciences, we find confirmation of the law discovered by Hegel in his *Logic,* that at a certain point, what have been purely quantitative changes become qualitative."[19]

17. Engels, *Dialectics of Nature,* English translation by C. Dutt, p. 26 (London, 1946).

18. Ibid., p. 30.

19. *Capital,* vol. 1, p. 319 (Everyman edition). In a footnote Marx writes: "The

It will thus be seen that this is another notion that Marxists have adapted from Hegel. In his discussion of the category of "measure" Hegel gives the following examples of the transformation of quantity into quality across what he calls "nodal lines": (1) The series of natural numbers is formed by the addition of units, so that each number has the same relation to its neighbors that any other number has. But nevertheless, according to Hegel, the series also generates at various points along it different, new relations, such that some numbers are the squares, or square roots, of others. (2) The notes of a musical scale ascend gradually, the interval between any two successive notes being the same as that between the first of them and the note that preceded it. At a certain point in the scale, however, the regular ascension is variegated by a sudden return, with a difference, to the keynote from which the series of notes began. Thus there is a gradual ascension from low C until the next higher C, at which point there is an abrupt return and a relationship to the starting note which the intervening notes did not have. (3) In chemical combination the substances that combine do so in certain definite proportions. Thus only from certain combinations of Oxygen and Nitrogen do the various oxides of Nitrogen result. (4) Water suddenly becomes ice when the temperature is lowered to freezing point. That is, water is gradually cooled down to freezing point—a nodal line—and then suddenly changes from the liquid quality to the solid quality. (5) Birth and death are each of them sudden changes succeeding the gradual changes of growth and decay. (6) By a sudden transition beyond a certain point, carelessness becomes crime, justice becomes injustice, virtue becomes vice. (7) The population of a state may gradually increase without causing any fundamental change in the character of the state. But if the population gets above a certain level the old institutions cease to be adequate, and the state changes its form. "The state," writes Hegel, "has a proportion relative to its size, such that if it grow beyond this it becomes unstable and collapses under the very constitution which, with another range of size, brought to it happiness and strength." This is illustrated in the note to § 108 of the *Encyclopedia* by the constitution of a Swiss canton

---

molecular theory of modern chemistry, first scientifically worked out by Laurent and Gerhardt, rests on no other law." (I understand that this is questionable.)

which "does not suit a great kingdom." (8) In the note to § 108 of the *Encyclopedia* Hegel also refers to puzzles about the number of grains it takes to make a heap, and the number of hairs that have to be plucked from a horse's tail to make it a bald-tailed horse. It is by these examples that Hegel illustrates his principle.[20]

Before we discuss the Marxist view, it will be as well, I suggest, to look at these examples a little more closely, since they differ from one another quite a lot. They are not easy to classify, but may conveniently be grouped into four classes.

The first class comprises (4) and (5), and, a little less obvious perhaps, (1) and (2). These are the examples that most clearly correspond to those employed by Marxists. In all these cases there is a series of regular changes, of temperature, of growth and decay, of number and of pitch, and at some point in each of the series a member emerges which is not merely the next in the series but has some peculiar characteristic over and above that of being next that differentiates it from the preceding ones. The water gets colder and colder and then, suddenly freezing, becomes a solid; the sleeping embryo wakes up and breaks from the mother; the man's body gradually decays and then collapses in death; the number 4 is not merely the one that follows 3 but is also the square of 2; the next higher note is not merely the one that follows B but is also the higher C. The general formula seems to be as follows: something has properties A, B, and C; the quantity of C is gradually changed and as a result A or B becomes D. (If the conception were to be fully analyzed we should have to distinguish between unspecific properties like color or physical state and specific ones like scarlet or solid, and between intensive quantity like the loudness of a noise and extensive quantity like size or population. But the scale of our work does not allow of such detailed treatment of this matter.)

The second class is exemplified by (3), the case of chemical combination. Here the notion is not that of a series of gradual changes leading to a sudden jump. Instead there are two (or more) substances which can be combined in all sorts of ways and proportions and yet retain their separate identities; but there is a definite proportion and way of combining them which results in their losing their separate identi-

---

20. The first seven examples are from the *Science of Logic,* I, III, 2, B.

ties and becoming a different sort of substance. Just as water suddenly becomes ice at 0 °C, so a mixture of Hydrogen and Oxygen suddenly becomes water when sparked under the requisite conditions. The general formula appears to be: A has properties P and Q, B has properties R and S; mechanically combined they retain their separate identities, but chemically combined they become C, with properties X and Y (or with properties P, S, and X, etc.).

Example (8), it seems to me, makes up the third class, although (6) could conceivably be grouped with it too. A few grains are not a heap, and a million grains are; hairless Harry is bald, and hirsute Horace is not; and so we suppose that there must be a definite number of grains beyond which a heap is attained, and a quantity of hair beyond which baldness lies. But in fact this sort of case is quite different from the first two. With them the "leap" was a leap in nature, from liquid to solid, from mechanical mixture to chemical compound. But with the present case the point of transition calls for human legislation, and it is for us to *decide* how little hair a man must have if he is to be *called* bald. If Horace loses a few hairs a day for a long period a time will come when his friends will say: "Horace is bald." But baldness did not flash on to his head in the way in which his wet hair might have frozen in the cold. There is an intermediate stage when some of his friends might have said he was bald and others might have said he was not.

The fourth class comprises the moral and political examples, i.e., (6) and (7). (7) might have been included in the first class, as the gradual increase of population is analogous to the gradual decrease of the temperature of the water. The "nodal line," however, is not nearly as definite in the political example. In normal circumstances water freezes at 0 °C, but we have no such knowledge of an exact level of population beyond which the constitution fails to operate. There are various reasons for this. The breakdown of a constitution is not something that can be apprehended by the senses, as the transformation of a liquid into a solid can be. Indeed, there is no very definite criterion of the failure of a constitution to work which could be correlated with the fairly definite notion of the population of a state. Temperature and freezing are notions with the same possibilities of precision, whereas the fairly precise notion of population does not consort very well with the rather rough notion of a constitutional breakdown. That Hegel's comparison of the two cases is suggestive cannot be denied, but it would be misleading (even within the confines of the Hegelian philosophy) to regard them as closely analogous. The importance of thus distinguishing between these different levels of precision (as we may call them) for the philosophy of the social sciences need hardly be emphasized.[21] The moral examples given in (6) are even less susceptible of quantitative treatment. It is not by the accumulation of quantitative changes that carelessness becomes crime and virtue becomes vice. It is true that there may be a transition from carelessness to negligence, and from negligence to criminal negligence, but it is not any *amount* of carelessness that leads to this transition but rather the circumstances in which it takes place and the precautions that might have been taken. There is a slight similarity with (8), since what constitutes criminality is in part a matter of legislation. But the legislation is not the fixing of a quantity, since there is no quantity such as numbers of grains or hairs on which the legislation is based. (Unless it be *de minimis non curat lex.*) Again, we say that providence is a virtue, but it becomes meanness or miserliness, not when the provident man gets more and more provident, nor when he saves more and more money, but when he saves what he ought to spend or give away. (This is the sort of criticism that is brought against Aristotle's doctrine that virtue is a mean between two extremes, a doctrine that Hegel, no doubt, had in mind when writing the section we are now discussing.)

We may now return to the Marxist interpretation of the Law of the Transformation of Quantity into Quality. The Marxists chiefly have in mind changes such as those exemplified in the first group of cases given by Hegel, in which there are natural jumps across "nodal lines." The first question we have to ask is: To what sort of natural changes is this law applied—to the evolution of nature as a whole, or to the changes that take place within the various parts of nature? If the intention were merely to say that some of the changes that take place in the

21. It should be noticed that in Hegel's writings the notion of the transformation of quantity into quality is first put forward in connection with *social* affairs—the series of gradual and almost unnoticed changes that lead to a sudden revolutionary outbreak. Nohl, *Hegel's Theologische Jugendschriften*, p. 220. Hegel also makes the point in the Preface to the *Phenomenology*.

world conform to this law, then it could hardly be contested, for water does freeze and boil. Some Marxists, perhaps, have been content with this, and have thought that if it be granted that such sudden changes occur in inanimate nature it follows that human societies must necessarily undergo revolutionary transformations. But there is no force in this argument. If some natural changes are across "nodal lines" and others are not, some special reasons must be given to show that social changes are of the sort that do occur across "nodal lines." Apart from such special reasons, all that can be legitimately concluded is that since some physical changes are of this nature, and since human society is a part of the physical world, it is conceivable that some of the changes that take place in human societies conform to this pattern. If *all* physical changes exemplified this law, there would be slightly more reason for expecting it to be of relevance to human societies, though again the inference would be shaky enough, since it might well happen that the human parts of nature are subject to different laws of change from those that apply in the purely physical parts. But it can hardly be maintained that *everything* in the physical world changes in the way that water changes into ice or steam. It is characteristic of glass, for example, that on being heated it reaches the liquid stage gradually, and can therefore be manipulated and molded in a way that ice cannot be. In advance of detailed enquiry, the melting of glass might just as well be regarded as a model of social change as the freezing or boiling of water.

The Marxist view appears to be, then, that the law in question is exhibited in the development of nature *as a whole*. Stalin, in the passage from which I have quoted, refers the laws of dialectics to "nature," and uses the phrase "the process of development" when he writes specifically of the Law of the Transformation of Quantity into Quality. If we turn to Engels' *Dialectics of Nature* we find that Stalin has been faithful to his tradition, since Engels writes: "It is, therefore, from the history of nature and human society that the laws of dialectics are abstracted. For they are nothing but the most general laws of these two aspects of historical development. . . ."[22] The scheme presented by the Marxists commences with a universe in which there was only one type or only

22. P. 26.

a few types of physical substance. Changes in the temperature or density or some other quantitative feature of this prime material resulted in the emergence of a greater variety of physical substances until life and mind and human societies have come into existence. This is the evolutionary picture of things that has been familiar since the middle of the last century. What differentiates the Marxist version is the emphasis on sudden leaps as, for example, liquid is considered to have brusquely distilled into a previously gaseous universe and so instituted a new type of being. From time to time something new emerges that is not merely a change of order or arrangement, that is no mere stirring up of the old ingredients.

At this stage we can see how the Law of the Transformation of Quantity into Quality combines the first two classes of example given by Hegel. The change of water into ice exemplifies the acquisition of new properties by the same chemical substance, whereas in chemical, as distinct from mere mechanical, combination, new substances with new properties are produced. In either event, materials come into the world that had not been there before. We can now see why Stalin, in language reminiscent of Herbert Spencer, says that there is a development "from the simple to the complex." The world is regarded as acquiring physical and chemical variety through stages of mere repetition punctuated by leaps into the hitherto non-existent. The new types of substance are "the natural results" of their components and predecessors, in the sense that we regard freezing and chemical change as normal and natural. The universe gets more various in as natural a way as water turns to steam. What can be meant by saying, then, that the more complex beings are "higher," and that the evolutionary movement is "onward and upward"? I do not wish now to discuss the tendency we have to prefer variety to monotony, but I have no doubt that we do all tend, other things being equal, to prefer a rich and varied world to one with little in it, and this, no doubt, is the explanation of the use of the word "higher" in this connection. Furthermore, inasmuch as human beings are the most complex of things, and the only ones that frame theories about the development of the world, they may take themselves as standards by which to judge the rest, both out of pride and convenience. Either the evolution of the universe is directed toward the production of man, who is thus the favorite, if not yet the lord, of creation, or else, man, once he has emerged, decides to use his species as the standard of the world's development. Clearly a Marxist would have to prefer the second alternative.

The view here summarized is substantially that which, in English philosophy, has come to be known as the theory of Emergent Evolution. On this view, there is no need to postulate a Creator of the world; the change and variety of things can be accounted for by supposing that new qualities have emerged from combinations and concentrations of a few original ones by processes we can come to recognize. Exponents of Emergent Evolution, like Marxists, stigmatize as "mechanistic" any attempts to maintain that complex beings are *really* only groups of simple ones to which they may be reduced. The process of the world is not, according to them, a combining and recombining of the old elements in manifold ways, but is rather a constant development of types of being that have not existed hitherto. The key word is "novelty." Thus on this view, life and mind are not merely certain re-arrangements of matter, but something that emerges when these re-arrangements take place. But for these re-arrangements there would be no life and mind, but life and mind cannot be reduced to them. Dr. John Lewis, the Marxist philosopher, gave several pages of his introduction to *A Textbook of Marxist Philosophy* to showing how Dialectical Materialism and Emergent Evolution are at one on this issue.[23] If, however, we turn to the part of this work that is translated from the Russian, we find what looks like vacillation. Mechanism, we are told, "arrives at an absolute monotony of nature,"[24] and this is what we should expect; but we are a little surprised to read a few pages later: "Breaks are never absolute."[25] Other Marxists have turned against Emergent Evolution with considerable emphasis. Thus Mr. Caudwell, in his *Further Studies in a Dying Culture,* writes: "Thus, instead of a world of becoming in which all unfolds itself with complete determinism, because all phenomena are materially real, we have a world unfolded in time and space by the Jack-in-the-box appearance of new and unpredictable qualities. Such a philosophy is incompe-

23. Pp. 12 ff.
24. P. 335.
25. P. 340.

tent to explain society or the generation either of itself or other philosophies."[26] A similar critical attitude toward Emergent Evolution is
adopted by Mr. Cornforth in his *Dialectical Materialism and Science.*

The reason for this modification of attitude is easy to see. Marxists
wish to emphasize two things, the occurrence of sudden leaps in nature, and the possibility of a science of society that will allow social
predictions to be made. They hold *both* that sudden leaps occur *and*
that they can predict what the future form of human society will be.
These two views, however, do not easily go together, as I shall now
endeavor to show. Both Marxists and Emergent Evolutionists criticize
mechanists for not allowing that there is genuine novelty in nature.
Now there is a sense of "new" according to which there is something
new whenever any change has taken place. In this sense of the word
there would be something new if some already existing elements were
merely re-arranged. What is new would be the re-arrangement, and
someone who knew what the elements were and had had some experience of their being re-arranged could conceive of all sorts of possible
re-arrangements that had never in fact existed. But someone might
say: "There is nothing *really* new when old elements are being merely
re-arranged. I mean by 'new' something of a sort that has never existed
before at all." In this second sense of the word, there is only something *really* new when something occurs which could not have been
conceived of in advance of its occurrence. Nothing that a blind man
smells or touches can give him, in advance of seeing, any idea of what
the color green is like, and therefore if a man born blind comes to see,
he will be seeing things new to him each time he sees a color for the
first time. It is possible that a man who has knowledge of some elements and of their re-arrangements will be able to predict how they
will be re-arranged in the future, for he knows at least what it would
be like for them to be re-arranged in certain ways. But no one could
possibly describe in advance of its occurrence a color or a sound which
no one had ever yet experienced. If something is new in this second
sense it cannot be predicted because no one is able to make or to
understand the prediction. Now it is clear that changes leading only
to new arrangements of the old units are the sort of change that Stalin

26. P. 233.

describes as "a movement in a circle" and as "a simple repetition of what has already occurred." It is such changes, however, which can obviously be understood in advance of their occurrence. It is not so obvious that predictions could be made of occurrences that (*a*) are not mere re-arrangements of elements that already exist, and (*b*) have never been experienced before. If such predictions are impossible, then two major theses of the Marxist philosophy, the thesis of sudden qualitative "leaps," and the thesis that at least one qualitative "leap" in the transformation of human society, viz., the transition to Communism, can be foreseen, are in contradiction with one another. This is probably the reason why the Leningrad philosophers say: "Breaks are never absolute," and why Mr. Caudwell refuses to accept aid from Emergent Evolutionists.

We must distinguish, I suggest, between qualitative leaps or breaks which have been observed on many occasions, like that of water to ice, and those major breaks with the past, like the emergence of liquid or life, which, according to the Marxist theory of evolution, have occurred on specific occasions. There was a time, we may suppose, when there was only gas, and then the first liquid emerged; there was a time when there was only matter, and then life emerged. Once liquids and life have come, it is possible that predictions will be made about when new liquids will emerge and about when new forms of life will emerge—for the man making the predictions will know in a general way what it is that he is predicting. It is conceivable that before such new things first came into existence someone might be able to predict that something very peculiar was about to happen—there might be circumstances analogous in some ways to those that preceded some earlier cosmic "leap"—but he could not, before it occurred, say what sort of thing it was going to be. If this be so, and if Communist society is a qualitatively different type of society from Capitalist society, then it is only possible to predict it if other societies have turned into Communist societies just as water has before now turned into ice. But Marxists do not believe that other societies in the past have turned into Communist societies. They think, rather, that the Communism of the future will be a break through to something that has not existed before. If, therefore, the "Communist quality" of the future society is a new sort of break with the past across a nodal line that we have not yet reached, we can have no idea of what is peculiar to it, and talk about it is talk about our ignorance. It may be said, of course, that according to Marxists there *has* been a Communist society in the past, viz., Primitive Communism, which is alleged to have existed before classes were instituted. If this were to be granted, then it could be said that prediction of the Communism of the future was comparable to prediction of some new liquid by someone who already has knowledge of liquids. This objection has some point, but it is in fact difficult for a Marxist to uphold, since the Communism of the future is, according to his theory, at several removes from Primitive Communism, and like it only to the extent that it would have no private property and no classes. These *formal* features cannot constitute what is *new* in the Communism of the future.

Marxists, it should be mentioned, rest their case in part on the fact that Mendeléeff, in the nineteenth century, was able, on the basis of his Periodic Table, to predict not only that certain hitherto unknown elements probably existed, but also what their properties would be. But Mendeléeff was not able to predict the discovery of properties that nothing had ever had before. The elements that were subsequently discovered (Gallium, Germanium, etc.) possessed, not properties that had never before been known of, but different groupings of qualities possessed by other already known elements as well. If, therefore, this conception is to be applied to the Communist society of the future, all that could be predicted would be that certain properties, A, B, and C, which had never before belonged to any single society, would co-exist in the future Communist society. But this would surely be "simple repetition of what has already occurred, a mechanistic or metaphysical circular change. For the dialectical change that Marxists sponsor is more than a re-arrangement of already existing entities, whether they be already existing units or already existing qualities.

In conclusion, it is perhaps worth pointing out that it is easy to confuse the emergence of new qualities with something that is quite different. The confusion arises when we fail to see the difference between Hegel's example that on page 75 I numbered (8)—the example about the number of grains it takes to make a heap—and his example about water changing to ice when the temperature is lowered to freezing-point. In the second case there is a marked observable difference; first there is liquid, and then there is solid. In the first case, however, there is no such marked difference at the point of transition, since there is an element of choice about whether we call a set of grains a heap or not. The addition of grain after grain is gradual and remains so, but in some circumstances (e.g., if we were buying or selling sand by the heap) we may have to decide quite definitely between what is a heap and what is not a heap. Now I am not at all sure that all of the "leaps" implied in the evolutionary picture of the world are of the water-into-ice sort rather than of the not-heap-to-heap, or bald-to-hirsute sort. If the world began as a gas, then the emergence of liquidity could be compared to the sudden freezing of water. But it is possible that the emergence of life has been no such abrupt occurrence. For it may be that the natural changes have been gradual, that we feel no hesitation in saying that certain things are without life and that others are clearly alive, but that the point at which we draw the line is one that we have to choose, not one that the facts press upon us in unmistakable fashion. Strictly speaking, indeed, every observable change is a change of quality. Each coldness that we experience as the water approaches freezing-point is a distinct coldness, though we have no separate name for each of them. This may be illustrated by the distinction we make between "warm" and "hot," for which there would seem to be no precise analogies in the degrees of coldness. Where there are very marked qualitative differences, we feel that a distinct name is needed, but it is unwise to assume that every different name for the stages in a transition corresponds to some marked leap or break.

Now the last paragraph needs to be supplemented by a further complication. Although the transition from grains to heap is one that allows us to draw the line between the two at various, more or less arbitrary points, the distinction has *some* analogy with the sudden transition from water to ice. For when the grains of sand are added, one after the other, a point is reached when the "look," of the grains becomes different. First there was a plurality of grains, and then, after a while, we see them as a whole. To begin with we should describe ourselves as adding grains to grains, and then as adding grains to *the heap*. Psychologists give the name "form quality" to the "look" that wholes have as distinct from the separate appearance of each of their parts. For example, if we look closely at the liquid in a glass we may see small particles swimming about in water, but if we look at it from further away we should say that the water is *turbid*. In this case turbidity is a form quality analogous to the form quality of being a heap rather than a collection of grains. These are qualities that can no more be described before they have been experienced than hitherto unseen colors could be, and they may thus be regarded as a sort of emergent quality. That they are different from transformations of quantity into quality of the chemical combination sort or of the water-to-ice sort may be seen from the fact that the grains of some substance that does not combine chemically with water, and is not even soluble in it, may have a turbid "look," though in fact they remain separate. However, there is no need here to take this matter further, now we have seen how unduly simplified the Marxist theory is.

8. Contradiction and the Negation of the Negation

We have now seen that, on the Marxist view, everything is changing, and that periods of gradual change are interspersed with sudden changes in which new types of being come to birth. Marxists regard it as a merit of their theory that it is also capable of explaining why nature changes at all. They hold that the driving force behind all change is an inherent contradiction in things. This is the fourth of the propositions in which Stalin summarizes the essentials of Dialectical Materialism. In expounding this view, he quotes the following phrase from Lenin's *Philosophical Notebooks:* "In its proper meaning dialectics is the study of the contradiction within the very essence of things." We may supplement this with a rather fuller statement from the same work of Lenin's: "The identity of opposites . . . is the recognition (discovery) of the contradictory, *mutually exclusive,* opposite tendencies in *all* phenomena and processes of nature (including mind and society). . . . Development is the 'struggle' of opposites. Two basic (or two possible? or two historically observable?) conceptions of development (evolution) are: development as decrease and increase, as repetition; *and* development as a unity of opposites (the division of the one into mutually exclusive opposites and their reciprocal correlation). . . . The first conception is lifeless, poor, and dry; the second is vital. The second *alone* furnishes the key to the 'self-movement' of everything in existence:

it alone offers the key to the 'leaps,' to the 'break in continuity,' to the 'transformation into the opposite,' to the destruction of the old and the emergence of the new. The unity (the coincidence, identity, resultant), of opposites is conditional, temporary, transitory, relative. The struggle of mutually exclusive opposites is absolute, just as development and motion are absolute."[27] Engels had argued that the fact that things moved at all was proof that contradiction was to be found in nature. "Motion itself," he wrote, "is a contradiction: even simple mechanical change of place can only come about through a body at the same moment of time being both in one place and another place, being in one and the same place and also not in it."[28] Other examples of "contradiction within the very essence of things" given by Engels and Lenin are: the plus and minus signs in mathematics, positive and negative electricity in physics, the class struggle in the social sphere.

All change, then, takes place through contradiction, opposition, struggle. What makes it evolutionary or progressive is that it proceeds by "the negation of the negation." Process A is opposed by its contradictory not-A, and, let us suppose, is succeeded by not-A. Not-A, in

27. *Selected Works,* XI, pp. 81–82. Lenin's *Philosophical Notebooks* (only a few extracts from which have been published in English) consists of extracts from philosophical authors read by him during the First World War, along with the comments he made on them. There are extracts from and comments on Hegel's *Science of Logic, Lectures on the Philosophy of History,* and *Lectures on the History of Philosophy;* Noël's *La Logique de Hegel;* Lassalle's *The Philosophy of Heracleitos the Dark, of Ephesus;* on Feuerbach's *Lectures on the Essence of Religion,* and *Leibniz.* Lenin read Hegel's *Science of Logic* very carefully, and it is possible from his comments to get a good idea of Lenin's philosophical ideas at this period of his life. Some students of Marxism have said that in the *Philosophical Notebooks* Lenin abandons the "copy" theory of perception which he had put forward in *Materialism and Empirio-Criticism,* and they quote such passages as the following: "The reflection (mirroring) of nature in human thought is not 'dead,' not 'abstract,' *not without movement,* but is an eternal process of movement, of the arising and resolving of contradictions" (Adoratski's edition, p. 115). But this, and other similar passages, in my opinion refer to *science* rather than to perception, and are in any case rather ambiguous. The passage I have quoted in the text comes from a brief essay in the *Philosophical Notebooks* headed *On the Question of Dialectics.* It may be seen in Adoratski's edition (V. I. Lenin, *Aus dem Philosophischen Nachlass: Exzerpte und Randglossen,* ed. V. Adoratski, pp. 285–86; Wien-Berlin, 1932).

28. *Anti-Dühring,* p. 135.

its turn, however, will be the pole of a further opposition, and so will be succeeded by its opposite, A. This second A, however, will not be merely the first A reinstated, for the first A was the opposite of a not-A that had not yet replaced it, while the second A is the opposite of a not-A which has already replaced the original A. Engels gives the example of a grain of barley planted in the ground. This is "negated" by the plant that succeeds it. This, in its turn, however, is negated (the negation of the negation) by its own decay. From its seeds, however, many new plants may arise. "As a result of this negation of the negation we have once again the original grain of barley, but not as a single unit, but ten, twenty or thirty fold."[29]

There is a great deal that might be said about all this, but as much of it would be more relevant to the theory of social development, I shall confine my remarks now to a few fundamental matters.

Dühring himself, and subsequent critics of Marxism, have criticized the whole view on the ground that contradiction and negation are logical notions which cannot be transferred without absurdity to the context of natural processes. The proposition "I am writing" is, for any given individual at any given moment, the contradictory of the proposition "I am not writing," such critics will say, but the process of writing is itself something happening in the world that cannot conceivably be in contradiction with anything else. On this view, contradiction is a logical, not a natural notion, and *it does not make sense* to say that one thing or event contradicts another. Such an objection, of course, would have to be elaborated in detail if it were to be pressed against Hegel, since Hegel, in his *Science of Logic,* held that logic and speculative philosophy were essentially one, and hence that logic is somehow involved in the world that exists beyond human thought. Furthermore, if the Marxist "copy" theory of truth were to be pressed, it might well be concluded that our contradictory notions must copy contradictory things, just as Lenin, in his *On the Question of Dialectics,* held that our ideas of "causality, necessity, natural law, etc." were "reflections in the human mind of the laws of nature and of the external world." My own view is that the Marxist theory of nature is anthropomorphic, and has become so by quite a natural, though misleading,

29. Ibid., p. 152.

sequence of ideas. It is true that the words "contradiction," "contrary," "opposition," etc., are used by logicians in ways that have to be explained to the plain man. For example, it is not immediately obvious to the plain man that the contradictory of "some men are not mortal" is "all men are mortal." But the ordinary senses of these logical words are nevertheless closely linked with social conceptions. If one man asserts a proposition and another man denies it, the logical relation of contradiction between propositions will be accompanied by conscious disagreement between men, and this may well arouse an opposition between them that is social as well as logical. Social opposition may show itself in more than merely verbal disputing, and then it becomes a maneuver, a struggle or a fight. Again, a frequent cause of struggle is that two people want the same thing and this thing is something that cannot be shared. One man's having it, we then say, is *incompatible* with another's having it, and in so saying we use a word which has logical as well as social import. Furthermore, if there is a struggle between two men, then if one has defeated the other, the other cannot have defeated the one. Logic settles this, but does not settle the issue of the fight. Such phrases as "incompatibility of temperament" and "contradictory aims" show how natural it is to describe human affairs in words that have logical senses. By a further analogical extension, however, it becomes possible to describe physical processes as "struggling," "opposing," and the like, as in Lenin's phrase "struggle of opposites." Thus, too, colliding or impinging particles may be described as opposing one another, and so there arises a vague picture of their being opposed in the way that men may be. According to Lenin, in a passage we have already quoted, if nature were free from contradiction it would be "lifeless, poor, and dry"; but since it is contradictory, it is "vital." (The German text has *lebendig*.) Now "vital" means "alive," and in thus opposing it to "lifeless" Lenin talks of nature as if it were a living being. This is not to be wondered at, since he borrows so much of his terminology from Hegel, who undoubtedly thought that there is no such thing as matter utterly divorced from mind. It should be noticed, in this connection, that one of the reasons that Lenin gives in his *Philosophical Notebooks* for holding that nature is always in movement and struggle is that if it were not *self*-moved, it would have to get its movement from God. He writes: "Linear procedure and onesided-

ness, woodenness and ossification, subjectivism and subjective blind-
ness, *voilà* the epistemological roots of Idealism. Priestcraft (= Philosophical Idealism) nevertheless has naturally gnoseological roots, is
not without some basis, is incontestably a *sterile* flower, but a sterile
flower, the blooms on the living tree of the living, fruitful, true, powerful, omnipotent, objective, absolute human knowledge."[30] Elsewhere
in the same work he comments: "Intelligent Idealism (*der kluge Ideal-
ismus*) is nearer to intelligent materialism than unintelligent (*dumme*)
materialism. Dialectical idealism instead of intelligent; metaphysical,
undeveloped, dead, crude, immovable instead of unintelligent."[31] (I
take it that in this last sentence Lenin is saying "Substitute 'dialectical'
for 'intelligent' and 'metaphysical, etc.' for 'unintelligent.'") What remains when such figures of speech are allowed for is that, according to
Marxists, there is nothing in nature that remains changeless, and this
may very well be true.

We must next observe that Engels thought that the existence of
movement proved that there are contradictions in nature, since if
something moves it must be in one place and the next adjoining place
at the same moment of time. Now the passage from the *Anti-Dühring*
to this effect that I quoted on page 86 follows very closely what Hegel
writes in his *Science of Logic,* book 2, section 1, chapter 2, C, which is
headed "Contradiction." Here Hegel says: "External sensible motion
is itself an immediate fact. Something is moving, not while it is in this
now *here,* and in another now *there,* but while it is here and not here in
the same now, while it both is and is not in the same here. We must
grant to the ancient dialecticians the contradictions they showed in
movement; but it does not follow from that that there is no movement,
but rather that movement itself is an *existing* (*daseiende*) contradiction."
Hegel is here referring to Zeno of Elea, who argued that to occupy
place A a moving thing has to be at rest there, and to occupy the adja-
cent place B, it has to be at rest *there,* and that therefore the thing
cannot be in movement at all. In his *Lectures on the History of Philosophy*
Hegel says that Zeno is not to be regarded as denying the existence of
movement; movement is as real as elephants. "The question concerns

30. *Aus dem Philosophischen Nachlass,* ed. Adoratski, p. 289.
31. Ibid., p. 212.

rather its *truth;* movement is untrue, for its idea contains a contradiction; thus he was intending to say that movement has no *true* being." It is therefore obvious that when Hegel says that movement is an existing (*daseiende*) contradiction he means something very different from what Engels means. When Hegel says that something exists, has *Dasein,* he is claiming very little for it, for he uses the word *Dasein* for what has immediate, merely finite being, not for what is ultimately real. Engels, therefore, has taken an argument from Hegel's *speculative* philosophy, and used it as if it could be comfortably housed in the Marxist *anti-*speculative philosophy. But it cannot, surely, belong there, for it is as clear as anything could be that things move, but to say that there could be no movement unless there was contradiction in the realm of fact is to draw a conclusion about matter of fact from a particular conception or notion of what movement *must* be. We observe things moving, and *therefore,* according to Engels, we *must* observe them contradicting one another. Could Dühring's phrase "arabesques of ideas" find a more striking application?

The notion of "the negation of the negation" is, in the Marxist system, primarily of social significance. It is easy to see that when movements of thought come into conflict with their predecessors the victorious system may well take up into itself features of the defeated system, just as legislation in the English Parliament is frequently (though not always) influenced by the criticisms of the Opposition. Thus, much of the paganism that the early Christians deplored has found its way into Christian thought and ritual. However this may be, the spectacle of such an intelligent Marxist philosopher as Plekhanov disputing whether it is the stalk of the barley, or the whole plant, or "the fertilized ovum," that is the negated negation of the barley seed, is one that can only arouse embarrassment. It is with some relief, therefore, that we read that barley (or is it oats?) will grow "according to Hegel," whether the sequence is triadic (seed, plant, seed) or tetradic (seed, stalk, flower, seed).[32]

32. G. V. Plekhanov, *In Defence of Materialism,* translated by A. Rothstein (London, 1947), pp. 112–14.

9. *Status of the Dialectical Laws*

We have not so far discussed the proposition that all things are "organically connected with, dependent on, and determined by each other." That things are *not* so connected is the thesis of "metaphysics," in Engels' sense of the word. What sort of unity of the world, then, do Marxist philosophers assert? It is easy to see that, on their view, nature is one, inasmuch as it is fundamentally material—there is nothing in nature that is not based in matter. A further suggestion of the view is that everything, including human societies, is subject to natural laws. Again, Marxists believe in universal determinism. Perhaps it is believed that all the sciences form a single continuous system, within which all scientific laws are of the same fundamental type. (Yet this would hardly be consistent with the theory of emergence.) "Dialectical materialism," writes Mr. Mitin, "is against one-sidedness in science, it insists on the examination of natural phenomena in all their connections and interactions."[33] The practical bearing of such a statement would seem to be that scientists should interest themselves in borderline problems, and aim at comprehensive views. Marxist philosophers also hold—as do non-Marxists too—that no single scientific truth is absolute, but is subject to modification in the light of later scientific developments. On the face of it, this might seem like Hegel's theory that "the truth is the whole," that only when Reason has completed the structure of philosophy can the partial truths of departmental knowledge be seen in their proper perspective. Hegel, however, was a speculative philosopher, and Marxists reject speculative philosophy. It is difficult not to conclude, therefore, that Marxists have used the language of speculative philosophy to express the methodological commonplace that any statement of empirical science is subject to the possibility of correction.

There is no doubt as to the Marxist account of the status of the laws of dialectic—the Law of the Transformation of Quantity into Quality, the Law of the Interpretation of Opposites, and the Law of the Negation of the Negation. The Marxist view is that these laws are scientific

33. M. Mitin, "Twenty-five Years of Philosophy in the U.S.S.R.," *Philosophy,* 1944, p. 80.

laws of a high degree of generality. According to Engels, "Dialectics is nothing more than the science of the general laws of motion and development of Nature, human society and thought."[34] "Nature," he also says, "is the test of dialectics."[35] That this continues to be the Marxist view may be seen from a recently compiled outline for a *Soviet History of Philosophy* where the "three laws of dialectics" are described as "Marx's and Engels' generalization on the data of natural science."[36] This being so, one would have thought that these laws would be subject to revision as the sciences progress, just as other generalizations are. One does not get the impression, however, that this is likely to happen. On the contrary, they appear to have got so deeply imbedded in the Marxist terminology that *any* future discoveries in the natural sciences would *have* to conform to them. This is not surprising when we consider the extremely wide range of cases to which the laws are already alleged to apply. The Law of the Negation of the Negation is already general almost to the point of evanescence when it is applied to such very different things as the formula $-a \times -a = a^2$, and the growth and reproduction of barley. When it is extended to include the passage from capitalist to communist society the only point of likeness appears to be the words employed. Indeed, it seems to me that the important thing about these laws is that they are formulae which may be used to express any state of affairs that it is desired to bring within their ambit. They are thus modes of expression rather than generalizations, etiquette rather than science. But they are a peculiar sort of etiquette, not of the drawing-room, nor even of the laboratory, but of the scientific journal or, more important still, of the scientific conference. Once these formulae are adopted as modes of speech which men of science are expected to use, then science itself may come to be regarded as absorbed into Marxist society. The conquest of a people's language becomes a conquest of their thought as etiquette develops into custom and custom into morals. *Allez à la messe; prenez de l'eau bénite.* Repeating the formula may transform scoffers into devotees.

34. *Anti-Dühring*, p. 158.

35. Ibid., p. 29.

36. *A Soviet History of Philosophy*, translated by William Edgerton, Public Affairs Press, Washington 8, D.C., 1950, pp. 38–39.

10. Marxism and Formal Logic

I will conclude this chapter with some very brief remarks on the Marxist view of logic. In Section 2 of the present chapter (page 48) I quoted a passage from Engels' *Anti-Dühring* in which he puts forward the positivist thesis that, as the various special sciences develop, all that is left to philosophy is "the science of thought and its laws—formal logic and dialectics." From this we may conclude that "formal logic and dialectics" are fairly respectable sciences and that they are distinguishable from one another, at any rate in thought. If, as seems very likely, "dialectics" consists of the sort of consideration we have just been examining in connection with the three "laws of dialectic," then formal logic would appear to be something different. Further on in the *Anti-Dühring* Engels says that "Even formal logic is primarily a method of arriving at new results, of advancing from the known to the unknown—and dialectics is the same, only in a much more important sense, because in forcing its way beyond the narrow horizon of formal logic it contains the germs of a more comprehensive view of the world."[37] In the same passage Engels goes on to say that "almost all the proofs of higher mathematics" go beyond formal logic into the realm of dialectics. In his *Dialectics of Nature* Engels contrasts dialectical *logic* with "the old, merely formal logic," saying that the former is not content with merely enumerating the forms of thought and "placing them side by side without any connection," but "it derives these forms out of one another instead of putting them on an equal level, it develops the higher forms out of the lower." He then goes on to give an outline of Hegel's account of the forms of judgment, and concludes the discussion with an attack on those who make a sharp contrast between deductive and inductive logic instead of recognizing that deduction and induction are not exclusive and opposite types of inference.[38]

We may notice four main points here. (*a*) Engels allows that formal logic is a part of philosophy that survives the overthrow of speculative philosophy. (*b*) Hegel had argued that where there is no development or advance in knowledge from premises to conclusion there is

37. P. 151.
38. *Dialectics of Nature*, p. 237.

no inference at all. On Hegel's view, that is, a mere tautology would not be a genuine inference. With these views in mind, Engels argues that since formal logic contains inferences it leads to new knowledge. (*c*) Like Hegel also, however, he holds that formal logic is somehow incomplete, and points the way to dialectical logic. In particular he complains that in formal logic the various types of judgment are regarded as fixed and as rigidly distinguished from one another, instead of being shown to be continuous and fluid. It would therefore be natural to conclude from this part of Engels' argument that he supposed formal logic to be (in his sense of the word) "metaphysical," and therefore false. He certainly considered that formal logic belonged to the domain of the Understanding and of the ability to abstract and to experiment which (he says) is common to men and animals, and that the dialectical procedures of the Reason are peculiar to mankind.[39] (*d*) It looks as if Engels would have approved of a sort of logic like that of Bernard Bosanquet or of some contemporary philosophers of "ordinary language" in which, for example, instead of the distinction being between, say, categorical and hypothetical *judgments,* it is between categorical and hypothetical *aspects* of them; or instead of there being a separate discussion of deductive and of inductive inference, the two are shown to be very intimately involved with one another; and so on for other well-known logical contrasts.

It will be seen that Engels left his Marxist successors with rather a difficult task, for on the one hand formal logic appears to have his support, and on the other hand he appears to stigmatize it as inferior to dialectics and as "metaphysical." In the Soviet Union the latter view was fashionable for some time, but since the Second World War formal logic has been defended by Marxist philosophers and its teaching reintroduced into Soviet high schools. Indeed, a textbook of the Tsarist period was re-published for this purpose. Soviet philosophers have in recent years been discussing whether there is one logic only, or whether there are two, formal logic and dialectical logic. From the passages I have referred to it will be seen that Engels contrasted formal logic with "dialectics" and with "dialectical logic," so that precise guidance cannot be obtained from him. However that may be, new text-

39. Ibid., pp. 203–4.

books of formal logic are now being produced in the Soviet Union in which it is stated that there are four basic principles of formal logic, the Principle of Identity, the Principle of Contradiction, the Principle of Excluded Middle, and the Principle of Sufficient Reason, and in which the Square of Opposition, the Syllogism, and the other parts of the traditional formal logic are treated in the traditional way. Thus by "formal logic" the Soviet philosophers mean the modified Aristotelian tradition that held sway in Europe and America until the innovations of Boole, de Morgan, Venn, and Peirce led to the development of what is now called symbolic or mathematical logic. It appears that the writings of Hilbert, Tarski, and other mathematical logicians have been circulated in the U.S.S.R., but they do not seem to have influenced Soviet philosophers (who have labelled them as "idealist"), whatever their influence on Soviet mathematicians may have been. It should be noticed, however, that there is no suggestion on the part of Soviet philosophers that self-contradiction is a feature of the dialectical thinking that they favor or that consistency and rigor are not desirable in all thinking. They consider that the laws of logic somehow copy or "reflect" the real world, and appear committed to this view so long as the writings of Lenin are accepted as authoritative, for in the *Philosophical Notebooks* he wrote: "The laws of logic are reflections of the objective in the subjective consciousness of men."[40]

40. *Aus dem Philosophischen Nachlass,* ed. Adoratski, p. 103. See also p. 110. The account of formal logic in the U.S.S.R. is summarized from the lucid description in G. A. Wetter, *Der Dialektische Materialismus: Seine Geschichte und sein System in der Sowjetunion* (Wien, 1952), pp. 544 ff. In the English translation of this work (*Dialectical Materialism,* London, 1958) Wetter brings his account of the controversy over the status of formal logic up to date. The view that formal logic is an independent science with universal validity is being vigorously upheld (pp. 531–35). But Bochenski (*Der Sowjetrussische Dialektische Materialismus,* 2nd edition, 1956, pp. 67–68) shows that the adherents of formal logic were accused of being "nihilists" and "vulgarizers" by influential writers in *Komunist* and *Voprosy Filosofic.* See also: *Logic and Dialectic in the Soviet Union,* by Alexander Philopov (Research Program on the U.S.S.R., New York, 1952). There is some interesting material in George L. Kline's review of Bochenski's *Der Sowjetrussische Dialektische Materialismus,* in the *Journal of Philosophy,* 1952, pp. 123–31.

Part Two

Scientific Socialism

I

Historical Materialism

1. Anti-metaphysical, Positivistic Aspect of Historical Materialism

We have now examined the most fundamental notions of the Marxist philosophy, and have seen what is meant by the assertion that Marxism is both a materialistic and a dialectical view of the world. We have seen, in particular, that Marxists deny the efficacy of speculative thinking and assert the all-sufficiency of scientific thinking in which theory and practice are conjoined. Now considered in its most general aspect, the Marxist version of Historical Materialism is the view that a scientific understanding may be—indeed has been—obtained of the development of human society. It is thus one of the several attempts at constructing a "science of history" that were made in the middle years of the nineteenth century and aroused those controversies that are associated with the names of Buckle, Froude, Spencer, and Droysen. That Marx recognized some kinship between his view of history and the "scientific" view expounded by Buckle in his *History of Civilization in England* (1857) may be seen from the letter—best known for the discussion of Darwin contained in it—he wrote to Engels on 18 June 1862. Referring to the announcement of the death of Buckle, he says: "Poor Buckle, whom a 'friend' slanders in today's *Times* by means of a *testimonium pietatis*." The friend was Mr. J. S. Stuart Glennie, who had been with Buckle when, a few weeks before, he had died in the Middle East (the letter is written from Beyrout), and the *testimonium pietatis*, I suppose, is Mr. Glennie's hope that Buckle was "now enjoying that immortality without the hope of which, as he once said to me with tears in his eyes, 'life would be insupportable,' and in the more immediate presence, and with deeper knowledge of that God in whom he firmly believed." Mr. Glennie, however, goes on to summarize Buckle's "science of history" in the following terms: "(1) Political economy—the science of wealth—is the deductive science through which the investigation of natural is connected with that of social phenomena, and thus the way is prepared for one universal science. (2) The laws of society are different from those of the individual; and the method of averages, with which has to be compared the mathematical theory of probability, is that by which the former are to be investigated. (3) In social phenomena the intellectual, in individual the moral, laws are chiefly or alone to be considered: all moral social changes are thus preceded by intellectual changes."[1] Although this is very different from the Marxist view, such points of kinship as the importance attributed to economics and the secondary character attributed to morals are striking enough. Buckle, too, like Marx, associated his "science of history" with an attack on speculative philosophy, which he calls "metaphysics." "In no other department," he had written, "has there been so much movement, and so little progress,"[2] but his conclusion was that as there are no means of settling the dispute, there would always be supporters of the two parties, "sensationalists" and "idealists."

Let us, then, make our transition from the fundamental notions of the Marxist system to the theory of Historical Materialism by considering the positivist, anti-metaphysical foundations of the latter. Marxists claim to give a scientific account, not only of the development of human society, but also of the human propensity to engage in theological and metaphysical speculation. That is, those who accept the theory of Historical Materialism both deny the theoretical efficacy of metaphysical speculation and also claim to show how it is that men come to misdirect their thinking by vacuously speculating instead of observing and experimenting. Perhaps it should be pointed out at this stage that to give a "scientific" account of how men come to adopt religious ideas and to work out theologies and metaphysical theories is not the same thing as to refute the religious, theological, and metaphysical theories in question. For these theories might be true even though men came to adopt them for some such reason as that belief in them rendered their lives more bearable. If such "scientific" accounts of religious and metaphysical theorizing are also to be refutations of it, then it must

1. *The Times,* 18 June, 1862.
2. *The History of Civilization in England* (3rd edition, 1861), vol. 1, pp. 150–51.

also be shown that metaphysical speculation is incapable of revealing truths about the world, that the methods of the empirical sciences are the only methods by which the world can be understood, and that these methods can be successfully applied to human and social affairs. Thus the fundamental Marxist thesis is identical with that of positivism, viz., that nothing can be known but what sense perception and the methods of science reveal. If this were rejected, then it would be possible to hold *both* that the Marxist account of the human origin of religion and theology was correct, *and* that certain religious, theological, or metaphysical propositions were true. That the Marxists unquestionably regard their account of the social origin of religion, theology, and metaphysics as showing the illusory character of religious, theological, and metaphysical "truths," is an added indication that they accept the positivist view about metaphysical speculation. Psychologists who give somewhat similar accounts of religious belief sometimes guard themselves against criticism by saying that they are speaking only as psychologists, not as theologians or metaphysicians. But on the positivist view, to speak as a theologian or metaphysician (i.e., as a speculative philosopher) is to speak idly, pointlessly, misleadingly. The theory of Historical Materialism is held to unmask the deception, but it can only claim to do so on the basis of the positivist theory of science.

It will be remembered that I illustrated Marx's positivism by reference to his jibe that metaphysical or speculative thinkers—he had Hegel particularly in mind—suppose that the particular things of the world are manifestations of the Idea, as if the various species of fruit such as apples and pears and strawberries were manifestations of Fruit Itself.[3] In the technical language of the philosophy of his day, Marx accused the metaphysicians of mistaking the predicate for the subject, the general characteristic ("fruitness") for the real thing (the particular apple). Now Marx accused Hegel of making this same mistake in his theory of politics. In § 263 of his *Philosophy of Right* (1821) Hegel had written: "The actual Idea is mind, which, sundering itself into the two ideal spheres of its concept, family and civil society, enters upon its finite phase, but it does so only in order to rise above its ideality and become explicit as infinite actual mind. It is therefore to these

3. See p. 47.

ideal spheres that the actual Idea assigns the material of this its finite actuality, viz. human beings as a mass, in such a way that the function assigned to any given individual is visibly mediated by circumstances, his caprice and his personal choice of his station in life."[4] This is extraordinarily obscure, and we need not enter upon a detailed interpretation. But from the context it appears that Hegel is asserting (among other things) that it is the Absolute Idea as manifested in the State which provides the rational explanation of the family and the economic organization of society—if we may thus roughly designate what Hegel called "civil society"—and that without these manifestations the Absolute Idea would not be infinite and real.

In commenting on this passage, Marx writes: "In this passage his logical, pantheistic mysticism shows itself very clearly. . . . The *real* relation of the family and civil society to the State is conceived as their inner imaginary activity. The family and civil society are preconditions (*Voraussetzungen*) of the State; they are the genuinely active beings, but in speculation it is the other way round . . . [in fact] the family and civil society form themselves into the State. They are the active element (*Sie sind das Treibende*). But according to Hegel they are made by the actual Idea; it is not their own life that unites them into the State, but it is the life of the Idea which has made them from itself (*die sie von sich dezerniert hat*) . . . the fact is that the State emerges from the masses (*aus der Menge*—from the individuals?) as they exist as members of the family and of civil society, but speculation announces this fact as a deed of the Idea, not as the Idea of the masses, but as the deed of a subjective idea different from the fact. . . . The fact that serves as a point of departure [for Hegel] is not conceived as such but rather as a mystical consequence."[5] Again, in commenting on § 270 of the *Philosophy of Right* Marx describes Hegel's method as follows: "The real interest is not the philosophy of right but logic. The work of [Hegel's] philosophy is not to embody thought in political determinations but to dissipate existing political determinations into abstract conceptions. The philosophical moment is not the logic of the real fact but a mere matter of logic (. . . *nicht die Logik der Sache, sondern die Sache der Logik*). Logic

---

4. Knox's translation (London, 1942), p. 162.
5. *Kritik des Hegelschen Staatsrechts*, 1843, M.E.G.A., I, 1, i, pp. 405–8.

does not serve to prove the State, but on the contrary the State serves to prove logic."[6] The next year Marx was to write in the Paris Manuscripts: "Sense experience (*die Sinnlichkeit*) (see Feuerbach) should be the basis of all science. Science is not real science unless it sets out from sense experience in its double form, sense awareness and sensed need (*des sinnlichen Bedürfnisses*)—unless therefore it sets out from nature. . . . The natural sciences will finally subordinate to themselves the science of man, just as the science of man will finally subordinate the natural sciences to itself; the sciences will thus become one."[7]

We have here to deal with a number of obscure comments on a very obscure author, but it is clear at least that Marx rejects the Hegelian plan of explaining certain facts of human society in metaphysical terms. Now in his Preface to the *Philosophy of Right* Hegel had written: "This book then, containing as it does the science of the State, is to be nothing other than the endeavour to apprehend and portray the State as something inherently rational."[8] Rationality, according to Hegel, is displayed in a whole the parts of which are intimately related with one another so that the whole is implicit in each part and each part is essential to the whole. Thus, his *Philosophy of Right* was, among other things, an attempt to show that families and civil society are not rational wholes of this nature, but that the State, and particularly a constitutional monarchy, is nearer to being a whole of this nature. Aristotle had attempted something of the same sort when, in Book I of the *Politics,* he had argued that individual men, families, and villages were incomplete beings by comparison with the city-state. It will be seen that Hegel's method is not only based on his metaphysical view of rationality, but is also one in which judgments of value are aimed at, for the less rational forms of social organization are judged to be defective by reference to the more rational ones, however unavoidable the defects may be. It is this whole metaphysical-evaluative method that Marx rejects in the writings that I have just quoted from. He is asserting that society should be studied by the methods of the empirical sciences. The *facts* of social life should, therefore, first be ascertained by obser-

6. Ibid., p. 418.
7. Ibid., I, 3, p. 123.
8. Knox's translation, p. 11.

vation ("sense experience"); among these facts will be the actual needs of men ("sensed needs"); the value of social institutions should then be assessed in terms of these empirically ascertained "sensed needs" rather than in terms of some logical or metaphysical ideal; and then it will be found that the nature of real men and their "sensed needs" will throw light on the ideal society and on the nature of metaphysical thinking, rather than *vice versa*.

Such, it seems to me, is a principal theme of these early essays of Karl Marx, a theme which already points toward what later came to be known as the Materialist Conception of History. The rejection of metaphysics leads to a demand for the "scientific" examination of human society, and this, in its turn, leads to the claim that any assessments or valuations of human institutions should be in terms of needs that can be ascertained by scientific methods of examination. Theories about human society, it is argued, should be based on observed facts ("sense experience"), and social institutions should be assessed in terms of human desires ("sensed need"). Social institutions may thus be observed with a view to finding more effective means of satisfying human needs, and since both natural and social science are human concerns for the satisfaction of human wants, both are really subordinate to a fundamental science of human wants which is social science *par excellence*. These, I might say, were also the views of Auguste Comte, which had been published in Paris in the form of lectures between 1829 and 1842.

Now there is a difficulty in this whole conception which we should notice before we pass on to further aspects of the Marxist view. The difficulty arises from a certain vagueness in the word "need." A man's needs may be understood in the sense of everything he desires. To satisfy his needs would then be to satisfy as many of his desires as possible. But what one man wants may conflict with what another man wants, and so the problem arises of deciding which wants of which men shall have precedence. It would be generally supposed that one man's desire to torture another one is a desire that ought not to be fostered, and we generally take it for granted that social science should find means for satisfying, not any and every desire, but *legitimate* desires. If this is taken for granted, then the notion of a "need" is not a purely empirical one based solely on "sense." On the contrary, it conceals a moral assessment behind its apparently purely factual façade. Anyone, therefore, who claims to show that men's moral ideals arise from their "needs," in this sense of the word, is misleading himself and others, since the "needs" on which moral ideals are allegedly based are already charged with moral meaning.

A second sense of the word "need" is that in which a man's needs are what he must have in order to keep alive (his "necessities"), as distinct from the luxuries and superfluities of his life. On this interpretation, to satisfy men's needs is to secure their necessities. Now the line of demarcation between a necessity and a luxury is a shifting one that varies, as Marx well knew, with the state of civilization. The cigarette that was a luxury in 1900 becomes, it is said, a necessity in 1950. Man's basic physical structure, however, has not changed during that period, so that the food and warmth and shelter that would have sufficed to keep a man alive in 1900 would also do the same in 1950. If by "being alive" we just mean "not dying," then the means that would just succeed in keeping men alive are fairly constant. But, of course, when we talk of "keeping alive," we often assume that living is living at the standard of life customary to the individuals in question. Thus this notion of "needs" generally relates to a standard of life regarded as customary or decent. Indeed, many people feel that it is *wrong* for anyone to fall below a certain level of life, so that a man's needs are the means to a standard of life in the determination of which moral considerations have played an essential part. Here again, therefore, the notion of a "need" is far from being the purely "scientific" or morally neutral conception that it was held out to be.

It might be argued that these difficulties which are, of course, commonplaces to students of economics,[9] can be avoided by assuming that the function of social science is to ascertain the means of satisfying most wants, or of satisfying the maximum of want in society as a whole. Now in the first place such a programme requires a means of counting and measuring wants. Methods would have to be devised, for example,

---

9. "By necessaries I understand, not only the commodities which are indispensably necessary for the support of life, but whatever the custom of the country renders it indecent for creditable people, even of the lowest order, to be without." Adam Smith, *Wealth of Nations*, V, chap. 2.

to show whether, or the extent to which, freedom to act on the desire to hurt someone else in fact leads to a diminution of the satisfactions of other people as a whole. In general, some instrument would have to be constructed for measuring the rise and fall of satisfaction in a society. This is not the direction that Marxist thought on social science has taken. In any case, there is a second difficulty in the view we are considering. "Why," the critic may ask, "*should* social scientists aim at increasing the number or amount of satisfied needs?" If the answer given to this is that it is *right* that they should do so, then social scientists are not mere scientists after all, but moralists as well, and so morality has not been reduced to science. If the answer given is that everyone in fact *does* aim at the maximum amount of satisfied need, then the answer is probably false. I say "*probably* false," because it is not at all clear what could be meant by "maximum amount of satisfied need." I say "probably *false*," because many people appear to prefer their own satisfactions to anything even remotely resembling the satisfaction of society as a whole.

We may conclude from this discussion that much of what we say about human beings, even when, on the face of it, it appears to be purely factual, contains implicit evaluations of them and their conduct. This should not surprise us, for human beings are normally regarded as capable of choice, as free, responsible agents whose conduct may be good or bad. Thus, when we talk about ourselves and our kind we usually assume that we are concerned with such free moral agents. This assumption is so ingrained in us that words that were originally coined for scientific use, such as "fixation" or "sublimation," rapidly acquire a moral flavor when they are constantly employed. We can, of course, set before us the ideal of extruding all moral assessment from some of our discussions of human beings. We should then find that we were discussing them as if they were animals unable to act freely or morally. We could, for example, discuss them in biological terms, as organisms or as a species that maintains itself. In this way many true things may be said about men, things of a character common to them and other living creatures. But such a manner of speech is singularly ill adapted to describe and explain what is specifically human. When, for example, the same word "response" is used for a moth's movement toward the light and a man's answer to a question, very little indeed is being said about the man's behavior.

If what I have just said is correct, then, whatever may be the case with the extrusion of metaphysics from it, the extrusion of ethical considerations from social science is seen to be fraught with difficulties.

We must now pass on to consider how the Marxist rejection of religion, theology, and metaphysics, and the Marxist account of what they are, arose from Feuerbach's treatment of the same theme. In doing this we shall, I hope, prepare the way for a more specific grasp of the Materialist Conception of History. The view that we are to discuss is the view that men's religious, theological, and metaphysical views are not true in the way that their adherents suppose them to be, but are fantasies and illusions based on their circumstances and experienced needs. According to the Marxists, the dogmas of religion and theology and the theories of metaphysics should not be discussed as if they were genuine views with evidence to support them, but should be traced back to the human wishes and desires from which they spring. Marxists do not normally argue against the religious and metaphysical theories of their opponents, but claim to "unmask" them as the expressions of class interests or socially determined wishes. Marxists do not, for example, give detailed "refutations" of the arguments put forward by theologians and philosophers to prove that God exists, or that the world is fundamentally spiritual, or that there are two main types of essentially different being, the physical and the mental. Instead of doing this sort of thing, they argue that this or that theological or metaphysical theory was developed in order to support this or that class interest. This is a feature of Lenin's discussion of phenomenalism that non-Marxist philosophers find both puzzling and disquieting. As we have seen, this method of discussion can only be accepted as a result of first accepting the positivist view that the *sort* of reasoning used both by theologians and their anti-theological but metaphysical opponents is beside the point and cannot possibly lead anywhere. It is a method that is obviously most unsettling for those against whom it is used. To be told not merely that your point of view is unacceptable, but that it is not even worth discussing in the way that you have been used to discuss it, is to be treated as a somewhat comic figure.

The character in the comedy thinks, let us suppose, that he is doing his duty with dignity and authority, but he is laughed at by an audience that sees the real point that, in being hidden from him, makes him ridiculous. Religious persons, theologians, and metaphysicians cannot but feel that they are being made to appear absurd when they are told that all their arguments count for nothing in themselves, but are a sort of squeaky noise given out by the grinding of their own axes.

Let us then see how the Marxist theory of "ideologies" arose out of Feuerbach's theory of the nature of religion, theology, and metaphysics expounded chiefly in *The Essence of Christianity* (1841), *Preliminary Theses towards the Reform of Philosophy* (1842), and *Foundations of the Philosophy of the Future* (1843).

2. Feuerbach's Theory of Religion and the Marxist Theory of "Ideologies"[10]

Fundamental to Feuerbach's argument is the proposition that to say something *exists* is not merely to say that it can be *thought* or *conceived*, but is to say that in addition to being thought or conceived it can also be *perceived* or *sensed*. "Existence, empirical existence," he wrote in *The Essence of Christianity*, "is proved to me by the senses alone."[11] It follows from this, Feuerbach argued, that God's existence can never be proved by arguments that do not lead up to some perception of him. Hence the arguments of natural theology fail because they remain *mere* argu-

10. There is a good account of Feuerbach's views in Sidney Hook's *From Hegel to Marx* (London, 1936). I have also found the following particularly valuable: Hans Barth, *Wahrheit und Ideologie* (Zurich, 1945); Karl Löwith, *Von Hegel zu Nietzsche: Der revolutionäre Bruch im Denken des neunzehnten Jahrhunderts* (Zürich-Wien, 1941); Nathan Rotenstreich, *Marx' Thesen über Feuerbach*, Archiv fur Rechts- und Sozialphilosophie, XXXIX/3 and XXXIX/4 (Bern, 1951).

11. Translated from the second German edition by Marian Evans (George Eliot), London, 1854, p. 200 (VI, 243). The references in parentheses refer to the collected edition of Feuerbach's works by Bolin and Jodl (Stuttgart, 1903–11). That George Eliot should have published this translation at the time when she was helping to edit the *Westminster Review* shows that Feuerbach's ideas had European influence. They fitted in, indeed, with the Positivism that George Eliot had adopted. "With the ideas of Feuerbach I everywhere agree," she wrote in a letter.

ments, *mere* thoughts, and do not lead to the only sort of situation in which existence can be proved, viz., perception. This is the foundation of the whole view.

"The fundamental dogmas of Christianity," wrote Feuerbach, "are realized wishes of the heart."[12] Belief in God, he held, arises from man's tendency to compare particular, imperfect human beings with the general notion of the highest conceivable human perfection. This latter conception, which is constructed from the particular admirable men we are acquainted with, is then "projected" outside the human sphere altogether, as though there really were a single particular being to which all the scattered human excellences belonged.[13] Human predicates are thus attributed to a divine subject, whereas subject and predicate are really both of them human. "The identity of subject and predicate is clearly evidenced by the progressive development of religion, which is identified with the progressive development of human culture. So long as man is in a mere state of nature, so long is his God a mere nature God—a personification of some natural force. When man inhabits houses, he also encloses his Gods in temples. The temple is only the manifestation of the value which man attaches to beautiful buildings. Temples in honour of religion are in truth temples in honour of architecture. . . ."[14] When they thus project or objectify human characteristics as a non-existent God, men frequently deny themselves real satisfactions and indulge instead in imaginary ones. The monk or nun who refrains from sexual enjoyment receives substitute satisfactions on an ideal plane: ". . . The sensuality which has been renounced is unconsciously restored, in the fact that God takes the place of the material delights which have been renounced. The nun weds herself to God; she has a heavenly bridegroom, the monk a heavenly bride . . . and thus in reality, whatever religion consciously denies—always supposing that what is denied by it is something essential, true, and consequently incapable of being ultimately denied—it *unconsciously* restores in God."[15] In a somewhat similar manner, Feuerbach goes on,

12. *E. of C.*, p. 139 (VI, 145).
13. Ibid., p. 13 (VI, 16).
14. Ibid., pp. 20–21 (VI, 25).
15. Ibid., pp. 26–27 (VI, 32–33).

belief in immortality and in the divine justice established in heaven compensates man in an imaginary fashion for the lack of justice in human affairs: ". . . The other world is nothing more than the reality of a known idea, the satisfaction of a conscious desire, the fulfilment of a wish"—and he illustrates this by quoting St. Augustine's moving epigram: *Ibi nostra spes erit res.*[16] ("There our hope will be a reality.") Feuerbach, indeed, maintained that there is an important affinity between religious belief and dreams. "Feeling is a dream with the eyes open; religion the dream of waking consciousness; dreaming is the key to the mysteries of religion."[17] But it is not only dreams that throw light on the nature of religion, for according to Feuerbach the aberrations of religious fanatics and the religious extravagances of savages call our attention to what is at the core of the most developed forms of civilized religions.[18] "The mystery of theology," he wrote in the *Preliminary Theses towards the Reform of Philosophy,* "is anthropology."[19] That is, religion and the more or less naïve theorizing of it that is theology, can be seen for what they are if we come to understand how they emerge from the emotional and imaginative life of man. Once he understands this, and sees his religious imaginings for what they really are, man will no longer be obsessed by them, and will cease to be divided in his nature, with his ideals in one world and his failures in another: ". . . only the perception of things and natures in their objective reality makes man free and devoid of all prejudices,"[20] he wrote in the *Preliminary Theses,* and in the *Essence of Christianity* he calls this freedom "the identity of the human being with itself."[21]

According to the speculative philosophy of Hegel, the Absolute Spirit is self-conscious spirit, and self-conscious spirit is free. Feuerbach, it will be seen, gave a naturalistic, materialistic version of this theory. The free man, according to Feuerbach, is the man who has no illusions about himself. To man's systematic study of his own nature Feuerbach gave the name "anthropology"—today we call it psychol-

16. Ibid., p. 177 (VI, 215).
17. Ibid., pp. 139–40 (VI, 169).
18. Ibid., p. 178 (VI, 216).
19. (II, 222).
20. (II, 231).
21. Ibid., p. 229 (VI, 279).

ogy—and Feuerbach's view was that as men came to know more about themselves religion would lose its hold on them and cease to play any part in their ordinary calculations. In the Preface to the second edition of the *Essence of Christianity* he claimed "that Christianity has in fact long vanished not only from the Reason but from the life of mankind, that it is nothing more than a *fixed idea,* in flagrant contradiction with our Fire and Life Assurance companies, our rail-roads and steam carriages, our picture and sculpture galleries, our military and industrial schools, our theatres and scientific museums."

This is by no means an adequate account of Feuerbach's views on religion, but it is sufficient, I hope, to show their importance, both in preparing the ground for the Marxist theory of ideologies, and in setting in motion the naturalistic psychology that was later to undermine the religious faith of whole generations. It is important to notice, in the first place, how, in Feuerbach's hands, certain of Hegel's metaphysical conceptions were transformed into allegedly empirical ones. I have already indicated that Hegel's conception of the free self-consciousness of the Absolute was the basis of Feuerbach's conception of the free man who had cured himself of religious illusions. It should also be noticed that Hegelian conceptions form the basis of Feuerbach's view that men attempt to cure their personal and social ills by unconsciously providing for themselves a projected compensatory world of imaginary satisfactions. Feuerbach talks of God as man "objectified" (*vergegenständlicht*). He says that religious satisfactions result from the "externalization" (*Entaüsserung*—literally "alienation") of feelings. And he stigmatizes the division in man between his real needs and their imaginary fulfillment as human self-estrangement (*Selbstentfremdung*). There can be no doubt that the origin of these notions is in Hegel's conception of nature as the Absolute Idea alienated from itself. Thus, in the *Logic* (Book III, I, i, B) Hegel refers to nature as "the 'outside-itself-ness' of the Notion." He also uses the conception in a more detailed manner in the *Phenomenology of Spirit,* where he writes of the individual mind which is conscious of its self-estrangement (*Selbstentfremdung*) when it sees the effects of human thought and effort in the products of human culture. The individual is here regarded by Hegel as a mind confronted by an objective world in which it seems to recognize something that is both akin and alien to it. The resulting tension,

Hegel holds, can only be removed by absolute knowledge in which the divorced aspects of mind are re-united. Whereas for Hegel man's self-estrangement was ended in an experience that was rationally religious, for Feuerbach it was ended when religion was seen to be self-estrangement and was replaced by a clear-sighted recognition of the earthly tasks to which embodied human beings were committed. Marx, in the Preface to the second edition of *Capital,* said that he had turned Hegel's dialectic, which had hitherto been standing on its head, the right way up, but Feuerbach had preceded him in this task.

No one who is acquainted with Freud's account of religion in *The Future of an Illusion* can fail to be impressed by the similarities between it and Feuerbach's views. There is the same refusal to believe that the existence of God—or of anything else—could be based on anything but the evidence of the senses. Like Feuerbach, too, Freud stresses three main tasks of religion: that of relieving men from their fear of natural forces they do not understand, that of reconciling them to their miseries, and that of "making amends for the sufferings and privations that the communal life of culture has imposed upon man."[22] Like him, again, Freud argues that as knowledge of nature develops, it is the last of these tasks that assumes the greatest importance. He is as unwilling as Feuerbach to accept the imaginary or substitute compensations that religion offers, and thinks that men could free themselves from this "universal obsessional neurosis" if they listened to the voice of the intellect—"in the long run nothing can withstand reason and experience." At the end of the essay, indeed, Freud more than once refers to "our God Λόγος." I suggest that these likenesses may even indicate that Freud was directly influenced by Feuerbach's writings on this subject. "I have said nothing," writes Freud, "that other and better men have not said before me in a much more complete, forcible and impressive way. The names of these men are well known . . . I have merely added a certain psychological foundation to the critique of my great predecessors." Whether or not Feuerbach was one of these "great predecessors" that Freud had in mind, there can be no doubt that Feuer-

---

22. *The Future of an Illusion* (English translation, second impression, 1934), p. 30. The other quotations from that work in this paragraph are from p. 76, pp. 94–95, p. 62.

bach's theory of religion contains ideas that adumbrate certain features of Freud's system of psychology. There is the suggestion that the ravings of insane people and the beliefs of savages may provide clues that help us to understand the workings of more civilized and normal minds; there is the idea of the satisfaction in imagination of essential desires of which the individual is unconscious; there is the association of this process with dreaming; and there is the governing principle that when someone comes to know himself more fully, he will be less obsessed with thoughts of an imaginary world, and will be able to deal more adequately with the real one. Feuerbach's observation that theology is *pathology* hidden from itself[23] is most significant in the light of later theories. It should also be observed that notions such as that of "projection"[24] and that of "self-consciousness" were metaphysical before they became scientific. Their history would suggest, therefore, not a metaphysical level of thinking followed by quite a distinct scientific level, but rather a development of one into the other. This, in its turn, suggests that perhaps science and metaphysics are more closely bound together than some positivists have allowed.

There is a further aspect of Feuerbach's view which should be emphasized before I pass on to show how the Marxist theory of "ideologies" is formed from it. I said above that according to Feuerbach men who worship God and believe in his providence are in fact (*a*) unconsciously glorifying the highest achievements of mankind, and (*b*) obtaining imaginary satisfactions for needs that are real. Now Feuerbach did not think that (*a*) and (*b*) involved quite the same sort of illusion. He thought that (*b*) was just the mistaking of the shadow for the substance, but (*a*) was the misplacing of values that were real. Feuerbach had no doubts whatever about the genuineness of the human values themselves, but thought that people deceived themselves when they

23. *Werke,* VI, 107.

24. Schopenhauer's metaphysical conception of the "objectification" of the will in the human body and in nature is also relevant here. Feuerbach had read Schopenhauer's *World as Will and Idea* (the first edition of which had appeared in 1819) before he wrote *The Essence of Christianity.* This is not the place to discuss the respective influence of Feuerbach and Schopenhauer on modern thought, but it should be mentioned that the latter was a *metaphysician* who regarded consciousness and the intellect as a sort of self-deception.

projected them on to a supernatural being. He emphasized this in *The Essence of Christianity* by saying that the true atheist is not the man who denies God as subject (i.e., the man who denies that there is a being with the divine predicates), but the man who denies the genuineness of the moral predicates that have been falsely attributed to God. "He alone is the true atheist to whom the predicates of the Divine Being—for example, love, wisdom, justice—are nothing; not he to whom the subject of these predicates is nothing. . . . It does not follow that goodness, justice, wisdom are chimaeras, because the existence of God is a chimaera, nor do they become truth because God exists."[25] Indeed, Feuerbach says, somewhat rhetorically perhaps, that when the divine predicates are seen to be really human ones, humanity is more deeply revered and human actions are sanctified. Feuerbach advocated disillusionment as regards God, immortality, and divine justice in heaven, but only so as to achieve a clearer insight into what love, goodness, justice, and wisdom are here below. He does not apply the method of disillusionment to our moral notions. On the contrary, he thinks that the destruction of religious faith will lead to a heightened sense of human worth and possibility.

Marx and Engels, as I have already pointed out, became enthusiastic admirers of what Feuerbach published in 1841–43. Marx's "Criticism of Hegel's *Philosophy of Right*: Introduction," which appeared in the *Deutsch-Französische Jahrbücher* in Paris in 1844, is obviously written in this spirit. It is in this article that religion is described as "the opium of the people." The whole sentence, however, reads as follows: "Religion is the sigh of the hard-pressed creature, the heart of a heartless world, the soul of soulless circumstances. It is the opium of the people." It is clear from this that Marx thought that religion was the opium of the people in the sense that they use it to help them to bear their misfortunes, not in the sense that their rulers deliberately keep them quiet with it. In this article, too, Marx refers to the religious viewpoint as a "transposed (*verkehrte*) consciousness of the world," and argues that it is thus misleading. "The criticism of heaven transforms itself into a criticism of the earth, the criticism of religion into a criticism of law, the criticism of theology into a criticism of politics." "It is evident," he goes on, "that the weapons of criticism cannot take the

25. P. 21 (VI, 26).

place of criticism of weapons; material force can only be overcome by material force, but theory becomes itself transformed into material force once it penetrates the masses. . . . The criticism of religion ends with the doctrine that man is, for man, the supreme being. It ends, therefore, with the categorical imperative of overturning all the relationships in which man is debased, enslaved, abandoned, contemptible. . . ." The lesson to be drawn, therefore, from the criticism of religion is the need for a revolution in the social conditions that produce the religious illusion, and in this article Marx asserts that it is the proletariat, a class which is "the complete loss of man, and cannot reconquer itself except through the complete victory of man," which will carry out this revolution. "Revolutions," he continues, "need a passive element, a material basis. A theory is realized in a people only in so far as it is the realization of the needs of that people. . . . It is not enough for thought to *seek* (*drängen zur*) realization, but reality itself must seek the thought." And so he concludes: "Just as philosophy finds in the proletariat its material weapons, the proletariat finds in philosophy its intellectual weapons."[26]

Now Feuerbach had recognized that a consequence of his view of religion was that men should concern themselves with improving their life on earth rather than with hopes of a divine justice hereafter. In 1842 he had written: "Only when you have given up the Christian religion do you get, so to speak, the right to a republic: for in the Christian religion you have your republic in heaven, and therefore do not need one here. On the contrary, here you must be a slave, otherwise heaven would be superfluous."[27] According to Marx, such revolutionary observations, although they do occasionally occur in Feuerbach's writings, "are never more than isolated surmises,"[28] and in the event Feuerbach devoted most of his subsequent career to the "anthropological" analysis of religious belief, to uncovering its human and social origin, in the hope, presumably, that this would lead to greater moral enthusiasm in the affairs of this life. The passages just quoted from Marx's article of 1844 show a very different attitude, since the

26. The quotations in this paragraph are from M.E.G.A. (I, 1, i) in the following order: pp. 607, 608, 614–15, 620, 615–16, 620.

27. *Werke*, II, 222.

28. *The German Ideology*, p. 34.

emphasis is on transferring the criticism of religion from the intellectual to the social sphere. The argument is that the thinker who has "seen through" the religious illusion must find allies among those who, because they suffer most, have the strongest motive to press for real rather than for merely imaginary alleviations. Philosophers will never achieve justice by merely pulling off the illusions that are draped over injustice. They must transmit their instructions to the men who will push it away. Thus the proletariat was to be the "passive element," the "material basis," for the realization of a just social order. The passage in question almost suggests that the proletariat happened to be the most convenient agency for the philosophical ambition of destroying religious illusion. The expressions used by Marx here give the impression that he felt that the proletariat was a likely instrument for the exercise of philosophical reform. I do not know that he expressed himself in this way elsewhere, but Lenin in *What is to be Done?* (1902) wrote: "We said that *there could not yet be* Social-Democratic consciousness among the workers. This consciousness could only be brought to them from without. The history of all countries shows that the working class, exclusively by its own effort, is able to develop only trade union consciousness. . . . The theory of Socialism, however, grew out of the philosophic, historical, and economic theories that were elaborated by the educated representatives of the propertied classes, the intellectuals." [29]

We have not so far made use of the word "ideology"—for the use of the word itself, as well as for discussion of the thing, we have to turn to *The German Ideology,* which Marx and Engels wrote in 1845–46, but which remained unpublished until 1932. What we have so far seen is that according to both Feuerbach and Marx religious and metaphysical ideas convey false views of the world, but that these false views arise from the aims and desires of men and from the social arrangements which prevent these aims and desires from being realized. Feuerbach thought that, once this was clearly recognized, men would free themselves from their obsession with another world, and would endeavor

29. *The Essentials of Lenin* (London, 1947), vol. 1, p. 170. Cf. pp. 176–77 where Lenin approves of Kautsky. The statements of Kautsky are "profoundly true and important" (p. 176). Kautsky is quoted as saying that "the Socialist consciousness" is introduced into the proletarian class struggles *from without,* and is not something that arose spontaneously within it.

all the more strongly to realize love, justice, goodness, and wisdom in the human world. Marx, in 1844, held further that the instrument by which freedom from religious illusion and the resulting improvement in human living would be achieved was the proletariat, a class which, if its material strength were fortified with a correct philosophy, would change the conditions in which they and most men were forced to live lives that were "debased, enslaved, abandoned, contemptible." At this time both Feuerbach and Marx held that religion resulted from human failure both in the intellectual and moral spheres, but that it was no delusion that men with physical bodies live on this earth trying to achieve ideals of human perfection. In *The German Ideology* Marx and Engels not only used the word "ideology," but also passed a long way beyond Feuerbach's conception of the thing it stood for. This was because they had by this time definitely established their materialist conception of history. In this book they criticize Feuerbach, and by implication themselves too, for having falsely supposed that there is such a thing as "man" in the abstract rather than the different sorts of men who exist at different times and places. Men, they argue, are social beings whose nature changes with the sort of life they lead, and the sort of life they lead changes according to the way in which they get their living, according to the tools and organization of labor they employ to get food and shelter and to satisfy their other needs. As men have improved their tools, a division of labor has developed, so that some men live in towns, others on the land, some organize production and others carry out manual tasks under the supervision of masters. The division of labor leads to class divisions, and at different times different classes have dominated human societies in accordance with whatever was the predominant mode of production. For what the mode of production is and what sort of division of labor this requires determine which class shall dominate. There is also a division of labor between material and mental work. When this division has taken place within a dominant class, there will be a sub-class who specialize in the production of ideas. Since these ideas are produced from within the dominant class, they will be imposed upon the whole society. They will in fact be expressions of the needs and aspirations of the dominant class, though they will seem, both to those who frame them and to many others too, to be of universal significance. It is not only religious and metaphysical ideas, therefore, which reproduce a false consciousness of things, but other ideas, too, produced by specialists at the behest of a given class or within the framework of a given historical epoch. A given historical epoch is a period during which a given mode of production prevails. "If in all ideology men and their circumstances appear upside down as in a *camera obscura,* this phenomenon arises just as much from their historical life-process as the inversion of objects in the retina does from their physical life-process."[30] That is, it is in the nature of things that men should get distorted views of the world, just as it is in the nature of things that they should receive inverted images on the retina.

The following passages may serve to illustrate the notion of an "ideology" developed in *The German Ideology.* On page 14, Marx and Engels refer to "morality, religion, metaphysics, all the rest of ideology and their corresponding forms of consciousness"; on page 16, they say that the French and the English, though they have been "in the toils of political ideology, have nevertheless made the first attempts to give the writing of history a materialistic basis by being the first to write histories of civil society, of commerce and industry"; on page 20, they say that the division of mental from material labor leads "to the formation of 'pure' theory, theology, philosophy, ethics, etc."; on page 23, they write that "all struggles within the State, the struggle between democracy, aristocracy and monarchy, the struggle for the franchise, etc., are merely the illusory forms in which the real struggles of the different classes are fought out among one another. . . ."; on page 30, they say that those who endeavor to understand any epoch of history in terms of political and religious issues "share the *illusion of the epoch*"; on page 40, they refer to the "active, conceptive ideologists" of a class "who make the perfecting of the illusion of the class about itself their chief source of livelihood"; on page 43, they write of "the illusion of ideologists in general, e.g. the illusions of the jurists, politicians (of the practical statesmen among them, too)" and to "the dogmatic dreamings and distortions of these fellows"; and on page 80, in criticizing the "true socialists," Marx and Engels say that those theorists of socialism "have abandoned the realm of real history for the realm of ideology."

---

30. *The German Ideology* (London, 1942, reprint), p. 14.

The first feature that emerges from these passages is that Marx and Engels regarded ideologies as systems of misleading or illusory ideas. But no one can justifiably describe something as misleading or illusory except by comparison with something he thinks is not misleading and not illusory. What, then, according to Marx and Engels, is it that is not misleading and not illusory? In *The German Ideology* they state quite clearly what they think it is. "We set out," they say, "from real active men, and on the basis of their real life-process we demonstrate the development of the ideological reflexes and echoes of this life-process. The phantoms formed in the human brain are also, necessarily, sublimates of their material life-process, which is empirically verifiable and bound to material premises." On the next page they say: "Where speculation ends—in real life—there real, positive science begins: the representation of the practical process of development of men."[31] That is to say, there is, according to Marx and Engels, a system of ideas ("the representation of the practical process of development") about man, his religions and his societies, which is not illusory, which is not ideology. This system of ideas is the positive science of man and society, a science based on observation of men as they really are in their day-to-day concerns. Thus the positive science of man in society is *contrasted with* "ideological reflexes." This is, of course, quite in accordance with Feuerbach. In his opinion, the only way to discover what exists is by means of sense observation, and since this does not lead rationally to a revelation of God, heaven, or immortality, the religious view of things needs to be explained in terms of what the senses reveal. Marx and Engels accept this, but proceed to argue that an empirical science of man must trace back all his other activities to the ways in which he gains a living, and to the social organization involved in this. This contrast between "ideologies" on the one hand, and "real, positive science" on the other, is clearly based, as was Comte's contrast between positive science and theologico-metaphysical thinking, upon a distinction between what is held to be unverifiable and what is believed to be verifiable. And lest it be urged that *The German Ideology,* an early work, was later superseded in this respect, I refer also to the famous Preface to Marx's *A Contribution to a Critique of Political Economy* (1859)—

31. Ibid., pp. 14–15.

frequently cited by Marxists as fundamental for an understanding of the Materialist Conception of History—where we find the view of *The German Ideology* repeated as follows: "In considering such revolutions the distinction should always be made between the material revolution of the economic conditions of production which can be accurately substantiated in the manner of the natural sciences, and the legal, political, religious, artistic or philosophical—in short ideological forms, in which we become conscious of this conflict and fight it out."[32] It should be noticed that the phrase I have translated by "accurately substantiated in the manner of the natural sciences" is, in the German *naturwissenschaftlich treu zu konstatierenden* and thus gives the idea of an accurate, honest *natural*-scientific procedure. "Ideology" was used in this sense right to the end of Engels' life, since he wrote to Mehring on July 4, 1893: "Ideology is a process accomplished by the so-called thinker consciously indeed, but with a false consciousness. The real motives impelling him remain unknown to him, otherwise it would not be an ideological process at all."[33] The fundamental idea is of a scientific procedure that enables its users to show what are the *real* aims of men who are conscious only of their own apparent aims.

A second important feature of the Marxist theory is that the "ideological" thinker is held to be not only theoretically, but also practically, misleading and misled. Feuerbach, Marx and Engels argued, was too sanguine about the results of unmasking the religious illusions. His books and lectures, they considered, opposed the religious false consciousness in a purely theoretical manner, whereas the only effective way of opposing it was to overthrow in deed as well as word the social conditions that give rise to it. I have already discussed, in Part One, the Marxist view that genuine science is a practical as well as a theoretical activity. Just as, on the Marxist view, the sciences of nature involve practice, in the form of experimentation and manufacture, so the science of society, properly understood, involves the transformation of human society, as well as understanding how it works. It should here

---

32. Second edition, ed. Kautsky (Stuttgart, 1907), pp. lv–vi. Also, translated by N. I. Stone (New York, 1904), p. 12. I have modified Stone's translation to bring out the force of "*naturwissenschaftlich treu.*"

33. *Selected Correspondence,* p. 511.

be observed that one of the problems that caused the most puzzlement to nineteenth-century thinkers was how the methods and teachings of empirical science fitted into a society that had hitherto seemed to be based on religious belief and Christian morality. Some of the theories of the natural sciences—in geology, for example, and in biology —appeared to conflict with Christian dogmas, while the technological changes associated with scientific advance seemed to weaken the whole religious attitude, causing many people to adopt spontaneously the view that nature must be a self-regulating mechanism. Thus the question arose whether the science which was undermining the Christian view of things could also provide standards for human conduct. Comte and his followers thought that science itself was a moral enterprise; the qualities that led to successful scientific research were moral qualities of humility and disinterestedness that would also lead to the regeneration of human society. Marx and Engels did not share this view, but they did believe that, as a scientific understanding of physical processes was at the same time a mastery over them, so a scientific understanding of human society would involve the subjection of social forces to human control. On their view, pure theory is an abstraction, not something that could really exist and be true. Genuine theory, on the other hand, they held to be at the same time a practical mastery over events. Thus Feuerbach's exposure of religion and metaphysics was, they held, an abstract, merely contemplative exposure, and therefore not fully scientific in the way in which the Marxist theoretical-cum-practical exposure is. It is clear, of course, that this view involves morality with empirical science as Comtism does, though in a different way, but before I can discuss the matter further, there are some other features of the Marxist theory of ideologies that need to be brought out.

A third aspect of the Marxist theory of ideologies concerns what is to count as an ideology. We began this account of the theory of ideologies with an exposition of the religious-theological-metaphysical one. The passages I have quoted from the writings of Marx and Engels show that they also included as ideologies, that is, as forms of "false consciousness," "morality," "ethics," "political ideology," and "legal," "artistic," and "philosophical" ideologies. We may suppose that the philosophical ideology is the same as the metaphysical, and that no important distinction is being drawn between morality and ethics. We must then ask in what sense ethics or morality, art, law, and politics are forms of false consciousness. The language used would suggest that we are as deluded when we make moral, aesthetic, legal, or political judgments as, on the Marxist view, we are when we make religious and metaphysical judgments, that, for example, the differences between right and wrong, beautiful and ugly, legal and illegal, constitutional and unconstitutional, are merely imaginary, and hide from us some real experienced need or desire. Feuerbach rejected God and heaven in favor, as he thought, of human love and justice, and for this was jibed at as "a pious atheist."[34] But Marx seems to have thought that moral ideas themselves were a sort of illusion the reality of which was something more fundamental in human life; and so too for art, law, and politics. People are only free from illusions, on this view, when their pronouncements on matters of morality, art, law, and politics are consciously related to the scientifically ascertainable realities which they reflect. But we cannot go further into this until we have looked more closely at the Marxist account of social reality.

Before we turn to this, however, there is a fourth aspect of the Marxist theory of ideologies that must be referred to. We have seen that Marx and Engels use the word "ideology" to refer to misleading or false views about the world of nature and society, and do not apply the word to scientific knowledge of things as they are. In contemporary Marxism, however, there is a tendency for the word to be applied to any sort of theory whatever, true or false. Thus, "Marxism-Leninism" is regarded as a scientific theory of nature and man, and would therefore, in the usage of Marx and Engels that we have been discussing, not be called an "ideology" at all. But in his report at the Seventeenth Congress of the Communist Party of the Soviet Union in 1934, Stalin referred to "our tasks in the sphere of ideological and political work," and said that one of them was "to intensify ideological work in all the links of the Party."[35] By "ideological work" he clearly means education in principles that are not, on his view, illusory. In *A Soviet His-*

34. Karl Löwith, *Von Hegel zu Nietzsche,* 2nd edition (Zürich-Wien, 1941), p. 363.

35. *Handbook of Marxism* (London, 1935), p. 945.

tory of Philosophy the authors write: "The struggle of the materialistic 'line of Democritus' with the idealistic 'line of Plato' was an ideological partisan struggle between a progressive slave-holding democracy and the reactionary landowning aristocracy."[36] Here, "ideological" seems to have the meaning given to it by Marx and Engels. On pages 43–44, however, they write: "It will be shown that Lenin and Stalin in their struggle against revisionism developed the materialistic conception of history and worked out the ideological foundations of the Party and questions about the mutual relation between spontaneity and consciousness in the workers' movement, about economic and political struggle, about the formation of the socialist ideology of the proletariat, about the role of revolutionary theory. . . ." It is clear that in this passage the word "ideology" stands for ideas that are held to be neither false nor misleading. Again, in the article "Ideology" in their *Handbook of Philosophy*,[37] Rosenthal and Yudin say it is "a term used during the past century to denote the whole complex of views, ideas, concepts, notions, functioning on a social level—a form of social consciousness. Political views, sciences, philosophies, ethical systems, arts, and religions are forms of ideology, in this sense of the word, regardless as to whether they are true or false, progressive or reactionary."

This development in the terminology is, in my opinion, very important. I suggest that the juxtaposition of "partisan" with "ideological" shows how the development has taken place. According to Marx and Engels, "ideologies" were false thinking determined by class interests, but they also held that the final victory of the proletariat would bring into being a society not divided into classes. In declining capitalist society the rising, progressive class is that of the proletariat, and its views of social questions, being those of the class that will end all classes, are not limited in the way in which other class theories are. The class character and partisanship of "Marxism-Leninism" make it natural enough to call the theory an ideology, but it is at the same time "scientific" be-

36. P. 8.

37. New York, 1949. Translated from the Russian. The English translation of this book is described as having been "edited and adapted" by Howard Selsam, but the passage I have quoted is referred to in I. M. Bochenski's *Der Sowjetrussische Dialektische Materialismus* (Berne, 1950), p. 138, and Bochenski made use of the Russian text.

cause it will ultimately cease to be limited to a single class, and will be accepted throughout a society the transformation of which will be the theory's verification. It will be observed, furthermore, that Marxists do not clearly state that *natural* science is an ideology except in the sense that it involves theorizing. They talk about "bourgeois" science, but when they do I think they are suggesting that elements of distortion, arising from class interests, enter *into* the natural sciences. They can hardly mean that bourgeois natural science *as a whole* is distorted, since, for example, Engels was at great pains to support the theory of dialectical materialism by reference to discoveries made by bourgeois scientists in the nineteenth century. Again, it may be that the wider use of "ideology" has been adopted in order to evade the conclusion that would appear to follow from Marx's account of ideological thinking, viz., that in communist society not only would religion disappear, but art and morality as well. (Politics and law, as we shall see, will, according to the Marxists, disappear in the classless society.) However that may be, a problem of very great importance for the understanding of Marxism emerges from our discussion of the theory of ideologies. For on the one hand Marx and Engels regard morality as an ideology and thus as involving false consciousness, and on the other hand they hold that a scientific understanding of human society would be at the same time its practical regeneration. But we cannot deal with this until we have considered in outline the social "reality" with which the ideological "reflexes" and "illusions" are compared. This brings us to the central ideas of the Materialist Conception of History.

3. The Materialist Conception of History in Outline

In this section I propose to deal with the fundamental elements of the Marxist theory of history, and to leave details of the theory of ethics and politics for discussion in the next chapter.

According to the Marxist theory of Historical Materialism, the form assumed by human society is *influenced* by such factors as geographical environment and the level of population, but is *determined* by what Marx, in the Preface to his *Critique of Political Economy*, called "the material conditions of life," in which the "legal relations and forms of state," as well as religious, philosophical, and artistic ideas, are "rooted." In order, however, to understand this very general statement of the view, we must first see how the Marxists analyze the notion of "the material conditions of life."

What, on the Marxist view, differentiates man from the other animals is that whereas the other animals keep themselves alive by making use of the physiological equipment they are born with so as to seek and find their food and shelter, men produce their food and shelter (their "means of subsistence") by the use of instruments (tools) which are not parts of their original physiological equipment. Even though other animals make such shelters as nests, hives, and webs, these works of theirs remain much the same from one generation to another. But human beings, through the use of tools, produce works which permit of indefinite improvement by succeeding generations. The tools which one generation has made and used are handed on to the next. The new generation starts where the previous one had left off, and may in its turn transmit improved tools to its successors. The skill, experience, and tools thus received and used Marx called "productive forces." "Productive forces," on his view, are not *individual* products. Any improvements made by individuals are made on the basis of what is already current in the society to which the individual belongs. The man who, for example, improves on a spade, is improving something which is itself the result of many men's work in past epochs. "The individual and isolated hunter or fisher who forms the starting-point with Smith and Ricardo belongs to the insipid illusions of the eighteenth century. They are Robinsonades. . . ."[38] Thus each generation of men inherits a set of productive forces which are social in their origin.

"Productive forces," however, are social in their use as well as in their origin. A man who digs with a spade may be digging his own field, but he is able to do this only because there is a social organization that permits individuals to own fields, and perhaps to sell what they produce in them. The individual who uses some socially inherited instrument of production to produce goods that he sells to others, is dependent upon the readiness of other people to buy from him or to barter with him. Thus an individual tool user does not merely use a particular instrument to change the parts of nature he applies it to; he uses it

38. *Critique of Political Economy*, trans. Stone, pp. 265–66.

within the context of a social organization. Spades, ploughs, canoes, or looms are not merely instruments by means of which an individual man breaks the earth, gets fish, or makes cloth. The breaking of the earth, the fishing, and the weaving involve relations of men to one another, in operating the tool (as with a large canoe), in disposing of the product (as with the wheat that the plough prepares for), or in both (as with the cloth woven in the cottage and sold to a merchant). Thus the men who brought the "blue stones" from Pembrokeshire to Stonehenge showed their mastery over natural forces, but their task could not have been accomplished without a most elaborate organization among the men themselves, though we do not know what it was. Associated with the "productive forces," therefore, are what Marx called "productive relationships." "Productive relationships" are the ways in which men are related to one another as they operate the "productive forces."

According to the Marxists, specific types of "productive relationship" are linked with each main type of "productive force." They hold that there are five main levels of productive force, and with these, it would seem, five main types of productive relationship must be associated. There was the era of stone tools, with which was associated a primitive communism in the means of production and in the distribution of the product. "Here," writes Stalin, "there was no exploitation, no classes" (*sic*).[39] When metal tools were first used, society divided into masters and slaves. ("It was iron and corn," Rousseau had written, "which civilized man and ruined the human race.") The windmill is mentioned by Marx on one occasion as the technological basis of feudalism. Corresponding to the production of goods in factories with power-driven machinery was the industrial capitalist order of society, though an earlier form of capitalism had existed prior to the introduction of such machinery. Capitalist society will be replaced by a socialist order as the highly elaborate productive forces that result from the application of modern science bring about control and ownership by the community as a whole.

Before I pass on to further aspects of the theory, it is necessary to make it clear that my outline of the Marxist theory is based on the

---

39. *Dialectical and Historical Materialism. History of the Communist Party of the Soviet Union*, p. 124.

belief that it is fundamentally a *technological* theory of history. Many but not all interpreters of Marx and Engels adopt this interpretation. There are, as Professor Bober points out,[40] serious difficulties in it. For example, Marxists do not show in detail precisely how technological changes bring each new epoch into being. Engels, in *The Origin of the Family,* appears to argue that it was the use of iron that caused the advent of the ancient slave society, but he mentions other causes, too, that are not technological. Marx, in a famous epigram in the *Poverty of Philosophy* says that "the windmill gives you society with the feudal lord," but I am not aware of any detailed attempt to substantiate this. Again, in *Capital,* volume 1, Marx says that in the earliest phase of capitalism men work for wages in small factories, but the difference between this and what went before seems to be one of scale rather than of technique. It is at a later stage of capitalism, that of modern industry, a phase that began toward the end of the eighteenth century, that technological changes had great influence. In explaining this Marx writes: "The machine that gives rise to the industrial revolution is one which replaces the worker handling a single tool, by a mechanism operating simultaneously a number of identical or similar tools, and driven by a single motive power, whatever the form of that power may be."[41] This would seem to be a more careful statement of the epigram in the *Poverty of Philosophy* that the steam mill gives you society with the industrial capitalist. Marx does, however, state the technological view very strongly, in general terms, in a long footnote in *Capital,* volume 1, from which I cite the following: "Technology reveals man's dealings with nature, discloses the direct productive activities of his life, thus throwing light upon social relations and the resultant mental conceptions. Even the history of religion is uncritical unless this material basis be taken into account. Of course it is much easier, from an analysis of the hazy constructions of religion, to discover their earthly core than, conversely, to deduce from a study of the material conditions of life at any particular time, the celestial forms that these may assume. But the latter is the only materialistic method, and therefore the only sci-

40. M. M. Bober, *Karl Marx's Interpretation of History* (2nd edition, revised, 1950, Cambridge, Mass.), pt. 1, chaps. 1 and 3.

41. *Capital,* p. 396.

entific one."[42] Stalin, in *Dialectical and Historical Materialism,* is rather vague about the matter. He gives a brief account of the development of technology and of its association with the various historical epochs, but he does not make it quite clear how the technologies and social systems are connected. However, he makes a point of arguing that technological innovators are unaware of how their inventions will affect society, that the men who introduced iron did not know that they were preparing the way for slavery, that the men who started "large manufactories" never imagined that royalty and aristocracy would be destroyed by them. This appears to support the technological interpretation, if we are prepared to regard "large manufactories" as technological innovations. In fact, they do not seem to be new *inventions,* in the sense in which metal tools or steam engines once were, but only expansions of something already in being. This, of course, may well be an example of the transformation of quantitative changes into a change of quality, and I shall discuss it as such later. My main reason for accepting the technological interpretation of the theory is that it does at least purport to provide a definite theory of history, whereas the alternatives are almost too vague to discuss. Furthermore, if we accept it, we are able to understand the importance in Marx's argument of his view that man is a tool-making animal. Anyone who reads part 4 of *Capital,* volume 1, will see that Marx attempted to investigate the origins of industrial society as a *historian,* trying to find out what really happened and to make some sense of it. This part of his work has value independently of the Materialist Conception of History.

The main point, then, of the Materialist Conception of History is as follows. The basis of any human society is the tools, skills, and technical experience prevalent in it, i.e., the productive forces. For any given set of productive forces there is a mode of social organization necessary to utilize them, i.e., the productive relationships. The sum total of productive relationships in any society is called by Marx its "economic structure." This, he holds, is the real basis on which a juridical and political superstructure arises, and to which definite forms of social consciousness correspond. Radical changes in the basis sooner or later bring about changes in the superstructure, so that the prime cause of

42. Ibid., p. 392.

any radical political or moral transformation must be changes in the productive forces. In effect, the idea is that human society has a "material basis" consisting of the productive forces and associated productive relationships. This is also called the "economic structure." This, in its turn, determines the form that must in the long run be taken by the legal and political institutions of the society in question. Less directly but no less really dependent on the economic structure of society are its moral and aesthetic ideas, its religion, and its philosophy. The key to the understanding of law, politics, morals, religion, and philosophy is the nature and organization of the productive forces.

There are three further aspects of the theory that must be briefly touched on before I come to discuss it in detail.

In the first place it must be emphasized that Marxists do not assert that the superstructure has no influence whatever on the development of a society. On the contrary, they hold that there is interaction between basis and superstructure, and that such interaction is only what would be expected in a dialectical system.

In the second place, the Marxist theory of classes forms an important element in the doctrine of Historical Materialism. Briefly, the theory is that each main arrangement of the productive forces calls into existence its own form of the division of labor, and that this, in its turn, leads to a division of society into classes. Corresponding to each form of the division of labor there is a division of society dominated by a single class—slave owners in ancient society, feudal landowners in the Middle Ages, the bourgeoisie in modern times. Both the political and intellectual life of society is dominated by the class that has the upper hand in making use of the productive forces and is thus able to *exploit* the rest. Furthermore, within each governing class there is division of labor between the thinkers and the men of action. The thinkers of each governing class are "its active, conceptive ideologists, who make the perfecting of the illusion of the class about itself their chief source of livelihood."[43] When the proletarian class, the class with the broadest basis, has finally consolidated its power, class divisions will have been overcome and the division of intellectual from physical labor will have been brought to an end. Then the ideological "false

43. *The German Ideology,* p. 40.

consciousness" will have disappeared, to be replaced by a permanent union of theory and practice.

In the third place, the theory of Historical Materialism is a theory of revolutions. The source of social revolution, on the Marxist view, is the qualitative "leap" to a new form of productive force, such as the "leap" to steam-powered machinery which was the real basis of the bourgeois revolution against the feudal system. When one of these qualitative changes in the productive forces has first manifested itself, the old forces of production and the old political and ideological forms continue to exist for a while. Hand-looms, for example, continue to exist alongside power-looms, Parliament remains unreformed, and landowners are still regarded with veneration. But as the new productive forces are developed, they render the old ones obsolete, and new ideologies develop critical of those that had prevailed earlier; at the same time the new class that is interested in the new productive forces begins to demand new political and legal institutions to give scope for its own development. The bourgeois capitalists, for example, dispute the political supremacy of the landowners, and do so in terms of the new ideology of *laissez-faire* economic theory. Conversely, widespread criticism of a given order of society is a sign that that order is in process of being replaced by a new "progressive" one. A "progressive" class is a class that controls the new productive forces that are ousting the obsolete ones. Thus the moral protests of "progressive" publicists are signs that the old order is *in fact* giving place to a new one. The "reactionary" defenders of the old order will, of course, cling as long as they can to their political power and to the moral and religious notions that go with it, but their plight is hopeless, since the ultimately determining social influences are the productive forces, and if qualitatively new productive forces have been brought into operation, the whole of society will be transformed in accordance with them.

It will have been noticed that Stalin, in his compressed statement of this theory of revolution, says that the new productive forces may for a time develop while productive *relationships* appropriate to the *old* productive forces continue in existence and so give rise to social "contradictions." This simplified view does bring out what is essential in the theory, but in fact the Marxist theory allows for various types of disproportion in social development. The new productive forces could conflict both with the political and legal relationships and with the moral, religious, and philosophical ideologies of the society in question. Or the legal and political relationships could be brought into line with the new productive forces while the ideological superstructure still remained unreconciled with them. It is conceivable, too, that the ideological superstructure might be brought into line with the new productive forces *before* the legal and political relationships had become so adapted—this last would be the condition in which men's minds and hearts already approved a new social order although the political revolution lagged behind. In our next section we shall have to consider how these different tiers or layers could be connected.

As I have been making a point of comparing the Marxist views with those of Comte and other contemporary nineteenth-century thinkers, it may be of interest to notice the theory of revolution that Comte had expounded in 1838. "By a necessity that is as evident as it is deplorable," writes Comte, "and is inherent in the weakness of our nature, the passage from one social system to another can never be a direct and continuous one; it always presupposes, for the space of at least several generations, a sort of more or less anarchic interregnum, the character and duration of which depend on the intensity and the extent of the renovation to be secured; thus the most marked political advances essentially consist in the gradual demolition of the old system, the chief bases of which had been constantly undermined beforehand. This preliminary upsetting is not only inevitable by reason of the strength of the antecedents that bring it about, but is also quite indispensable, both to allow the elements of the new system, which up to this point had been slowly and silently developing, to receive, little by little, their political establishment, and to give a stimulus toward reorganization by means of knowledge of the inconveniences of anarchy. . . . Without this prior destruction, the human mind would never be able to reach a clear conception of the system that is to be brought into being."[44] The notion that is clearly common to Positivism and to Marxism is that of a new society starting its growth within the old one that it will finally destroy. Comte's "anarchic interregnum" corresponds to the Marxist "leap," though Comte, as I understand him, does not re-

44. *Cours de philosophie positive*, leçon 46 (edition of 1864, Paris), pp. 35–36.

gard this as such a clear-cut affair as Marx appeared to do. Comte brings to light also the most important problem of how the members of one type of society could foresee the type of society that is to replace that in which they themselves live. His view seems to be that as men come to dismantle the old society they will find a new one developing in which will appear in embryo form the lineaments of that which is to come. It was, he thought, from an examination of the essential features of science and industry, already existing in dying feudalism, that an idea of the future could be obtained. This conception is clearly most important for the Marxist view, since if there were an absolute novelty the other side of a "leap," then it could not possibly be predicted, whereas a new society, once it has found its way, by whatever means, into the old one, may conceivably bear marks that the whole society may some day exhibit. I should also mention that Comte, in the section from which the above passage is quoted, also argued that the dying feudal society was unsettled by "fundamental inconsistencies"; for once it made any compromise with the new scientific ideas, and once it allowed some scope to modern industry, it had abandoned the only basis from which they could be consistently attacked. This is an earlier version of the theory that their "contradictions" bring dying societies to their destruction.

4. Examination of the Materialist Conception of History

We have now described in outline the social reality with which Marxists compare the false views of society that they call ideologies. Our next step must be to consider the reasons they give for holding that the Materialist Conception of History is a true account of social reality. This is not easy, however, since Marxists tend to regard the theory as one that any candid person is bound to accept as soon as he understands it, or as one that the whole creation conspires to proclaim, or as one that immediately illumines the dark places of history. But there are one or two specific arguments that can be examined.

Stalin, following Lenin, argues (1), that if matter is primary and mind derivative, then "the material life of society, its being, is also primary, and its spiritual life secondary," and (2), that if mind "reflects" an objectively existing material world, then "the spiritual life of society"

reflects "the material life of society," which is "an objective reality existing independently of the will of man."[45]

Let us then consider (1). The contention is that from the materialist thesis that matter existed first and mind evolved from it; it follows
that it is changes in "the material life of society," that is, in the productive forces, that bring about the major changes in social life, and in
art, religion, and philosophy. More briefly still, the contention is that
philosophical materialism entails historical materialism. It is not difficult to see, however, that this is not so. The matter that is "primary"
in the doctrine of philosophical materialism is such things as gases,
seas, and rocks, but "the material life of society" consists of tools, inventions, and skills. The alleged *social* primacy of "the material life of
society," therefore, is quite a different thing from the alleged primacy
of matter over mind, for the "material life of society" that determines
the political and ideological forms itself contains mental components,
whereas, on the Marxist view, it is from mindless matter that mind has
sprung. From the premise that mind sprang from matter, nothing can
be concluded about the causes of social development. The fact that
Frankenstein had made his monster did not prevent the monster from
destroying Frankenstein, and if the monster had made Frankenstein,
Frankenstein might still have had the power to control it.

No one who is convinced by my argument against (1) will accept
(2) either, for (2), like (1), rests upon an equivocation between "material" in the sense of "purely physical" and "material" in the sense of
"technological." "The material life of society" is, indeed, something
that individual men are born into and have to accept much as they
do the physical world itself, but it depends upon mankind as a whole
in a way that physical nature does not. Once it is clear that "the material life of society" includes socially inherited skills and experience,
then the difference between the Materialist Conception of History and
theories such as Comte's, according to which intellectual development
is the cause of social progress, is very much diminished. The Marxist
theory might, indeed, be reworded so as to state that social advance
depends in the first instance upon the success with which men solve

---

45. *Dialectical and Historical Materialism*, p. 115. Lenin argues (2) in *M. and E-C*,
p. 278.

their technological problems. But among the factors involved in the solution of such problems are the intelligence and persistence of the human beings concerned. Intelligence and persistence are, in a broad sense, moral as well as physical or physiological qualities. Another way, therefore, of putting the Marxist view would be to say that the application of a given amount of intelligence and energy to technological problems has an enormously greater influence on social development in general than the application of that same quantity would have if it were directed to political, moral, and other ideological problems. I do not know whether this is true, but its truth or falsity cannot be decided by reference to the view that mind came from matter or that individual men have to submit themselves to already existing ways of life.

The above arguments show that Lenin and Stalin thought that the Materialist Conception of History was seen to be obviously true once philosophical materialism was accepted. Both Marx and Engels thought that there is something *obvious* about the theory. In the *Communist Manifesto* Marx wrote: "Does it require deep intuition to comprehend that man's ideas, views, and conceptions, in one word, man's consciousness, changes with every change in the conditions of material existence, in his social relations and in his social life?" And in his speech at the graveside of Marx, Engels said that Marx "discovered the simple fact, hitherto concealed by an overgrowth of ideology, that mankind must first of all eat and drink, have shelter and clothing, before it can pursue politics, science, religion, art, etc." Marx's view thus is that it does not require "deep intuition" to see that the Materialist Conception of History is true, and Engels refers to it as "a simple fact." What is this "simple fact"? The simple fact seems to be that in order to pursue politics, religion, and art men must keep alive, and that in order to keep alive they must eat and drink. This, surely, has never been denied, unless by someone who argues that angelic politicians, priests, and artists operate beyond the grave. And no one, surely, would deny that people's ideas change as the things and situations change about which the ideas are ideas. Such truisms hardly seem to establish the Materialist Conception of History. They are held to be relevant, I suppose, to an evolutionary theory of the origins of human society, according to which the first men are supposed to have been a sort of animal that could keep themselves alive but were ignorant of politics, science, and religion. There was a time, it is supposed, when these creatures were only just able to keep themselves alive, and during this time influencing one another, thinking, and praying were activities that they could not afford. First there had to be the activities that kept them alive, and only then could they start on these less vital ones. Now let us leave aside the question of prayer, and consider only the activities of influencing one another—or any other political activity—and thinking. Are we to suppose that these do not play a part in keeping men alive? Do men think only *after* they have found food and shelter? Do they quarrel with one another and maneuver with friends and enemies only when the day's work is done? On analysis, I suggest, this sort of argument can do no more than say that early men must have found it very hard to keep alive and succeeded in doing so only in so far as they found food, drink, and shelter. To say that success in these directions must have preceded politics, science, and religion is like saying that eggs must have preceded hens, or that hens must have preceded eggs.

In the *Communist Manifesto,* however, Marx puts forward what looks like another argument in favor of the Materialist Conception of History when he writes: "What else does the history of ideas prove than that intellectual production changes its character in proportion as material production is changed?" Here he seems to be supporting his case by reference to history. But to say that the Materialist Conception of History is a *historical* theory is not to say anything very precise, for there are different sorts of historical enquiry agreeing in little except the claim to report or explain the human past. Now when Marx supports the Materialist Conception of History by historical considerations one of the things he does, I think, is to construct what Dugald Stewart, writing early in the nineteenth century, had called "Theoretical or Conjectural History," and what French writers of the eighteenth century had called *Histoire Raisonnée.* Dugald Stewart, in explaining what "Theoretical or Conjectural History" consists of, wrote: "In examining the history of mankind, as well as in examining the phenomena of the natural world, when we cannot trace the process by which an event *has been* produced, it is often of importance to show how it *may have been* produced by natural causes."[46] Now Marx, it seems to me, arrives at the Materialist Conception of History in this way, except that he seems to claim to know how the events *must have been* produced. This may be seen from *Capital,* volume 1, chapter 5, § 1, which is entitled "The Labour Process." Here Marx endeavors to explain what human labor is. Men are parts of nature who act on the rest of nature with their bodily organs so as to make it supply their wants. They thus change the rest of nature, and in doing so they develop their own potentialities. (I imagine that an example of this would be the development of human skill through agriculture so as to produce new tastes and such works as Virgil's *Georgics.*) Bees just build cells, but men transfer to nature cells that previously had existed in their heads—their works are realizations of themselves. Unlike other animals, men use tools to transform nature into something that they have previously conceived. As they use tools to do this, and as the use of tools is a specific characteristic of men, Franklin was right to call man "a tool-making animal." It therefore follows that the various sorts of tool that men have made and used in the past enable us to distinguish one human epoch from another, as with the stone, bronze, and iron ages. Just as we can from an examination of fossil bones discover what sorts of animal once inhabited the earth, so, from an examination of tools left behind by them, we can reconstruct the nature of men and societies that are now extinct. The types of tool enable us to discern "the social relations amid which labour was performed."[47]

It will be noticed that this argument has two strands. In the first place it is argued that tool making and tool using (technology) are the specific human characteristic. In the second place, variations in the use of tools are regarded as evidence for fundamental variations in the societies and men that use them. As to the first strand in the argument, it is as if Marx had agreed with Aristotle that man has an essence but had disagreed with him about what that essence is. Whereas Aristotle had said that man is a rational animal, Marx said he was a tool-making and tool-using animal. Thus the argument fundamentally is

46. This account of "Theoretical or Conjectural History" is based on Gladys Bryson's *Man and Society* (Princeton University Press, 1945), pp. 88 ff.

47. *Capital,* vol. 1 (Everyman edition), p. 172.

that since men are essentially tool makers and tool users, their society is the necessary outcome of their tool-making and tool-using activities. It is also worth noticing that the proposition that men, in transforming nature, develop their own potentialities, is obviously suggested by the thesis of Hegel's *Phenomenology* that men, in changing the natural world by their labor, gain a fuller consciousness of their own nature. Indeed, Hegel's metaphysical observations on human labor are transformed by Marx into a theory of society and of human progress according to which men discover and unfold their powers in the process of controlling nature.

Let us start our examination of this view by seeing how it is linked with the Aristotelian theory of essences. Very briefly, an essence is that without which something could not be what it is, that which makes the thing the sort of thing it is. To take an example, the essence of a knife is to cut by means of a blade fixed into a handle. Something without a blade or handle would not be a knife, for knives cut, and cannot do so without these parts. On the other hand, however, knives may have handles of different colors and blades of different shapes without ceasing to be knives. These features that knives may cease to have without ceasing to be knives are called their *accidental* features in distinction from the *essential* features they must have if they are to be knives. Now there are different sorts of knife, such as paper-knives and carving knives. These, too, have their essential and their accidental features. It is essential to the paper-knife to cut paper, and to the carving knife to cut meat, and as these are very different operations, different sorts of blade and handle will be needed if they are to be these sorts of knife. Paper-knives, for example, will have to be smaller than carving knives, carving knives broader-bladed than paper-knives. Again, it does not matter what color their handles are. Now Marx's view, so far as it is that tool making and tool using are the essence of man, is that, just as all knives must cut by means of a blade fixed into a handle, so all men must be tool makers and tool users; that just as there are paper-knives and carving knives, so there are men who make and use stone tools, and men who make and use metal tools; and that just as cutting paper requires one sort of blade and cutting meat requires another, so making and using stone tools requires one sort of politics, law, and ideology, and making and using metal tools requires another. On the basis of the theory of essences, therefore, the analogy between man and a knife is as follows. Technology is an essential feature of man, as cutting by means of a blade fixed in a handle is essential to a knife. Having a stone age technology or a bronze age technology corresponds to being a paper-knife or a carving knife. Stone age politics, law, and ideology correspond to the blade and handle essential to a paper-knife, and bronze age politics, law, and technology correspond to the blade and handle essential to a carving knife. But when we draw out the analogy in this way we see that it cannot be fully maintained from the Marxist point of view. For it is a well-known Marxist contention that politics, law, and ideology belong only to class societies, and will not exist in the future communist society after the withering away of the state and the rise of social self-awareness. But, if we follow our analogy, this would be as though there could be a specific sort of knife that had no specific sort of blade and handle. But there could not be any such thing. Hence, the Marxist view that technology is of the essence of man and determines the different sorts of society and ideology is not consistent with the other Marxist view that there will be no politics and no ideology in the communist society of the future.

In noting this, we discover, I suggest, a most serious flaw in the Marxist view of history. If man is to have an essence in anything like the way in which knives have essences—and this is what is implied by the view that he is a "tool-making animal"—then this essence sets a limit to the possibilities open to him, so that he cannot evade or transcend anything that the essence necessitates. But if the various types of technology involve various types of politics, law, and ideology, by what right can we say that one particular type of technology gets rid of all politics, law, and ideology? There can be little doubt, I think, that Marx felt this difficulty and endeavored to meet it by the theory that men develop their own powers as they work on the natural world. This last view may be interpreted as a theory of progress rather than as a theory of essences. Knives must always be knives, and we know pretty much what sort of thing they are. There is nothing about knives, as knives, that can ever cause more than a slight or momentary astonishment. They go on cutting, perhaps better and better, but it is still cutting that they do, and we know just what that is. Progress in knives is progress in the same rather simple thing. It is approaching nearer and nearer to an already clearly conceived end, the perfect cut. But human progress is not like this. It does not consist in getting closer and closer to some foreseeable perfect consummation, but rather in developing new possibilities that can only occur to men in the course of their attempts to develop those already known to them. This is so even if we admit that technology is the essence of man, for the purposes and types of machines can only be foreseen a stage or two ahead, and the technology of even the fairly near future is quite unpredictable by us.[48] To say that man has an essence is to suggest that he is a fairly simple and predictable sort of thing like a knife, or even an oak tree. To say that his essence is tool making and tool using is to modify this suggestion somewhat, but still to restrict the sphere of his development to one only of his activities. If someone is bent on talking of the human essence, then I think that rationality is more suitable than technology, since it is more fundamental and manifests itself more widely. However that may be, it was by committing himself to the view that technology is the essence of man that Marx convinced himself and others that the Materialist Conception of History is obviously true.

In the passage I am discussing, Marx gives what appear to be archaeological reasons for holding that technology is of the essence of man. From its fossilized remains, he argues, the structure and mode of life of a prehistoric animal can be reconstructed. Similarly, he goes on, from the tools of a vanished people the organization of its society can be inferred. But we cannot infer from the fact that certain parts of its body have survived that these were its fundamental or essential parts when the animal was alive, and so too, I should have thought, we cannot conclude that the tools that survived from an extinct culture were more essential to it than other things that have completely disappeared. The archaeological argument only has force if we *already* believe that technology is the determining feature in human life. From the fact that something survives of an extinct animal or culture it does not follow that it must have been the essential feature of that animal or society. The Stone Age is so called because the men of that time were unable to work metals and so left only stone implements behind

---

48. More will be said about this later.

them, not because everything else in their lives was determined by or depended on the stone that they worked. The Stone Age was not stone in the way in which Old Red Sandstone is red.

We have now considered the principle behind the conjectural history involved in the Materialist Conception of History. We have seen that Marx's account of it is based upon his view that the essence of man is his technology. We have argued that man is not the sort of being that has an essence, since, unlike such things as knives, whose structure is determined by a single end, such as that of cutting, men are complex beings who constantly discover new aims as they achieve or fail to achieve their old ones. We have argued, furthermore, that Marx's appeal to archaeology does not show that technology is the fundamental determining force in history but only presupposes that technology is the essence of man. We have also argued that Marx, in saying that man has an essence, was implying that human progress is a much more simple and limited thing than in fact it is, and that in saying that man changes himself in changing the world he is in effect denying that man has an essence at all. Our next step must be to consider the claim that the Materialist Conception of History is not conjectural history at all, but a comprehensive view based on the facts of history. For when, in the *Communist Manifesto,* Marx said that his view was supported by "the history of ideas" he may well have meant something of this sort. The Materialist Conception of History, that is, would be an account of social development supported by the facts of history, much as the geological theory of the formation of the earth's surface is supported by the nature and position of rocks and fossils. That Marx held such a view may be seen from his constant references, in *The German Ideology,* to the empirical nature of his view of history, as well as from his general criticism of Hegel's speculative philosophy of history.

The Materialist Conception of History has undoubtedly had a great influence on historical study in the twentieth century. Many non-Marxists are prepared to admit that it suggests a fruitful method for historical investigation, and it has been held to be of value as "a sort of recipe for producing empirical hypotheses."[49] It would, indeed, be foolish to deny that since the theory was first formulated there has

---

49. W. H. Walsh, *An Introduction to Philosophy of History* (London, 1951), p. 162.

been, at least in part under its influence, a good deal of interesting research into the technology and economic life of past societies. It should not be forgotten, however, that Marx had been preceded in this by Adam Smith and others. The growth of economic science, quite apart from Marx, naturally led historians to look with new eyes at the commerce and industry of past ages, while the growth of inventions in the eighteenth and nineteenth centuries aroused interest in the technologies of the past. But all this relates primarily to historical description, i.e., to discovering and recording economic and technological facts in addition to the political and religious and literary ones that had interested previous historians. The Materialist Conception of History, however, is a theory of historical *explanation*. It is one thing to admit that historians have done well to consider the commerce, industry, class structure, competing interests, and changing outlooks of past societies, but quite another to say that the technological factors determine all the rest. If this last is a coherent hypothesis, then it should be possible to test it, to see whether those things are which would have to be if it were true. If, on the other hand, it is not a coherent hypothesis, then we do not know how to test it, and any good that comes from considering it will be accidental. It is my view that it is not a coherent hypothesis, and that therefore historical research cannot confirm it, but on the contrary is likely to be led by it into confusions. This is not to say that it may not *also* help in the advancement of historical knowledge; incoherent hypotheses, such as Kepler's astrological ones, have often led to important discoveries, though they get rubbed away and lost when their work is done. Marxists, however, do not regard the Materialist Conception of History as an expendable hypothesis but rather as a truth which reveals why history happened as it did and what is next to come of it. It would be impertinent for a philosopher to criticize the coherence of a hypothesis that was being used in a provisional way in the course of some particular investigation. The examination of eternal truths and established dogmas, however, is his proper business.

In the Materialist Conception of History three main sorts of notion appear. There are, in the first place, those such as "matter," "contradiction," "dialectics," "nodal lines," which I have called metaphysical and which Marxists themselves would prefer to call philosophical or fundamental. In the second place, there are those that relate primarily to the Marxist *analysis* of society, such as "productive forces," "productive relationships," "division of labor," "classes," "revolution." And thirdly, there are the various historical epochs recognized by Marxists, such as "primitive communism," "feudalism," "capitalism." The first two sets of notions are used to explain how the epochs distinguished in the third set have emerged and developed, and to predict the coming epoch. In brief, the Marxists claim to have established the outlines of a science of history which, in its general structure, is not unlike the science of geology. Just as the geologist, by interpreting his observations in the light of physics, chemistry, and biology, is enabled to establish a sequence of geological epochs, so the Marxist claims to utilize his analysis of society in terms of division of labor, classes, productive forces, etc., in order to plot the series of past social epochs and to predict the coming of the next.

In what follows I shall say something about the principal notions in each of these three main classes.

In the first class I select for discussion (*a*) the notion of "contradiction" and (*b*) the notion of "nodal lines."

(*a*) When I discussed the notion of "contradiction" as applied by Marxists to the material world, I suggested that it is primarily a logical notion and agreed with those critics of Marxism who have said that physical events or things cannot contradict one another. But I also pointed out that a man who asserts what another man denies is contradicting that other man, that in contradicting him he is, in a sense, *opposing* him, and that it is only a short step from opposition to struggle. To say that physical events contradict or oppose one another is to speak anthropomorphically. That being so, we cannot say out of hand that "contradiction" is not a suitable notion for applying to human societies. The contradictions that hold between propositions or statements are involved in the assertions and denials that form part of the social interplay of human beings. Now the social contradiction most frequently cited by Marxists is probably that which they say holds between "social production" and "capitalist appropriation." This is explained by Engels as follows. Before the advent of the capitalist system, the workman, owning his own tools and raw materials, produced commodities that were his property until he sold them. He was the owner, that is, of the products of his own individual labor. Under capitalism, however, the workman is a member of an elaborately organized group; his labor is no longer individual but social. The plant and tools he works with and the raw material he works on belong to the capitalist, and the commodities so produced belong to the capitalist also. The capitalist, that is, becomes the owner of the products of other people's labor. But, Engels argues, individual ownership of a commodity presupposes that the commodity has been individually produced, so that to have individual ownership of a socially produced commodity is to treat what is socially produced as if it were individually produced. This, according to Engels, is a contradiction.[50] There are many points at which this argument might be criticized, but what I am concerned with is the notion of contradiction involved in it. Engels believes, I suggest, that the social production of commodities cannot go on indefinitely in association with the individual ownership of the commodities so produced. He seems to be arguing that the organization of production under capitalism is so very different from the organization of production under the system that preceded capitalism that capitalism cannot for long retain the pre-capitalist system of ownership of the commodities produced. This must be because there is something about the capitalist, social, method of production that will ultimately make private ownership of the commodity unlikely or impossible. A simple example of a social change which makes the retention of an old social arrangement *unlikely* is that of the adoption of printing. Once books came to be printed, it was unlikely, though not impossible, that books would continue to be copied and illustrated by hand. It was unlikely, because printing is so much cheaper than hand copying; it was not impossible, because the copyists might have had sufficient social or political influence to induce the community to continue paying a higher price for a proportion of its books. It might be quite naturally said, therefore, that there was a contradiction involved in wishing to have *both* cheap printed books *and* hand-produced books, though it might be better to say that these two things were *incompatible* with one another. A simple (and simplified) example of a social change that makes the retention of an existing state of affairs *impossible* is the following. In a community where the level of production is not rising and cannot rise it is

50. *Anti-Dühring*, pp. 296 ff.

decided that there shall be an increase of investment abroad without affecting the level of consumption or of investment at home. But it is impossible that this should take place, for it is impossible that something should be taken from a finite quantity and for that quantity to remain the same. Yet it might well happen that people should unthinkingly try to do both these things, or to do other things that were really logically impossible. Perhaps Engels' use of the word "contradiction" means that he thought that "capitalist appropriation" and "social production" are contradictory in this last, most stringent, sense, though his use, in the same discussion of the word "incompatibility" (p. 298) and, in an analogous discussion, of the word "antithesis," may suggest the first sense. However that may be, it cannot be justly argued that the Marxist use of the term "contradiction" in social contexts is open to the objections that are rightly made to its use as descriptive of physical events.

There is a good deal that might be enquired into about contradictions in human affairs. For example, when A seeks to be superior to B, and B to be superior to A, they cannot both be superior to the other in the same respect, though each may succeed in achieving *equality* with the other. The relationship between A and B has then some analogy with that between contradictory and contrary propositions in the Aristotelian logic, where, of contradictories one must be true, and of contraries both can be false. Only one man can win, but both may fail to win. Again, the man who makes contradictory statements succeeds in saying nothing, but the man who unwittingly pursues a policy and the negation of that policy may undo each of the things he sets out to do, but he cannot be said to do nothing as the man who contradicts himself says nothing. Some philosophers, furthermore, have argued that just as there is a logic of propositions, so there is a logic of imperatives. Of these, some have argued that the logic of imperatives is similar to the logic of propositions, while others have said that there must be great differences between them—that, for example, while from the conjunctive proposition "He put on a lifebelt and jumped into the water" we may validly infer either of the conjuncts, e.g., "He jumped into the water," we cannot, from the imperative "Put on a lifebelt and jump into the water," infer the single command "Jump into the water." These considerations show that there are some interesting problems to be investigated here, and it is to be regretted that Marxists, whose theory of social contradictions raises some of them, have, as far as I am aware, left them unexplored.

(*b*) There is, then, some merit, or at least some philosophical suggestiveness, in the notion of contradictions in society, but I am afraid that the theory of qualitative leaps across nodal lines, when applied to social affairs, can bring little but confusion. Now we saw in Chapter II that Hegel and, following him, Marx and Engels, lumped together a number of different things under this heading. One of these was the sort of change that occurs when substances form a new substance by chemical combination as distinct from mere mechanical mixture. Most people have seen that sort of change take place in a test tube. When the chemicals are mixed there is a striking change of color or condition. I do not imagine that we need spend long in disposing of the suggestion that social changes are at all like this. For the individuals who make up society do not get fused or transmuted, as in chemical combination, but remain, changed perhaps, but still recognizable, as in mechanical mixtures. And if it be argued that it is organizations, or institutions, that coalesce in this way, then it is clear that they are being metaphorically regarded as substances like sulphuric acid or sodium chloride. The important conception, for our present discussion, is clearly that of a series of gradual quantitative changes terminated by a sudden qualitative leap, as in the cooling of water and its transformation into ice. We have to consider whether there is anything to be gained by applying this notion to the changes that take place in human societies. And it is not without interest that Hegel seems first to have thought of this in connection with human affairs and only later applied it in his reflections about nature. In the Marxist theory, the most important nodal lines are, of course, those that run between one historical epoch and another. If we take technology as basic, we must suppose that a form of technology that is the foundation of a certain social system for a time develops in ways that contain nothing new but are merely variations on a single technological theme; then the economic, political, religious, and other ideological changes that result from this will be of the same gradual, unoriginal sort; next, there is a technological revolution, and instead of another variation there is an absolutely new theme—there is now a new technology imbedded in the old society; new ideologies and a new social system will ultimately follow. What we have to consider is, first, the nature of this technological leap, and secondly, the nature of the social changes that result from it.

That there is a difference between gradual technical improvements and new inventions I am fully persuaded. Once the working of iron, for example, has been introduced, it is natural and not very difficult to foresee the working of other metals. The thing that was not natural, and could not have been foreseen, just was the working of metals. We must distinguish, that is, between *routine* inventions and *creative* inventions. The latter are unpredictable though their routine development can be foreseen. No *particular* invention can be predicted, for to predict it in detail would be to make the invention. But it is often easy to see, in a *general* way, the directions in which a new invention may be developed. If what is the other side of a nodal line is an unpredictable novelty, then creative inventions are the other side of nodal lines. But not every creative invention starts a new social system. The invention of the wheel seems not to have had this effect, yet it is surely as much of a technological leap as the invention of metal-working. Furthermore, while the invention itself may be described as a leap, its acceptance may well be so gradual as to be describable as a crawl. As the new technology comes to be adopted, the society which adopts it is gradually changed. What is sudden or abrupt, I suggest, is the noticing rather than what is noticed—the new order surprises people because their main concern was with the old things that they were used to rather than with the new thing that was creeping up behind them. If we turn our attention again to the invention itself we may ask whether it is preceded by a series of gradual changes that correspond to the gradual lowering of temperature that precedes the freezing of the water. There does not seem to be any such thing, for the gradual changes are seen in the development *of* an invention rather than in the preparation *for* it. It may sometimes happen that a new idea was, as we say, "in the air" for a time before it took definite form, but the analogy between this and the dropping of temperature over continuous degrees is obviously very slight. There is an analogy, however, between this and the gradual increase in size of the workshops in which workmen were employed for wages—the growth of what Stalin calls "large manufactories." *Fairly* large factories, it is argued, existed in the pre-capitalist era, but when many of them got beyond a certain size the change of scale was at the same time a change in the *nature* of the system, and hence quantity has become transformed into quality. But on the face of it this is an example, not of the water-ice transformation, but of the grains-heap or not-bald-bald transformation, which, as I pointed out in Chapter II, involves a decision on our part about how many grains we are going to *call* a heap, or about how great a lack of hair we are going to *call* baldness. This does not mean that between not-heap and heap, or between not-bald and bald, there had been a tremendous jump, but only that different words are going to be used for the different sides of an almost invisible division. We are going to *call* it capitalism when there are a lot of very large workshops—a verbal leap does duty for a factual crawl, and justifiably so because the opposite ends of the crawl are so very different from one another. We can now see one of the reasons for the obscurities in the technological aspects of the Materialist Conception of History. The transition from primitive communism to slave society, and from the earlier phase of capitalism to *industrial* capitalism, was by means of sudden, unforeseeable inventions, the use of iron and the use of power-driven machinery respectively. The transition from the slave society to feudalism, and from feudalism to the first phase of capitalism, however, was by means of cumulative improvements that at a certain stage suggest a change of name. The expression "transformation of quantity into quality" is used to cover both, and hence is here a source of confusion.

It would be most misleading, of course, to suggest that Marx's own account of the coming of capitalism is vitiated by this confusion between a qualitative change in the things described and a decision to draw a line between the application of the words "feudalism" and "capitalism." When we consider his description of how "co-operation," the first phase of capitalism, came about, we find him saying such things as that the employer of a large number of workmen has more assurance of getting an average performance from them than the employer of only a few, since these few may happen to be unusually stupid or unskillful. Again, he points out that it is likely to be cheaper to provide a single building for a large number of workmen than to provide several separate buildings for small groups of them. He says, furthermore, that when a considerable number of men work together under the same roof, their output may increase because of "emulation" and "a certain stimulation of the animal spirits."[51] Now here are three different reasons for the spread of larger workshops than had hitherto been favored, viz., that the employer of a considerable number of workmen is less dependent on the abilities of any one of them than a small employer is; that it is less costly to construct a large factory for, say, one hundred men, than to construct ten factories each housing ten men; that men working together in large groups feel the urge to work harder than they would work if they were alone or in small groups. How miserably inadequate to this sort of discussion is the "quantity-quality" formula. Here are three different reasons that lead in one direction. The first reason concerns the number of men, regardless of whether they work in a factory or not. The second concerns the costs of building and their effects on the price of what is produced in them. The third concerns an alleged principle of group psychology applied to men who have not yet formed trade unions. There is no single category here, such as temperature, that permits of measurable degrees of increase or decrease, nor is there a single quantity that all three factors move toward—for there is no reason to suppose that the number of men required to avoid having too many useless workmen is anything like the number required to get the most economical building or to stimulate the "animal spirits." The "quantity-quality" formula gives rise to the misleading picture of feudalism being lowered in degree, unit by unit, until it is replaced by the first unit of capitalism, icy but exhilarating. But the difference between feudalism and capitalism is most dissimilar from the difference between a liquid and a solid, and not very like the difference between the "look" or "form quality" of a number of grains and a heap of grains. It may at first sight appear, to take Hegel's example, that there is some analogy with the case of the constitution that works well for a small state and then breaks down when the state grows beyond a certain size. But when we look into the matter, we find that the constitution broke down because there was too much work for the officials, or because they failed to adapt themselves to the new jobs they were called upon to do, or because the population lost inter-

51. *Capital,* vol. 1, p. 341.

est, or for a combination of these and other reasons, just as there were a number of very different reasons, according to Marx, for the development of feudal workshops into capitalist factories. When Hegel put forward this view of a right proportion between population and constitution he was not only influenced by Montesquieu's explanation of the decline of Rome, but was concerned to show that there was a degree of truth in Pythagoras's theory that "things are numbers." The social theorist is not bound to accept such speculations.

So much, then, for the main metaphysical notions involved in the Materialist Conception of History. We must now turn to the most important part of the theory, the part that comprises the Marxist *analysis* of society. Certain of the conceptions used by Marx, Engels, Lenin, and Stalin are common to Marxism and to non-Marxist social theory, and I need not, therefore, discuss them here. But basic and essential in the Marxist analysis are the notions of "productive forces," and "productive relationships," which together constitute "the material conditions of life." If these are coherent conceptions, then the theory may still be coherent in its main outlines, but if they are not, then the Materialist Conception of History cannot be coherent. Now I have already shown very briefly what is meant by these terms, basing my interpretation on the Preface to the *Critique of Political Economy* (the most frequently quoted text) and on Stalin's *Dialectical and Historical Materialism.* The distinction between the "productive forces" and "productive relationships" is also drawn, though not always in the same words, in the early pages of *The German Ideology,* and the following passages from the *Communist Manifesto* are of importance: "The bourgeoisie cannot exist without constantly revolutionizing the instruments of production, and with them the whole relations of society." The bourgeois productive forces are listed as ". . . subjection of nature's forces to man, machinery, application of chemistry to industry and agriculture, steam navigation, railways, electric telegraphs, clearing of whole continents for cultivation, canalization of rivers, whole populations conjured out of the ground." Unfortunately, in no passage known to me is the distinction between productive forces and productive relationships illustrated by detailed examples, and I must therefore make my own attempt to repair this omission, and develop my criticisms in doing so.

Now a relationship between a number of different men is involved in the use of most large tools and machines. A fishing vessel, for example, needs several men to operate it, and we should therefore be prepared to say that the vessel itself is a productive force, and that the relations of its crew to one another as helmsman, cabin boy, crew, and captain, are productive relationships. It might be said that this does not hold for small tools, since, for example, an individual can make and use a spade all on his own. This objection, however, is what Marx called a "Robinsonade." Just as, on his view, there are no isolated hunters or fishers, so there are no isolated agriculturalists. Unless the man with the spade could expect that the land he was digging would be left alone for the crops to grow, there would be no point in his digging. Although his fellow men may not be physically present when he digs, his behavior is part of a system of social relationships in which he, as an individual, is playing a recognized part. He and the people who do not trample down his crops are co-operating, though not so obviously, just as the cabin boy and helmsman are.

The examples of the fishing vessel and the spade may be used to call attention to yet a further element in the notion of productive relationships. If we suppose that the fish and the agricultural produce in question are not merely consumed by the families of the actual producers but are exchanged or sold, then the men who fish and the men who dig are in fact involved in still wider relationships. For their work is done largely with a view to supplying other people with what they want, and getting from these other people things other than fish and farm produce. We see, therefore, that there are three main types of productive relationships: (*a*) those involved in the very operation of the instruments of production (e.g., steering a ship while someone else looks after the sails); (*b*) those wider relationships that grow up in order to allow production to go on without interruption (e.g., the explicit or tacit agreement that land that has been dug shall not be trampled); (*c*) the economic relationships that exist when the objects produced are *commodities* for exchange (e.g., the fisherman throws away, or consumes himself, some sorts of fish he knows he will not be able to sell). If only (*a*) were in view, the theory could hardly be called anything but the Technological Theory of History, but with (*c*) in mind it is natural to think of it as an *economic* theory of history. A mingling of all three may be seen in the following passage from the Preface to the *Critique of Political Economy:* "The aggregate of these productive relationships constitutes the economic structure of society, the real basis on which a juridical and political superstructure arises, and to which definite forms of social consciousness correspond. The mode of production of the material means of existence conditions the whole process of social, political, and intellectual life."

The passage quoted above from the *Communist Manifesto* appears to stress the technological element of the theory, for the bourgeoisie are represented as "revolutionizing" the relations of production as a result of "revolutionizing" the *instruments* of production. What does such a view amount to? We can best decide, I suggest, if we consider in turn what connections there are between changes in the instruments of production on the one hand, and those sorts of productive relationship that we have labeled (*a*), (*b*), and (*c*).

It seems to me that to say that changes in productive forces bring about changes in productive relationships in sense (*a*) is to utter a sort of tautology. Let us imagine a society of fishermen who fish from small canoes each of which is paddled by one man. The productive forces are the men paddling their individual canoes, and individually fishing from them. The productive relationships are their putting to sea individually and working as independent individuals. Now let us suppose that someone invents and constructs a large sailing vessel. This will be a new sort of productive force. But it will bring with it a change in the productive relationships, for the new craft will require someone to man the sails, someone to steer, and perhaps several men to cast large nets. Now in what way does the new invention bring with it new productive relationships in sense (*a*)? It seems to me that in talking of the new invention we are talking of new job-relationships. In designing the large sailing vessel, the inventor was also arranging for new functions to be performed. What he invents is not only a new physical structure, but also the system of working it. Vessel and crew, contrivance and workmen, are elements in a single design. In designing the fabric the inventor has also designed the working functions. His invention *is* a new division of labor. When, therefore, it is said that any considerable changes in productive forces must bring about changes in productive relationships, and when "productive relationships" is understood in sense (*a*), the "must" indicates a tautology, for new machines are not merely differently constructed machines but machines that have to be worked in new ways. I do not call this proposition a tautology in order to disparage it, for it is often a most important thing to bring tautologies to light, and I think that the present one is by no means unilluminating. What we have to beware about with tautologies, however, is the tendency to transfer the certainty that they possess to other propositions that are not tautologies at all. That this has happened in the Materialist Conception of History I hope to show in a moment. First, however, let us give the name "technological relationships" to productive relationships in sense (*a*).[52]

Suppose, then, we understand "productive relationships" in sense (*b*), in the sense of wider relationships than those involved in actually operating the tools or machines but necessary if they are to be worked at all. Let us call such relationships "para-technological relationships." It is easy to see in general what these are. No one would dig if the crops were constantly trampled down; no one would take a trawler to sea if it were liable to be taken from him. If the instruments of production are to be operated at all, there must be rules about who operates them and what happens to them when they are not being operated. There must be some law or custom of property. One way of settling these matters would be to have private property in land and trawlers, and this, according to Marxists, involves a division into classes, classes, according to Lenin being divisions among men arising from their different relations to the instruments of production. On this interpretation, then, the Materialist Conception of History is the theory that corresponding to each main type of productive forces there is a set of property relations and class divisions, and that important changes in the former are necessarily followed, sooner or later, by important changes in the latter. (We must emphasize "sooner or later," for it is an important part of the theory that *for a time* the old productive relationships can linger on, hampering the new methods of production.) What sort of connection is this, between the productive forces and the para-technological relationships? Not the same sort of

---

52. Some of the sentences in this paragraph are from my paper entitled "The Materialist Conception of History," published in the *Proceedings of the Aristotelian Society*, 1951–52, pp. 207 ff.

connection as that between the productive forces and the technological relationships. That sort of connection, it will be remembered, was simply that a change in the form of a tool or machine is at the same time a change in the form of the jobs performed by the men who use it. Hence it could not possibly be the case that the new type of machine was being used and the old type of productive relationships survived. But when "productive relationships" is understood in the sense of para-technological relationships, it is expressly maintained that old para-technological relationships can, for a time, exist alongside the new productive forces. On the face of it, therefore, the connection between productive forces and para-technological relationships is a fairly loose one. There are many conceivable ways, for example, in which the newly invented vessel might be guarded between voyages or controlled in the course of them, but on the Marxist view, although there are many logical possibilities, only one of them is *in fact* possible at any given time. If a sufficiently important change is made in the forces of production, there is only one way of dealing with the resultant indirect problems of social organization that could in fact be adopted in the long run—once the new productive forces have been set in motion, there is only one possible way open for dealing with their indirect effects.

I have not been able to find in the writings of leading Marxists any reason for this social fatalism, but from what has already been said, it is easy to see how they came to adopt it. For it is easy to see how the constraining necessity that holds between productive forces and technological relationships should be transferred in thought to para-technological relationships also. The notion of "productive relationships" is left vague, and the devil of confusion enters in and confounds two different forms of it. And a further confusion arises as follows. When agriculture was first introduced, the hunting or pastoral people who had discovered it must have had to devise some land regulations that would enable cultivation to go on unhindered. A modern example is the need for new sorts of international treaty when aircraft comes to be widely used. Nomads need no land law, and earth-bound people need no air law. Failure to develop a land law or air law would have prevented the development of agriculture or air travel. In the absence of suitable para-technological arrangements, the technological innovations would have been nothing but ingenious dreams. Luck might have preserved a season's crops or enabled the aircraft to make some flights, but as agriculture or aviation were pursued more persistently, either chaos would have ensued or else some para-technological rules would have had to be accepted. These rules, of course, need not have been promulgated by anyone, but may just have "grown" in the course of action. To say, therefore, that agriculture and aviation flourish is to imply that suitable para-technological rules have been adopted. Looking at the matter retrospectively we see that the para-technological relationships "had to be," since those things exist that could not have existed without them. But *before* they were adopted it was by no means certain that they would be. Furthermore, all sorts of possible para-technological relationships are consistent with any given type of productive force—all sorts of systems of land-tenure, for example, with the early techniques of agriculture—so that there is no justification for supposing that those actually adopted were necessarily adopted.

Before we consider productive relationships of type (*c*), there is an important point to notice that arises from what we have just said. For it has now become apparent that para-technological relationships *comprise* moral, customary, and legal ones, and that therefore law and morals cannot properly be regarded as superstructures. Our previous examples serve to illustrate this. If a hunting people become agriculturalists, the land and its preservation, *ipso facto*, acquire a new importance. Rules for allowing or preventing access to the land are necessary. Conduct that had previously been permissible is now frowned on or prohibited. Trespassing is a new crime, respecting one's neighbor's landmark a new virtue. New sorts of disputes arise between agriculturalists and hunters—there are still farmers who resent the hunting pack—and between agriculturalists themselves. These new types of dispute will require new types of judgment, and these will have to be enforced. Hence, productive relationships, in the sense of para-technological relationships, *are* moral, legal, and political. The Marxist scheme is of a material basis comprising productive forces and productive relationships, of a legal and political superstructure forming the next layer, and of an ideological superstructure, comprising morals, as well as religion, art, and philosophy, at the very top. We now see, however, that an analysis of the Marxist distinctions uncovers moral and legal and

political relationships as aspects of the productive relationships themselves, and hence as aspects of the material basis of society. Since the
theory itself is thus confused, attempts to verify it are like trying to
carry water in a sieve.

We now come to the third type of productive relationship, the type
involved when what is produced is produced for barter or sale. As I
mentioned earlier, it is this type that sometimes secures for the whole
Marxist complex of "material conditions of life" the epithet "economic." Let us call such relationships "market relationships." Then
according to the Materialist Conception of History important technological changes bring with them important changes in market relationships. This view is obviously correct. When goods are exchanged,
improved means of producing them may lead to their becoming
cheaper, to their producers making a higher profit, or to both. In
terms of people this means that more people enjoy more of the goods
in question, that some producers are able to enjoy more other things
than they could before, or both. The technological changes have
changed people's lives. The extent of such changes becomes even more
apparent if the technological innovation is a means for producing a
type of commodity, such as a television set, that had not existed before. A new activity of living has then been introduced. But it is equally
obvious that market considerations influence the course of technological change. In a society where money is used, the producers aim at
producing more or different goods partly because they think that the
goods would be bought if produced. This, surely, is an influence of
market relationships, via men's conception of them, on the productive forces. Once there is production for sale, then the producers' esti-
mates of what the buyers want will influence the producers' thought
about their tools and machines. Productive forces on the one hand,
therefore, and productive relationships of type (*c*) on the other hand,
are distinguishable in thought, but are not so distinguished from one
another in fact as to permit observations to be made, in societies where
money is used, of productive forces that are not also elements in productive (i.e., market) relationships.

This brings us to a further fatal weakness of the Materialist Conception of History as a theory for which the support of factual evidence is claimed. The theory concerns the relationship of various so-

cial elements to one another. These elements are: productive forces, productive relationships, a political and legal superstructure,[53] and an ideological superstructure. The theory is that the productive forces are the prime causal agency. If there is to be evidence for such a theory, the elements must not only be distinguishable in thought, but must be met with apart from one another. Or alternatively, if they cannot be found, each of them, in a pure state, it must be possible to assess the influence of each by some sort of statistical device, as psychologists have endeavored to do with certain factors of the mind. For if the elements are never found apart, and if there are no means of separating them out statistically, there is no means of deciding whether the theory is true or false. The elements of the Materialist Conception of History are distinguishable neither in thought nor in fact. We have already shown that men using their instruments of production *are* men in social relations with one another. It is not a case of men using their productive instruments and of this *causing* social relations between them, as though there could *first* be something purely technological and *then* something social. Perhaps the use of the word "material" in the expression "material conditions of life" has led people to think of productive instruments as purely physical things, like rocks or rivers, the purely physical changes of which produce social changes. Marx himself, before his dogmas took possession of him, had no such idea, but emphasized how tools and machines are socially inherited. We may refer to his letter of December 28, 1846, to P. V. Annenkov, in which he says that society is "the product of man's reciprocal activity" and mentions "the productive forces won by the previous generation." But if the instruments of production are like that, then it is not possible to say: "Here is a purely technological, productive, *material* change that is the cause of those *social* changes." For the technological is not really distinguishable, even in thought, from the social, nor production from co-operation. In their early days, again, Marx and Engels saw this very clearly when they wrote: "It follows from this

---

53. Harrington, in *Oceana,* used the term "Superstructure" in this sense, contrasting it with the "Center or Basis of every Government" which contains "the Fundamentall Lawes," which concern "what it is that a man may call his own, that is to say, Proprietie."

that a certain mode of production, or industrial stage, is always combined with a certain mode of co-operation, or social stage, and this mode of co-operation is itself a 'productive force.'"[54] Our analysis of the notion of "productive relationship" has shown that this involves law, morals, and politics, and we can see that it is not fanciful to regard them as parts of the means of production. For good laws, good morals, and good government can help production, as bad laws, bad morals, and bad government can hinder it. The "material or economic basis" of society is not, therefore, something that can be clearly conceived, still less observed, apart from the legal, moral, and political relationships of men. Since this is so, there is no definite hypothesis to which evidence is relevant, and this is why discussion of the Marxist theory of history is apt to become a futile beating of the air. I venture to suggest that it is a merit of the analysis I have given of the Materialist Conception of History, that it serves to explain why that theory has seemed so obviously true to so many well-informed and intelligent people. It has seemed obviously true because of the tautologies concealed in the language in which the theory is formulated. The theory gives the appearance of being based on facts, and of being subject to the verdict of facts in the way that, say, Boyle's Law is. On the one hand, the theory seems to say, there are productive forces, and on the other there are productive relationships which carry, poised one on top of the other, like the baskets of a Billingsgate porter, political and legal relationships and ideologies. Analysis of what is being said, however, shows that the porter is not separable from the baskets, and the baskets are not separable from one another, so that what had seemed a wonderful feat of balancing turns out to be as commonplace as walking with one's head on one's shoulders.

I will conclude this critical discussion of the Materialist Conception of History with a few comments on the third aspect of it, the division of history into epochs. As this is a part of Marxism that Professor Popper has dealt with very fully in his *Open Society and Its Enemies* under the title of "historicism," I shall only make some brief remarks of my own.

(1) I have already pointed out that it is natural enough to compare the Marxist series of epochs with the series of geological strata. In-

54. *The German Ideology,* p. 18.

deed, the early writers on geology regarded themselves as a sort of historian. Thus the subtitle of Leibniz's *Protogaea* refers to "the first appearance of the earth and the traces of its most ancient history in the very monuments of nature." In the eighteenth century, fossils were compared with coins discovered in ancient ruins from which their date and origin may sometimes be re-constructed. (*Sunt instar nummorum memoralium quae de praeteritis globi nostri fatis testantur, ubi omnia silent monumenta historica.*) The phrase "medal of creation," used, I believe, in the *Bridgewater Treatises,* illustrates this view. Geology, we might say, is the most historical of the natural sciences. But its full success is due to the existence of other, non-historical, natural sciences. Fossils provide the information they do largely because of what biologists have discovered. Chemistry and physics make their essential contributions to the geological accounts of rock strata and their relations to one another. If these other sciences could not be brought to its aid, geology would not be an explanatory science at all but a mere chronicle. Now if I am right in arguing that the fundamental conceptions of the Marxist theory of society are incoherent, then they are incapable of bringing the sort of order into the events of human history that has been achieved for the physical development of the earth and of the living beings on it.

(2) When Marx and Engels began their careers, geology was already attracting the attention of the intellectual world. In the *Paris Manuscripts* Marx writes that *geognosis,* as he calls it, makes it unnecessary to appeal to creation to account for the development of the earth and of animal species.[55] His archaeological references in *Capital,* volume 1, show how he was influenced by the geological analogy. "The relics of the instruments of labor," he writes, "are of no less importance to the study of vanished socio-economic forms, than fossil bones are in the study of the organization of extinct species."[56] In itself this observation is valuable, but I think it is important to see that the analogy of geological with historical epochs can be most misleading. (*a*) Clearly there is an analogy between geology and archaeology. With geology there are two definite sets of data, fossils of a certain type and rocks of a certain

55. M.E.G.A., I, 3, p. 124.
56. *Capital,* p. 172.

composition. It is thus possible to ascertain which fossils are found in which rocks, and thus to date the appearance of various types of living being. With archaeology there are also two sets of data, tools, buildings, or ornaments of a certain type, and soil at certain depths, though this last is not nearly as definite as are the different sorts of rock. Still, it is possible to say such things as that paleolithic remains are likely to be found at lower levels than neolithic remains. It is possible that remains of our own civilization will be dated by future archaeologists in terms of their depth in the soil or even in terms of the type of soil they are found in. Now the method of correlating types of life with certain sorts of rock may well exaggerate the definiteness of the break between one pre-human epoch and another, since in some cases at any rate the division between one epoch and another was not as abrupt as the division between one stratum and another. The strata are our means of discovering about the epochs, not the epochs themselves. But however this may be with geological epochs, epochs of human history certainly should not be regarded as so definitely delimited one from another. Even archaeology does not present us with a series of earth strata to correlate with types of tool, and when we come to consider the living civilizations themselves there are no clear-cut divisions in them that we can associate with types of tool. Of course, someone might *decide* to distinguish historical epochs from one another by the type of tool used in them, but this would be like *defining* geological strata in terms of the fossils found in them instead of finding a correlation between fossils of a certain type and strata of a certain composition. And we could also decide to distinguish historical epochs in terms of religions or of political organizations. We distinguish pre-historic periods in terms of material objects such as tools because they are all we have to go on. (*b*) This brings us to a different but associated point. We know that, once the various geological epochs have been distinguished from one another, they will remain so distinguished for all time unless there is an enormous unnoticed mistake in the theory. It has been established as well as anything of the sort can be that the earth has passed through such and such phases of development. But it is difficult to believe that the epochs of human history distinguished at one time will be the same as those to be distinguished later on, even though the earlier historians had not made any enormous unnoticed mistake. There are two main reasons for this. One is that new sorts of knowledge develop that enable us to look back on the past with new eyes. There is no doubt, for example, that the development of economics in the eighteenth and nineteenth centuries led to a fruitful re-examination of the past. The Reformation, and the Puritan Revolution, for example, can now be seen differently and more perspicuously than before. I have no doubt that future scientific developments will have similar effects, and that such re-assessments could only cease if knowledge ceased to grow. But it is not only the growth of science that will lead to constant re-assessment. As one event succeeds another, we are able to use more and more recent experiences to throw light on earlier events. For example, the taking of the Bastille, the September Massacres, the Committee of Public Safety, present a very different appearance when seen as steps toward Napoleon and nineteenth-century demagogic nationalism, from that presented even to the coolest and most rational observer in 1796. As the stream of history is prolonged new vantage points are constantly set up from which its higher reaches can be the better surveyed. A fixed series of historical epochs could only be established and believed in by a people whose science had stopped developing and whose experience was atrophied. To use Marxist jargon against the Marxist view, the theory that there is a series of definite epochs of mankind is unprogressive and undialectical.

(3) The Marxist theory of epochs is not only an account of the past, but is also, and mainly, a prediction of the end of capitalism and of the coming of communism. Now it is important to notice at this stage that there are certain sorts of prediction of human affairs that could not possibly be made. These are, to make a rough list, predictions of what I have called *creative* inventions, of new scientific discoveries, of new social devices and techniques, of new religions, and of new forms of art. It is particularly important that the student of Marxism should be aware that creative inventions and scientific theories cannot be predicted, since science and technology are regarded by Marxists as fundamental features of society. If the rest of society depends on technology and science, and if the future of them is not predictable, then the future of society as a whole is not predictable. Now we have seen that it *is* possible to say, with good reason, that a certain sort of invention is likely to be made—for example, that there will soon be color television. What

is not possible is the prediction of a radically new invention, for to predict such an invention would be to make it. Mother Shipton is said to have predicted airplanes, and Erasmus Darwin mentioned them in a well-known poem. But such unfounded and vague speculations do not deserve to be called predictions. What a queer thing science would be if hypotheses and formulae flashed into the minds of scientists and were then verified or falsified by reference to facts. It is not just prediction that makes science, but rational prediction, and science itself, as well as technology, is only in part subject to rational prediction. There is often good reason to say that further members of a certain range of problem, earlier members of which have already been solved, will be solved before very long, but it is never possible to do more than this. If we could specify the scientific discovery, we should have made it.[57] This holds, too, of such social devices as joint-stock companies and life insurance. That it holds also of types of religion and art is, after what has been said, obvious. Indeed, it was in connection with such matters that the principle was first enunciated, in rather vague terms, in the nineteenth century, by such writers as J. A. Froude and F. H. Bradley. Froude, for example, in his lecture on the "Science of History," given at the Royal Institution on 5 February 1864, said: "Well, then, let us take some general phenomenon, Mahometanism, for instance, or Buddhism. These are large enough. Can you imagine a science which would have *foretold* such movements as those?"[58] In all such fields an act of creation is achieved from time to time. When it has happened, we can sometimes see how it has come about, but the signs that are afterward seen to lead toward it are not signs at all before it happened. When Marxists speak of "leaps" in history, they ought to mean something like this. But when they suppose they can predict the future of society as a whole, they have abandoned this view for a "scientism" that is incompatible with it. Rational prediction would be possible of a whole society only if it was no longer progressing. "For a people only in the period of their stagnation," writes Bradley, "for a person only

57. I have discussed this in "Comte's Positivism and the Science of Society" (*Philosophy*, vol. 26, no. 99, Oct. 1951), pp. 9–12, where I give references to recent discussions.

58. *Short Studies in Great Subjects* (1894 edition), vol. 1, pp. 17–18.

when the character and the station have become fixed for ever, and when the man is made, is it possible to foreknow the truth of the fresh achievement; and where progress has its full meaning, and evolution is more than a phrase, there the present is hard, and the future impossible to discover."[59]

5. The Ideological Superstructure

We have seen in Section 2 of this chapter that Marx and Engels used the word "ideology" for false conceptions of the world which men come to adopt for reasons they themselves are unaware of. We have seen further that Marx distinguished legal, political, moral (or ethical), artistic, religious, theological, and philosophical ideologies, and contrasted ideological thinking with thinking that can be "faithfully substantiated in the manner of the natural sciences." It will thus be seen that it is not a valid objection to Marxism to argue, as is often done, that Marxism makes science an ideology and therefore, in claiming scientific status, stultifies its own position. We have now considered, in outline, the view of society which Marx, Engels, and Stalin believed was thus "substantiated in the manner of the natural sciences," and we must now return to consider somewhat more carefully the Marxist notion of an ideology.

A first point to notice is that the list of ideologies must have been suggested by the philosophy of Hegel. Hegel regarded morality, law, and politics as aspects of the State, and the State he regarded as Spirit manifesting itself as freedom, and as the highest form of "objective spirit." It was not his view, however, that the State was the highest manifestation of Spirit altogether. He held that other, and higher, manifestations of it were art, revealed religion, and philosophy, philosophy being the rational working out of what in revealed religion is still not fully conscious of itself.[60] It will be seen, therefore, that, whereas in Marx's system the legal and political ideologies are closer to "the material conditions of life," i.e., to social *reality*, than art, religion, and philosophy are, in Hegel's system art, religion, and philoso-

---

59. *The Presuppositions of Critical History. Collected Essays*, vol. 1, p. 5.
60. *Encyclopedia*, §§ 553–77.

phy are closer to the reality of Absolute Spirit than law and politics are. It was with these views in mind that Marx attempted to show that law and politics distort the real less than art, religion, and philosophy do, and that his social science of industry and warring classes, being faithfully substantiated in the manner of the natural sciences, does not distort the real at all. Furthermore, the Materialist Conception of History, since it is thus scientifically established, is, he believed, more than a mere theory—it is a step in the transformation of society, just as natural science is a practical activity of controlling nature. This follows from the view that science is a union of theory and practice. Since the Materialist Conception of History is a science, Socialism is a science, and science is something practical.

A further point to notice is that Marx and Engels applied the term "ideology" to systems of ideas, outlooks, or theories. Ideologies, in their view, are more or less misleading conceptions of the world. Religious and philosophical ideologies, i.e., theology and metaphysics, distort our view of nature as a whole, including society, and ethical, legal, and political ideologies distort our view of society. What artistic ideologies are, and what they distort, is not made clear in the works that Marx published.[61] But we still need to consider what sorts of systems of ideas

61. In the unpublished Introduction to the *Critique of Political Economy,* Marx briefly discusses Greek art. He says that it "presupposes Greek mythology, that is, nature and the form of society itself worked up in an unconsciously artistic way by the imagination of a people" (Kautsky's edition, p. xlix. I have altered Stone's translation, which is misleading here). He says further that Greek mythology cannot be taken seriously in an industrial age, and that the delight that ancient Greek poetry gives us today is comparable with the delight that adults have in "the artless ways of a child." "Why," he asks, "should the social childhood of mankind, when it had obtained its most beautiful development, not exert eternal charm as an age that will never return?" We may note here (*a*) the significant reference to the *unconsciously* functioning imagination of a people (*Volksphantasie*), (*b*) the assumption that because the ancient Greeks had an inadequate conception of the physical world and a comparatively undeveloped technology, their social arrangements and cultural productions are childlike by comparison with those of 1859, and (*c*) the confusion of aesthetic appreciation with a sort of nostalgia for what can never be again. As to (*a*), we see Feuerbach's observations on the religious imagination being applied to art, so as to suggest what we may call a Freudian-cum-Jungian view of it. As to (*b*) and (*c*), it should be observed, in fairness to Marx, that it was not he who published this Introduction.

these ideologies are. Are the moral, legal, and political ideologies, for example, such *practical* systems as the Christian or Buddhist ethics, Roman or English law, or the political outlooks of Toryism and Liberalism? Or are they *philosophical* systems of morals, law, and politics, such as Utilitarianism or Intuitionism, Neo-Kantian jurisprudence, and the Idealist theory of the State? I think that both sorts of system were regarded by Marx and Engels as ideologies, and that the various *philosophies* of morals, law, and politics were not usually classed as elements of the philosophical ideology, but were associated with their respective subject-matters. An example of this may be seen in Engels' letter to Conrad Schmidt of October 27, 1890, where he writes: "The reflection of economic relations as legal principles is necessarily also a topsy-turvy one: it happens without the person who is acting being conscious of it; the jurist imagines he is operating with *a priori* principles whereas they are really only economic reflexes." A practicing lawyer, I imagine, does not often consider whether or not the legal principles he uses are *a priori*. That is the sort of problem that might occur to a philosophizing lawyer. Hence it seems that "jurist" here refers to philosophers of law, unless, indeed, Engels means that lawyers regard the law they practice as having an authority like that of logic or arithmetic and as being fixed like them, and, like them, quite distinct from the economic life of their society. This, surely, could not have been the case in Engels' day, since the law was then constantly being changed, and a very large part of it, as always, related to industry and trade. Lawyers of all people, I should have thought, must always have been well aware of the importance that people attach to money and property.

However this may be, the Marxist view, so far as one view can be extracted from the texts, is that both systems and philosophies of morals, law, and politics, and religious systems, and theology, and philosophy itself, are or involve systems of ideas that represent in a distorted form the real things they purport to relate to, the distortions resulting from the social situation of their framers and concealing from them what is really going on. People who accept systems of ideas like the Christian morality, Ethical Intuitionism, the law of their country, Toryism, Liberalism, the theory of sovereignty or of political pluralism, Platonism, Idealism, etc., do not know what they are really doing. They are all, in varying degrees, deceived. The Christian thinks he is trying to worship God and serve his fellow men, whereas in actual fact he is helping to perpetuate those false views of the world that make it easier for the bourgeoisie to exploit the proletariat. The Ethical Intuitionist—the philosopher, that is, who holds that there is a quasi-mathematical knowledge of moral principles—thinks he is showing precisely what ethical judgments are, but really he is arguing for the retention of the current morality and for the continuing supremacy of the class that it favors. Tories or Liberals, thinking they hold their political principles because they believe them to be for the good of their country, really hold them as a result of the unconscious promptings of their class interests. Platonist and Idealist philosophers believe that they have followed the argument whithersoever it led, but in fact their philosophies are thinly disguised theologies, theologies are justifications of irrationally accepted religious practices, and religious practices, with their "fanes of fruitless prayer," are futile gesturings arising from illusory hopes. Feuerbach had thought that if religious illusions were exposed by means of "anthropology" they would lose their attraction and shrivel up. Those psychiatrists who suppose that the neurotic's self-knowledge may cure his neurosis have had a similar idea. Marx did not suppose that ideologies would disappear once their adherents had seen through them, if "seeing through" is taken in the ordinary sense that would distinguish it from practical activity.

With this in mind, then, let us consider, in a way that Marx does not, some of the principal ways in which men might be related to their ideologies. In the first place, we have to distinguish between (*a*) those believers in an ideology who belong to an exploited class whose interests the ideology does not serve, and (*b*) those believers in the ideology who belong to classes whose sectional interests are both marked and promoted by it. On the assumption that most people are more than ready to accept points of view which harmonize with what they believe are their interests, we may suppose that believers of type (*a*) will tend to abandon their ideology if they come to think that it is a means of exploiting them. For, it can be argued, they have no strong vital urge for holding it, but have only come to accept it as part of the stock of ideas of their class-divided society. I suppose a Marxist would hold that because their interests incline them that way, believers of type (*b*) are unlikely ever to see through it. Our deep-rooted desires cunningly keep us from thinking thoughts that are too dangerous. Nevertheless, Marx and Engels were certainly members of the class that they called the exploiting class, so that it has to be admitted that *sometimes* people can see through an ideology from which they might expect to profit. It would seem that exploiters who have seen through the exploiting ideology have two main courses open to them: either to renounce their origin and attach themselves to the proletariat, or to uphold their sectional interests *consciously,* by not attacking or by actually promoting ideas they no longer believe in themselves, much as a wealthy atheist might give financial support to a church which he thought helped to maintain public order. When Marxists accuse their opponents of hypocrisy (perhaps "deceit" would be a better word), it is some such conduct they have in mind. But in so far as, on the Marxist view, science is a union of theory and practice and Marxism is a scientific view of society, no one who does not actively promote the proletarian cause has succeeded in gaining a scientific understanding of society. If the criterion of practice be insisted on, therefore, only those members of the bourgeois class who actually work for the Communist Party can claim to have seen through an ideology scientifically, "in the manner of the natural sciences." In this way the Marxist is enabled to argue that no one who does not work on behalf of the Marxist Communist parties can really understand what Marxism is. Once more the similarity with Pascal's advice to learn to be a Christian by going to Mass is obvious.

Earlier in this chapter I distinguished between the politico-legal superstructure and the ideological superstructure. This is in accordance with Marx's account of the matter in the Preface to the *Critique of Political Economy.* In that same Preface, however, he speaks of legal and political *ideologies,* and I have not so far considered this apparent discrepancy. Is it merely that terminology was not tidied up, or is there some fundamental confusion? In my opinion the latter is the case, and the confusion is the same as the one we exposed in the previous section. No doubt Marx was drawing a distinction between legal and political *behavior* and legal and political *theories.* Legal and political behavior was superstructural by comparison with "economic" behavior, but legal and political theories were superstructural by comparison with legal and political behavior as well as by comparison with "economic" behavior. Now we have already argued that there is no such thing as *purely* "economic" behavior, but that moral, as well as legal (or quasi-legal) and political factors are involved in production and exchange. It is now necessary to point out that, in saying this, we are saying that moral, legal, and political ideas, outlooks, theories, are involved in production and exchange, for moral, legal, and political behavior is conscious behavior that requires thought and talk. A man's conduct is right or wrong in terms of some system of moral assessment that guides his conduct; lawyers are occupied all their working lives with the interpretation of legal principles; and even the most unprincipled political adventurer is aware that there are various systems of political ideals that he must take account of. All conscious human action is in terms of standards and principles of some sort, however dimly conceived they may be. When Engels quoted the aphorism: "In the beginning was the deed," he should have added that the deeds of men, unlike those of the beasts, are conceived in, and sometimes perpetuated by, words. Thus, the distinction between the politico-legal superstructure and the relevant ideological superstructure can only be a distinction between behavior in which ideas and theories are neither explicit nor the prime object of attention, and explicit theorizing about such behavior.

We now come to a matter which leads on to the subject of the next chapter. It will be remembered that in the first section of the present chapter I showed that the Materialist Conception of History was meant to be an anti-metaphysical theory based on the evidence of our senses. The facts and "needs" revealed by our senses were, as we have seen, to be examined "in the manner of the natural sciences." Now it is commonly supposed that one important characteristic of the method of the natural sciences is to be free from any preconceptions about the value, the goodness or badness, the perfection or defect, of what is being investigated. At one time the heavenly bodies were regarded as divine or quasi-divine beings whose special essence (or "quintessence," as it was called) rendered them superior to the things here below. One of Galileo's many contributions to experimental science was to apply to the movements of earthly bodies mathematical principles which had previously been regarded as specially applicable to the moon, sun, and other planets. Under his inspiration physics ceased to distinguish between grades or orders of being, and became, as it is put today, "value-free." It is natural, therefore, for anyone who aspires to be the Galileo of the social sciences, to suppose that they, like the natural sciences, must be value-free. In the generation after Galileo, Spinoza was already making this demand. In our own day we are told, in the same spirit, that there must be no preconceptions about what people *ought* to want, or how they *ought* to act, but they must be studied to ascertain what they *do* want and how they *do* act. In this spirit, therefore, the material or economic basis of human society is human behavior as revealed to observers who seek to find out how people in fact desire, behave, and believe. Ideological thinking, part of which is moral thinking, is always the outcome of the thinker's wishes and interests, however much disguised they may be. The scientific thinking, however, to which Marxists aspire, would be undisturbed by such extraneous factors, and would seek to discover how society works in order to predict what it will become. Adherents of ideologies are, on this view, people who, because of their class situation, have failed to free themselves from emotional hindrances to scientific observation. The scientific observer of society, through his microscope of Historical Materialism, sees such people as they really are—as people whose view of both physical and social reality is distorted by their wishes and interests. The Materialist Conception of History, it is held, is not just another new view, but is the view which corrects and explains all other views, and differs from them in that, as scientific, it is not influenced by sectional prejudices. As a scientific theory of how things in fact happen, it claims to call the moral bluffs of mankind by showing how moral outlooks depend on class interests. At the same time, as a genuine scientific theory in which theory and practice are combined, it claims to provide a practical solution to our social difficulties. We must now consider the details of these remarkable claims.

Marxist Ethics

1. Marxist Social Science as a Form of Social Regeneration

It is well known that one of the problems that nineteenth-century thinkers found most disturbing was that as natural science developed it appeared to overthrow religion and morality by demonstrating the subjection of mankind to a natural order of things where strife ruled and the weak were thrust aside. Thus Tennyson asked whether the conclusion to be drawn from geology was that man

> Who loved, who suffered countless ills,
>> Who battled for the True, the Just,
>> Be blown about the desert dust,
> Or sealed within the iron hills?

About the same time Clough wrote:

> Ashes to ashes, dust to dust;
> As of the unjust, also of the just—
>> Yea, of that Just One too!
> This is the one sad Gospel that is true—
>> Christ is not risen.

Clough remained perpetually in a somewhat distressed unbelief, but Tennyson thought that scientific knowledge could be supplemented by a higher wisdom in which love and faith were comprised. What is mere knowledge, he asked

>> cut from love and faith,
> But some wild Pallas from the brain

Of Demons? fiery hot to burst
   All barriers in her onward race
   For power.

Comte and his followers thought they could meet the situation by finding both religion and morality, faith and love, in science itself. Humanity replaced God as an object of worship, the earth became the Great Fetish, and honesty, patience, disinterestedness, and justice were held to be virtues inseparable from the pursuit of scientific truth. Comte, indeed, argued that in the last resort all science was absorbed into sociology, the science of society, and that sociology was at the same time a complete code of morals.

I have already shown, in Section 1 of the previous chapter, that in 1844 Marx, too, had played with the idea of a social knowledge which, in becoming scientific like the natural sciences, would "subordinate them to itself." But the main line of argument used by Marxists is that just as natural science is the progressive mastery of nature by man, so social science is man's mastery over his social conditions. There is a sort of Promethean pride about this view, and it is worth noting that at the end of the preface to his Doctoral Dissertation Marx had written: "Prometheus is the chief saint and martyr of the philosophical calendar."[1]

In presenting this view, Stalin writes: "Hence the science of the history of society, despite all the complexity of the phenomena of social life, can become as precise a science as, let us say, biology, as capable of making use of the laws of development of society for practical purposes. Hence the party of the proletariat should not guide itself in its practical activity by casual motives, but by the laws of development of society, and by practical deductions from these laws. Hence Socialism is converted from a dream of a better future for humanity into a science. Hence the bond between science and practical activity, between theory and practice, their unity, should be the guiding star of the party of the proletariat."[2] Many years before, he had written, in his *Anarchism or Communism,* "Proletarian Socialism is based not on sentiment, not on abstract 'justice,' not on love for the proletariat, but

1. M.E.G.A., I, 1, i, p. 10.
2. *History of the Communist Party of the Soviet Union* (Moscow, 1939), pp. 114–15.

on the scientific grounds quoted above."[3] Engels had written in the *Anti-Dühring* that the earlier socialism criticized the existing capitalist mode of production and its consequences, but could not explain them, and hence "could not get the mastery over them; it could only simply reject them as evil."[4] And he went on to say that with the "discovery" of the Materialist Conception of History and the Theory of Surplus Value "socialism became a science. . . ." Some such view appears to be expressed, though not very clearly, in the eighth of Marx's *Theses on Feuerbach*, where he writes: "All social life is essentially *practical.* All the mysteries which urge theory into mysticism find their rational solution in human practice and in the comprehension of this practice." The following passage, however, from Marx's Preface to the first edition of *Capital,* volume 1, is somewhat clearer. "When a society has discovered the natural laws which regulate its own movement (and the final purpose of my book is to reveal the economic law of motion of modern society), it can neither overleap the natural phases of evolution, nor shuffle them out of the world by decrees. But this much, at least, it can do; it can shorten and lessen the birth-pangs."

Tennyson, we have seen, thought that the pursuit of science apart from moral considerations necessarily became a pursuit of power. I am not sure that this is so, since a man of science might desire knowledge itself quite apart from the power it brought him. But on the Marxist view of science as a union of theory and practice, natural science just *is* power over nature, and social science just *is* power over society. Engels' word "mastery" is significant. The science that is theory and practice combined is power over, mastery or control of, nature and society, and as such is held to be good. The obvious objection to this is that control over nature and society may be good or bad according to the use that is made of it. The chemical knowledge that enables disease to be cured may also enable enemies to be poisoned, and knowledge of social mechanisms may be used by some only all too enlightened despot for purposes of enslavement. Why did Marx admire Prometheus? For his defiance of the gods? This could only be good if there were gods and they were bad. For his courage? Courage can be exercised in a

3. Foreign Languages Publishing House, Moscow, 1951, p. 66.
4. Pp. 32–33.

bad cause, as the career of Dr. Goebbels shows. For his power of invention? Certainly, knowledge and ingenuity cannot fail to evoke our admiration, as do the gait of a tiger and the marking of a snake, but as these examples show, admiration is no proof of the *moral* excellence of its object. Perhaps, then, he admired Prometheus as a benefactor of mankind. If so, it would seem that the cause of his admiration was that Prometheus courageously defied the envious gods and suffered for it in the service of mankind. The intelligence and inventiveness that enabled him to bring fire to the earth would, unless they had been used for the benefit of others, have had no more moral significance than the song of a bird. That mastery of nature does not, in itself, connote any desirable moral qualities, is recognized in the modern mythology of demon scientists such as Professor Moriarty and Doctor Moreau. The superiority over physical nature and the animal world that man shows in his intelligence and skill is not, in itself, morally desirable. This I take to be the defensible element in Rousseau's criticisms of civilization.

The Marxist, no doubt, will attempt to meet this difficulty in the following manner. As science and industry develop, he will argue, man too develops morally, for in developing his technology he necessarily changes his productive relationships, and with them his law, politics, and ideologies; morals, therefore, as ideology, are linked with science and industry. It should be observed, however, in answer to this argument, that according to Marxism the development of technology (i.e., of science and industry) is basic and real, whereas the development of ideologies, including the moral one, is nothing but a shadowy transformation of one illusion into another. The argument provides no means of passing, therefore, from the practice of science and industry to a non-illusory moral outlook. The Marxist is bound to the dogma that morality is parasitical on science and industry, though the non-Marxist will readily admit that science and industry, being human activities, are subject to moral assessment as all human activities are, and cannot themselves provide the standards in terms of which they may all be judged.

Let us now consider somewhat more closely Marx's contention that a knowledge of Marxist social science enables us to know that certain events—notably, the proletarian revolution—are bound to happen, and that when we know this we can use our knowledge to make their coming less unpleasant than it otherwise would have been ("to shorten and lessen the birth-pangs"). There is clearly a comparison with the way in which science can help us to soften the impact of physical disasters. We must all die, but with the help of medical science we can defer death and lessen its pains. We cannot abolish hurricanes, but meteorologists can forecast them, and we can strengthen our houses accordingly. We foresee death and storm, and make use of science to go through with them as comfortably as may be. This, clearly, is the analogy that Marx is working with. Capitalism will break down, the proletarian revolution will come, and, armed with this foreknowledge, we can make the interim less miserable than it otherwise would have been. The two examples I have given, however, are not of exactly the same type. The meteorologist can predict the hurricane, but we can do nothing to stop it or to slow it down. It needs no scientist to tell us we all must die, but scientists can help us to defer our deaths. It would seem, from the passage I have quoted, that the breakdown of capitalism and the proletarian revolution are thought by Marx to be more like death than like a hurricane—that they cannot be prevented altogether, but can be delayed or hastened. No one wants hurricanes, and most people want their death delayed. But some people will want to delay the breakdown of capitalism, and others to hasten it. Marx, in this passage, appears to suppose that everyone will want to get through with it as quickly as possible. Now since there is a remarkable agreement about what are physical evils—such things as death, disease, cold, hunger, and physical injury—there is also agreement about the proper function of science in foreseeing, mitigating, delaying, and preventing them. With social breakdowns and revolutions, however, it is very different, for some will be opposed to the very things that others look forward to. Mark Pattison, like Marx, though for different reasons, thought that socialism was inevitable, but his comment was "I hate it." Furthermore, as physical science has developed, some things that at one time were thought to be inevitable have been found to be preventable. Diseases are the best example of this. Marx should not have considered it impossible for other social scientists, to whom the breakdown of capitalism was unwelcome, to discover, perhaps even with the aid of his diagnosis, means of keeping it indefinitely in being. Against this it may be argued that all previous social systems have ultimately broken down and that capitalism can hardly be an exception. This, however, is not a clear-cut argument like the argument that as all previous generations of men have died we shall too. Social systems or historical epochs cannot be instances in an induction in the way that men or ravens can be. We have a very clear notion of what it is for a man to die, but we have no such clear notion of what it is for a social system to break down. Indeed, as I have already argued, the distinctions between one historical epoch and another are unlike those between geological strata, and therefore still less like those between individual men or animals. Blurred notions such as that of a historical epoch do not permit of the definite sort of predictions that can be made when there is a number of clearly distinguishable individuals. We are all agreed as to the tests to ascertain whether a man is dead, but how do we decide that capitalism has broken down? We deceive ourselves with almost empty phrases if we suppose that we can make predictions about such things as societies, civilizations, revolutions, classes, social orders, and constitutions, as we can about men, genes, gases, and stars. If anything even approaching this is to be possible, these terms must be given definitions that will allow precise differences to be recorded.

It is not without interest, perhaps, in this connection, to mention that in 1857, two years before Marx published his *Critique of Political Economy,* a body was founded known as the National Association for the Promotion of Social Science. Its *Transactions* were arranged under the following five heads: Jurisprudence and the Amendment of the Law; Education; Punishment and Reformation; Public Health; and Social Economy. The sort of topics discussed in each section may be seen from the following examples, one from each section, taken from the first volume of the *Transactions:* Judicial Statistics; An Inquiry on Early Withdrawal from School in Swansea and Its Neighbourhood; Crime and Density of Population; Houses for Working Men—Their Arrangement, Drainage, and Ventilation; the Early Closing Movement. The papers submitted vary greatly in merit, but the prevailing manner of approach is to provide information on the topic chosen, to analyze the information provided, and to make suggestions about remedies for any evils brought to light in this way. The notions employed are seldom so general as "society," "capitalism," "revolution," etc., but are rather of the relative particularity of "convictions," "sentences," "bankruptcies," "adulteration of food," "drainage," and "penny banks." It is true, of course, that at some stage enquiries of this sort need to be linked together, and the policies they suggest have to be co-ordinated. But this would seem to be the sort of approach to social science that is most likely to ensure that its exponents know what they are talking about. Furthermore, since these men made no claims to a godlike detachment from human affairs, they did not easily disguise their prejudices from one another, as can be seen from the reports of their discussions.

To return, however, to our theme—the idea that just as science and history enable men to master nature, so Marxist social science enables us to control society. Mastering nature is discovering its laws of operation and making use of this knowledge to serve human ends, as men do when, discovering that friction causes fire, they are enabled to keep themselves warm and to cook food. One form of controlling society is for some people to discover how others can be threatened and cajoled and to use this knowledge to control these others. This is the sort of control that can be got by skillful use of propaganda, and it presupposes a division into enlightened (i.e., scientific) masters and ignorant followers. Just as mastery over nature is manipulation of physical things for the satisfaction of human desires, so mastery over society would be the control of the many by the few for the prime satisfaction of the few. Clearly this is not the sort of control over social processes that the Marxists consciously advocate. Whatever control over social processes is, it is regarded by them as something opposed to class domination, and something which would readily appeal to unprejudiced people. The view they are endeavoring to put forward is, I think, something to the following effect.

If we did not know some of the causes of disease or cold or storm we should be pretty much at their mercy, as savages still are. When we know some of their causes we can prevent them from happening or protect ourselves against them when they do happen. Similarly there are social disasters, such as unemployment, slumps, and wars, which come to men ignorant of their causes just as if they were physical catastrophes like epidemics. If we could discover what causes them, they too could be prevented, or at least guarded against. Such social occurrences are like purely physical occurrences in one very important respect—no one wills them or decides that they are to happen. They are by-products of what people do decide. Thus someone invents a new machine, and men are put out of work though neither the inventor nor the employer aimed at this; a number of company directors decide to postpone capital developments, and there is a slump which they would have paid a lot to avoid; or two governments make a completely mistaken assessment of one another's intentions and find themselves involved in a war that neither of them wanted. There are, of course, important differences between these examples, notably the difference between a slump, which is never declared, and a war, which generally is. But in all these cases individuals, and even governments, find themselves, as it is popularly expressed, in the grip of forces they cannot control. The unemployment, slump, and war result from many decisions on other matters by people aiming at other things. ("Warmongers" are characters in Marxist propaganda and do not feature in Marxist social theory.) We may say that such occurrences are unwilled and impersonal, unwilled because no one aims at producing them, impersonal because to their victims they seem like such natural catastrophes as storms and epidemics. Now one thing that Marxists mean by mastery over social processes is the knowledge of what causes such phenomena, and the resulting ability to prevent them from happening. (Incidentally, we can prevent some, but not all diseases, but storms and death we cannot prevent at all, so that Marxists are more optimistic about the possibilities of "social control" than experience of the natural sciences justifies.) The result would be that only those things would happen in human society that men had decided should happen. Fear of slumps is like fear of epidemics, and as no one now fears the Black Death, so no one in a society from which the unwilled and impersonal had been eliminated would have to fear unemployment, slumps, and war.

It should be noticed in the first place that the contrast between what is willed and what is unwilled is not necessarily a contrast between what is good and what is bad, for some people deliberately aim at harming others. The removal from human society, therefore, of what is unwilled may not mean the removal of all that is evil, for intended evil would still remain. This being so, the improvement of human society depends on the aims of those who direct the improvements as well as upon the knowledge they may have of social forces. We may ask, in the second place, whether everything in society that is unwilled is bad like storms and epidemics. Marxists appear to assume that it must be, probably as a result of some trace, in Marx's thought, of the Hegelian view that "self-consciousness" was the perfect condition of spirit. But surely employment (supposing it to be good, in contrast to unemployment), booms, and peace are often as little the result of deliberate effort as are their less welcome contraries. The New York skyline is no less to be admired because no one designed it, and not all the effects on society of educational systems that were left to take their own way, or of haphazardly competing outlooks and theories, have been regrettable. Control over nature, we may observe, is a small area of control in an immense desert of uncontrol. The background of human effort is still an untamed accumulation of seas, mountains, and planets. Nor, unless we are in a particularly "Promethean" mood, do we regret this. Is there any reason why we should want something radically different in society? That we should wish to see nothing there but what has been deliberately put there? Before answering "Yes" to this question, we should consider what it implies. Its chief implication is that there should be no conflicting aims at all, for as soon as aims conflict, circumstances grow up which neither of the conflicting parties had aimed at, that is to say, unwilled circumstances. If A wants policy X, and B, who wants policy Y, opposes him in this, then perhaps X, perhaps Y, or perhaps neither X nor Y, will result. This, in its turn, implies that if there are to be no unwilled circumstances, *everything* that *anybody* does must be willed in accordance with some universally accepted or imposed set of co-ordinating principles. It is only by successful total planning that unwilled social by-products can be completely eliminated. The qualification "successful" is, of course, very important, since if in any respect the plan breaks down, things will happen that no one has intended. For if the single authority aims at X and fails to achieve it, then whatever results is something that was not planned. When we consider how little of intention there is in an individual personality or the spirit of a people, how the structure of scientific truth and the evolution of artistic styles have provided mankind with a succession of not altogether unwelcome surprises, and how most languages proliferate from uncontrolled sources, the idea of achieving a self-conscious mastery over all social processes is seen to be as impracticable as it is depressing. It may be argued that it is only necessary to plan to prevent *bad* unwilled events, such as unemployment and slumps, and that therefore I have exaggerated when I said that the Marxist's aim requires total planning of society. But it is characteristic of Marxism to stigmatize as "reformism" the removal of particular evils one after another. It is true that there is every reason to suppose that mistakes will be made by those who carry out particular, limited reforms, so that as the reforming process continues, new, unwilled difficulties will present themselves. This, I suggest, is a good reason for not expecting any human arrangements to be perfect. But the Marxist's response is to conclude that "reformism" is necessarily bad and that its evils can be avoided by "revolution," that is, by a complete overthrow of the old system of things and its replacement by a new one decreed by the revolutionaries. This is to substitute total re-modeling for piecemeal improvement, and requires those who do the re-modeling to be very clever indeed if they are not to be confronted by a much more formidable array of unintended evils than face the reformers. For if so very much is risked on one venture, the penalty of failure is correspondingly great.

From Marx's earliest writings there has been, in the Communist movement, an emphasis on basic human wants or needs. The idea seems to be that Marxist social science has become morality, or rather has become a more desirable substitute for morality, in that it teaches how the basic wants and needs of men can and will be satisfied. This will come about as the power of the proletariat is extended until it becomes a ruling class and finally brings classes to an end. In a classless society all basic wants will be satisfied because there will be no exploiters. But an account of social policy in terms of wants or desires must suppose both that satisfaction is better than frustration and that some wants or desires are more worthy of satisfaction than others. If this were not so, there could be no reason why most men should not be slaughtered to allow the rest to live in luxury in the ruins of civilization, nor why widespread happiness should not be induced by universal indulgence in opium. In any case, the words "needs," "basic," and "exploitation" introduce moral conceptions. I have already discussed the ambiguities of the word "needs," and the word "basic" introduces similar difficulties. Clearly, by basic needs Marxists mean amounts and kinds of food and shelter which every person in a highly developed society like our own is *entitled* to, or *has a right to*. Again, by "exploitation" they do not mean merely the making use of some social opportunity, but the *wrongful* use of it to the detriment of others. This moral use of the word is particularly likely to predominate in the German language, since the German word—*Ausbeutung*—is formed from *Beute,* which means loot, prey, spoil, plunder, much as the English word "booty" does. The Marxist can derive moral precepts from his social science only to the extent that they already form, because of the vocabulary used, a concealed and unacknowledged part of it.

In the course of his account of Historical Materialism in his *Karl Marx,* Mr. Isaiah Berlin says that the theory cannot be rightly objected to on the ground that in it moral recommendations are illicitly derived from mere matters of fact, since "Marx, like Hegel, flatly rejected this distinction. Judgments of fact cannot be sharply distinguished from those of value: all one's judgments are conditioned by practical activity in a given social milieu: one's views as to what one believes to exist and what one wishes to do with it, modify each other. . . . The only sense in which it is possible to show that something is good or bad, right or wrong, is by demonstrating that it accords or discords with the historical process, assists it or thwarts it, will survive or will inevitably perish."[5] Now it is true that Hegel objected to the procedure (characteristic of the Understanding, and, on his view, needing correction by the Reason) of making clear-cut oppositions such as that between what is matter of fact and that which only ought to be but is not. It is true also that he maintained that social institutions were moral creations as well as matters of fact, and that he concluded his *Philosophy of History* with the following words: "That the history of the world, with all the changing scenes which its annals present, is this process of development, and the realization of Spirit—this is the true *Theodicaea,* the justification of God in History. Only *this* insight can reconcile spirit with the History of the World—viz., that what has happened, and is happening every day, is not 'without God,' but is essentially His Work."[6] It cannot be denied that Marx was influenced by such views. They do

5. *Karl Marx* (2nd edition, London, 1948), p. 140.
6. Translated by Sibree (New York, 1944), p. 457.

not, however, form part of, and are, indeed, inconsistent with, the Materialist Conception of History. If I am right in my interpretation, that theory is established "in the manner of the natural sciences." It is held by its exponents to be a *science* of morals, aesthetics, and religion, but moral, aesthetic, and religious judgments are shown, by means of this "science," to be ideological distortions of social realities. Therefore for Marx to say that judgments of fact and value are necessarily mixed up with one another would be for him to say that no science of society is possible. Indeed, it would involve him in a skepticism about the truth of natural science too, which, as I judge, he would have found most shocking. It seems to me that an important feature of the Materialist Conception of History is the attempt to show that valuations are superstructural forms of "false consciousness" which Marxist social science enables us to "see through." Mr. Berlin, I suggest, implicitly acknowledges this when he interprets Marx as holding that "The only sense in which it is possible to show that something is good or bad, right or wrong, is by demonstrating that it accords or discords with the historical process, assists it or thwarts it, will survive or will ultimately perish." Hegel's view was that the course of history, taken as a whole, is divinely good; historical events, he held, were at the same time divine events, so that whatever happened was, in its degree, good; facts were more than *mere* facts, they were elements in the goodness of things. But the view that Mr. Berlin is attributing to Marx in the sentence beginning "The only sense . . ." is the view, not that facts are *also* valuable, but that value is reducible to fact, that to say that Communism is right is *merely* to say that it will prevail, and that to say that liberalism is wrong is *merely* to say that it will disappear from the world. The contrast may be seen if we compare the broad outlines of the two theories. Hegel's *Philosophy of Right* is, in effect, a comprehensive system of political philosophy in which no attempt is made to avoid moral assessments, and in which even titles of divine honor are openly bestowed on the state. Marx, on the other hand, set out to explain, in terms of what he considered to be natural facts, how the institutions of society come to be decorated with pretentiously misleading moral and theological coloring.

2. *Ethics and the Materialist Conception of History*

So far my discussion of Marxist ethics has been confined to the Marxist attempt—which, historically considered, is a branch of the nineteenth-century Positivist attempt—to derive principles of right conduct from some alleged science of society. We must now, however, look somewhat more closely at what Marxists say about moral beliefs, remembering that in their view morality is an ideology. In the present section I shall be concerned with the most general aspects of the theory, the account, we might put it, of what morality itself is held to be. In later sections I shall discuss some of the chief Marxist proposals for the *reform* of morality. For the texts show that, inconsistent as it may appear to be, Marxism is a program for the reform of morality as well as an attempt to reduce it to science. All students of Marxism must at some stage have felt that there is at the very least a difficulty in reconciling the Marxist attack on class divisions and "exploitation" with the view that moral ideals are masks that cover interests. This is a problem to be kept in mind throughout all that follows.

The chief account of the matter is that given by Engels in chapters 9, 10, and 11 of his *Anti-Dühring*. Here Engels argues that there are no "eternal truths" in morality, but that moral codes must vary with changes in the conditions of human life. Engels held that at the time when he was writing (1877) there were three main moralities being preached, "the christian-feudal morality," "the modern bourgeois morality," and "the proletarian morality of the future." The first of these was based on economic forces that were rapidly dying; the second was the ideological construction of the capitalist ruling class; the third was emerging as capitalism produced the proletariat, and would replace the other two when the proletarian revolution had been effected. Although he does not say what they are, Engels admits that there are likenesses between these three moral systems. These likenesses have two main causes: in the first place, the feudal, capitalist, and emerging proletarian society are different stages of a single economic development; and in the second place, the economic fact of private property requires recognition in all non-communist moral systems, although "Thou shalt not steal" would be quite unnecessary in "a society in which the motive for stealing has been done away with."

Engels argued, furthermore, that as one class has succeeded another in the conflicts of the past "there has on the whole been progress in morality, as in all other branches of human knowledge," and that "a really human morality which transcends class antagonisms and their legacies in thought becomes possible only at a stage of society which has not only overcome class contradictions, but has even forgotten them in practical life." It is the proletarian morality that "contains the maximum of durable elements" and "in the present represents the overthrow of the present, represents the future." The chief element of the morality of the future, it appears, will be equality: ". . . the real content of the proletarian demand for equality is the demand for the *abolition of classes.* Any demand for equality which goes beyond that of necessity passes into absurdity."[7]

When we read that moral codes depend upon conditions of life, that these vary with changes in the economic basis of society, and that each class has its own morality, we are tempted to conclude that Engels was arguing for what is called a relativist view of morality, i.e., a view according to which there are many different groupings of men each with *its own* standards of moral conduct, but that there is no *universal* standard of moral conduct in terms of which the manifold particular codes can be rationally assessed. It might seem, furthermore, that the Marxist version of Relativism is somewhat as follows: The differences between human groupings are all, in the last resort, differences between their economic structures; all non-communist societies are class-divided and therefore all moral codes in them will be class codes; when an economic system is firmly established, the generally accepted morality will be that of the exploiting class, and justice will be, as Thrasymachus the Greek Sophist said it was, "the interest of the stronger"; but when a new economic system is in process of development, the rising class whose interests are tied to it will develop a moral outlook that will bolster its own interests as opposed to those of the class that has hitherto ruled supreme, and in this way a conflict of class interests will manifest itself as a clash of moral codes. From all this it would follow that moral fervor is a disguise for class interest, and that, since classes judge one another in terms of incompatible

---

7. This last quotation is from p. 121; the previous passages are from pp. 106–8.

standards, conflict between them can never end by their submitting themselves to some commonly accepted rule; their interests may conceivably bring them to a truce, but they can never submit themselves to the tribunal of an agreed morality. That this is Engels' view seems to be suggested by his remark that "the proletarian demand for equality" is "an agitational means in order to rouse the workers against the capitalists on the basis of the capitalists' own assertions."[8] Lenin, too, has let fall a number of phrases which suggest this form of Relativism, as when, in his "Address to the Third Congress of the Russian Young Communist League," he said: "When people talk to us about morality we say: for the Communist, morality lies entirely in this compact, united discipline and conscious mass struggle against the exploiters. We do not believe in an eternal morality, and we expose all the fables about morality."[9]

Nevertheless, however much relativist arguments may be used to confute and discourage those who accept the traditional codes, there is in Marxist ethics a claim to absoluteness. It has already been pointed out that Engels held that there are elements common to the feudal, bourgeois, and proletarian moralities, and that "there has on the whole been progress in morality, as in all other branches of human knowledge." So too Lenin, in the sentence following the passage I have just quoted from his speech to the Russian Young Communist League, said: "Morality serves the purpose of helping human society to rise to a higher level, and to get rid of the exploitation of labour." Rosenthal and Yudin's article on "Ethics" in their *Handbook of Philosophy* concludes with these words: "Communist morality takes the position that only that which contributes to the abolition of human exploitation, poverty, and degradation, and to the building and strengthening of a system of social life from which such inhuman phenomena will be absent is moral and ethical." And Mr. Shishkin is quoted as having written as follows in an article entitled "The Decay of Anglo-American Ethics" in the Soviet periodical *Voprosy Filosofii:* "The chief struggle [in Anglo-American ethics] is against Marxist ethics, and its objective and rigorous norms and principles derived from a scientific understanding

8. *Anti-Dühring*, p. 121.
9. *The Essentials of Lenin* (London, 1947), vol. 2, p. 670.

of society; ethical relativism was important in the thought of Rosen-
berg and Goebbels."[10] From all this it will be seen that moral standards
are not held by Marxists to be merely *different* from one another, but
are said to have progressed as the earlier codes gave way to others that
were closer to the Communism of the future. How, then, in view of
what has been said in the previous chapter about the nature of ideologies, can we understand the claim that Communist morality is *superior*
to the morality that went before it?

From the passages I have quoted it will be seen that there are four
main respects in which Marxist ethics differs from ethical relativism.
In the first place it is held that there are elements common to the feudal, bourgeois, and proletarian moralities. Little is said about these
common elements, but undoubtedly the view is that no society could
survive in which there was no respect for human life or for personal
possessions, no loyalty, no courage, no care for the helpless. These
"conditions of human peace," as Hobbes called them, are referred to
by Lenin as "the elementary rules of social life that have been known
for centuries and repeated for thousands of years in all school books."[11]
To call attention to such principles, however, is not sufficient, on its
own, to eliminate ethical relativism, since, although a rule such as
"murder is wrong" may be universal in the sense that every society
recognizes it as binding within itself, it may not be universal in the
sense that every society regards it as applying to its conduct toward
foreigners as well as within its own bounds. The universal acceptance
of a rule such as "It is wrong to murder fellow-tribesmen" (or "non-
backsliding fellow party-members") is compatible, therefore, with the
belief that it is right to kill anyone else. The Marxists' references to
elements common to all moral codes, although they *may* be meant to
constitute a rejection of Relativism, do not conclusively show that they
are this.

In the second place, however, it is quite clear that Engels wrote
of *progress* in morality, and that this implies some standard in terms
of which the various stages are estimated. He speaks, too, of "a truly
human morality which transcends class antagonisms," and asserts that

10. *Soviet Studies*, vol. 1, no. 3, Jan. 1950.
11. *State and Revolution* (London, 1933), p. 69.

this will be achieved when classes have been abolished. We should note, too, Lenin's phrase "helping human society to rise to a higher level" and Rosenthal and Yudin's talk of getting rid of such "inhuman phenomena" as "human exploitation, poverty, and degradation." Thus, those societies are the better ones in which there is the least exploitation, the least poverty, the least "degradation." "Human," in this context, has two meanings. A "human" morality is, in the first place, one in which religious and theological elements play no part. In the second place, it is a morality which extends to *all* human beings by requiring the abolition of *all* poverty and *all* exploitation. It is "human" in the sense of being both atheistic and applicable to all men.

In the third place, the emerging proletarian morality is held to be superior to all those which preceded it. This is because the proletariat is the class which, exploited as it is in capitalist society, will surely bring capitalist society to an end, and in so doing will abolish classes, exploitation, and poverty. It does not seem that proletarian morality is preferred by Marxists solely because it is the morality of the class that has a future, of the class that will become the ruling class. They also prefer it because it is the morality of the class that will bring classes to an end. They appear to have the picture of a morality that extends the ambit of its respect as it spreads from a few feudal lords to the more numerous bourgeoisie, and thence to the proletarians who will finally be the whole of mankind.

It must be said in the fourth place, however, that the standard of moral assessment is itself held by Marxists to depend upon the level of economic (or technological) development of society. Here we come to the central, and most difficult, aspect of Marxist moral theory. There can be no doubt that capitalist industrial society is much more effective, from an industrial point of view, than any society that has gone before it. The standard of comparison between it and its predecessors in this regard is the quantity and quality of goods producible during any given time, "quality," of course, being understood in a sense that excludes artistic excellence or moral suitability. It is obvious that a society in which wireless sets and cyclotrons are produced is industrially more advanced than one in which steam power has not yet been employed. Now the Marxists maintain the following theses: (*a*) that moral codes are parasitic on industrial achievement; (*b*) that private ownership of the means of production is a hindrance to the industrial progress of modern society; (*c*) that when this hindrance has been removed by the abolition of capitalism, industrial progress will be vastly accelerated; and (*d*) that the classless morality of the new society will show a corresponding advance on that of the class-divided societies of the past. The view is summarized in an article in *Soviet Studies* as follows: "Just as each stage of human development possesses a certain level of consciousness which is the highest attainable in the historical conditions, so it also possesses an understanding of good and evil which is the highest attainable in the same conditions. Since we needs must love the highest when we see it, it is the duty of each individual not to aim lower than the ethical ideals of his society; and a society or social group which falls short in its ethical ideal of those ideals previously established is morally retrogressive. It follows from the general propositions of historical and dialectical materialism that a community in a higher stage of organization will reflect its social attainments in its higher stage of morals; and consequently ethical studies may be closely related to, and based on, the exact knowledge ("science") which is provided by sociology."[12]

What is the relation between (*a*) and (*d*) above? Surely it does not follow that, because moral codes depend upon industrial systems, the more advanced the industrial system, the higher the moral code. If "industrial progress" is understood in a sense that is independent of "moral progress," then no amount of industrial progress can give the slightest ground for supposing that there has been any moral progress whatever. Moral progress must be understood in moral, not in technological, terms. One is tempted to suppose that Marxists, having relinquished the view that morality is strengthened by divine support, have nevertheless felt the need for something else to support it when there is no God to do so, and have picked on technology for the role of substitute deity. The Marxist view must be either that industrial progress is *the same thing* as moral progress, or else that industrial progress is *a sure sign* of moral progress. We have rejected the first suggestion, and if there is to be anything in the second it will have to be possible to know what moral progress is independently of knowing what indus-

12. *Soviet Studies,* vol. 1, no. 3, Jan. 1950, p. 227.

trial progress is. For to know that changes in one thing are a sure sign of changes in another, *both* things must have been observed changing. For example, thermometers can only be used to measure the temperature of a room because we have been able to experience both the changes from hotter to colder and colder to hotter, and changes in the height of the column of mercury. The Marxist is rather like a man who, disgusted at the idea of feeling hot or cold, will refer only to the "objective and rigorous norms" on the temperature scale, and asserts that they are what hot and cold really are. Indeed, there is a further analogy between the use of thermometers and the Marxist correlation of industrial with moral progress. Once a scale of temperature has been established, the scale can "register" both discriminations and quantities that no one can have experienced. For example, no one is conscious of a change of temperature of (say) half a degree Fahrenheit, and no one has ever been conscious of a heat of 2000° Fahrenheit. Once the scale has been established it acquires a certain independence and appears to measure things that are quite beyond the range of human experience. The initial correlation between the marks on the scale and what people feel gets lost sight of. The Marxist use of the notion of industrial progress appears to have broken loose in a somewhat similar way from its initial conjunction with moral progress. First it was correlated with a norm, and then it became a norm itself.

According to the French Hegelian scholar M. Jean Hyppolite there is in Marx's *Capital* a conflict between two inconsistent points of view, the one Darwinian and the other Hegelian.[13] There is a similar conflict, it seems to me, between the ethical implications of the Materialist Conception of History and Engels' and Lenin's view that there has been and will be moral progress. For, as I have pointed out, the Materialist Conception of History is held to be "faithfully established in the manner of the natural sciences," and must therefore, like them, be amoral. It purports to show that the struggle between classes will in fact cease with the victory of the proletariat. Each class has its morality, the victory of the proletariat will be the victory of proletarian morality, and

---

13. "La Structure du 'Capital' et de quelques présuppositions philosophiques dans l'oeuvre de Marx," *Bulletin de la Société Française de Philosophie*, Oct.–Dec. 1948. Reprinted in Hyppolite's *Etudes sur Marx et Hegel*.

the dissolution of classes will bring the dissolution of class morality. This is the amoral Darwinian theory which is held to explain the genesis of moral standards and their role as weapons in the class war. On this view, the superiority of a moral standard consists in its replacing the standards of vanquished classes, and the superiority of a classless morality consists in its having ousted all others, just as, for Darwin, the fittest are those who succeed in surviving, not those who, in some moral sense, ought to survive. When Marxists talk of moral progress, however, they desert this amoral Darwinism for something not unlike the Hegelian theodicy. Out of the clash of classes, they suppose, superior forms of society are developed which would never have existed at all if the clashes had been mitigated or suppressed. In spite of apparent retrogressions man is progressing. His earliest stage was one of primitive, almost innocent communism. His fall from this state was necessary if he was to advance to a developed, self-conscious (i.e., planned) industrial communism. Industrial civilization, thinks the Marxist when he is in the Hegelian frame of mind, makes possible the mastery of man over himself so that, want and exploitation having been abolished, free men can each develop, without hindrance from others, the latent powers which class-divided societies had inhibited. In the progress of man what, to use Hegelian language, was merely implicit and ideal becomes explicit and real. Such a state of things would not be merely the latest in the succession of social orders, but would be both their consummation and the standard in terms of which their shortcomings would be judged.

We have now seen some of the Marxist attempts at making these inconsistent views go along together. The least Darwinian element in the first amoral theory was the view that the struggle between classes would come to an end through the abolition of classes altogether. (Darwin did not suggest that one species would oust all the rest.) Now the abolition of classes is a conception that readily gives rise to *moral* judgments. In so far as class differences involve exploitation, that is, the unjust use of power, the disappearance of classes may be supposed, rightly or wrongly, to lead to the disappearance of exploitation. (It is by no means certain that other forms of injustice would not arise after class injustices had been removed.) A classless society, again, is readily conceived as one in which moral respect is given to all men instead of only to some. It is easy, that is, to pass from the amoral conception of a classless society to the moral conception that Kant described as a Kingdom of Ends, i.e., a society in which everyone is an object of moral respect. The link, I suggest, is the notion of universality; it is supposed on the one hand that if classes are abolished *all* men will belong to a single society, and it is supposed on the other hand that moral progress consists in more and more men being accepted as members of a single moral world. In combining the two views, however, Marxists inconsistently hold both that morality is mere ideology and that it is capable of real improvement.

At this point it will be useful to revert for a moment to the Marxist discussion of phenomenalism. The exponents of phenomenalism, we said, generally deny that they are saying that there are no physical objects. They claim instead to be providing an *analysis,* in terms of actual and possible sense data, of what it is to be a physical object. Now it might be suggested, at this stage of the argument, that the Marxist account of morals as ideology is really an analysis of what morality is rather than a denial of the validity of moral judgments. It might be said, that is, that the theory of ideologies, as applied to morals, is the view that when people make moral judgments they are really giving expression to their attitudes and endeavoring to get other people to share them. This is a view held today by a number of philosophers who are not Marxists at all. The chief difference between the Marxist analysis of morals, therefore, and these "attitude and persuasion" theories would be that the Marxists have a lot to say about how the attitudes are formed, whereas these philosophers ignore that side of the matter as altogether irrelevant to what they call "philosophy." On this interpretation, then, when Marxists say that morality is an ideology they are saying (*a*) that moral judgments are expressions of people's attitudes and at the same time attempts to get other people to have the same attitudes toward the same things, and (*b*) that these attitudes arise from class situations, and that these, in their turn, arise out of economic circumstances. Now Marxists *object* to the phenomenalist analysis of physical objects on the ground that it is idealism in disguise. Might we not have expected them to have objected to the "attitude and persuasion" theory of morals on the ground that it is a disguise for all that is arbitrary and unprincipled in human conduct?

(Mr. Shishkin, it will be remembered, seems to have taken this view, though in an inconsistent way.) That is how the Stoics, whom I earlier compared with the Marxists, looked at the matter, but in this regard Marxism is more like ancient skepticism than it is like Stoicism. The reason why they treat ethical subjectivism differently from how they treat perceptual subjectivism is, I suggest, that they think they can find scientific evidence for the existence of men with various wants, but feel that there is no evidence at all for such things as moral values. If this is so, then Marxists think they can "reduce" morality to wants and persuasions in a way in which physical objects *cannot* be reduced to sense data. Now I criticized phenomenalism on the ground that its view of physical objects was based on such things as reflections in mirrors and the images of dreams and delirium, whereas the status of these last can only be understood in terms of real things that are not reflections, not dreams, not delirium; the phenomenalist assumes, in saying what sense data are, that physical objects are not sense data and his alleged analysis of matter is a hollow, painted substitute for it. Now I suggest that the "interest and persuasion" analysis of morals suffers from an analogous defect. There is the same zeal for immediately perceived ultimates—in the case of morals these are wants, desires, and persuadings. But there is also the same failure to notice that these "ultimates" are not real existences at all, that wants, desires, and persuadings are themselves moral, or are understandable by relation to or in contrast with what is moral. We have seen this sort of false abstraction in another context, when the attempt was made to describe a "material basis" of society that was supposed to have in it none of the features that belonged to the "superstructure." Phenomenalism, the Materialist Conception of History, and the "attitude and persuasion" analysis of morals are all of them, in their different ways, results of misleading abstraction, a misleading abstraction that fabricates unreal units, sense data, the "material basis" of society, and "wants, desires, and persuadings." A further point to notice in this connection is that, just as the phenomenalist bases his theory on illusions, hallucinations, images, so the moral subjectivist bases his analysis on moral divergences, and as the realist bases his view on developed and successful perception, so the moral objectivist bases his analysis on developed and successful moral conduct.

It will be remembered that in Chapter I of Part One of this book I called attention to the fact that one of Lenin's arguments against phenomenalism was that phenomenalism is a form of idealism, that idealism is a disguised form of religion, that religion is dangerous to communism, and that therefore phenomenalism should be rejected. Basic to this argument is the assumption that it is legitimate to reject a philosophical theory on the ground that it appears to be a hindrance to the victory of the proletariat under Communist Party leadership. In still more general terms, Lenin's argument assumes that it is legitimate to reject a philosophical theory on the ground that it appears to conflict with a political movement supposed to be working for the long-term interests of mankind. Now that we have discussed the Materialist Conception of History and the moral theory that goes with it, we are in a better position to discuss this assumption of Lenin's than we were when our chief concern was the Marxist view of nature. We can now see that when Lenin dismisses phenomenalism on the ground that it is dangerous to communism, he regards it, as he regards all non-Marxist philosophical theories, as an ideology, i.e., as an expression of some class-interest. His view seems to be that, if the arguments its supporters put forward can be intellectually refuted, well and good, but that if they appear for the time being to be too subtle for this, then Marxists must try to prevent them from being accepted by such means as scorn or moral indignation or expulsion of the heretics. From Lenin's procedure it can be seen that he regarded it as necessary both to deal with arguments on the intellectual plane, and also to unmask the ideologies that produce them. It will, of course, be remembered that Marxists consider that they themselves are being scientific when they expose the ideologies of other classes. They believe, too, that in doing this they are helping on the ultimate good of all mankind.

It cannot be reasonably denied that beneath the surface of philosophical argumentation there is often the desire to gain acceptance for a way of living and appreciating as well as for a way of thinking. There is no doubt that most of those philosophers who have accepted idealism have sought, in this philosophy, to justify some form of rational religion. Again, it is obvious that most positivists have the practical aim of getting rid of what they consider to be superstition. The idealist endeavors to show that religious hopes are not all in vain, the positivist to show that they are illusory and should be replaced by the clear-cut expectations that he imagines the natural sciences provide. Idealist views, as with Hegel, tend to be respectful of tradition, Positivist views, as during the French Enlightenment, to be contemptuous of it. (Hume and Comte, it is true, are very notable instances to the contrary.) Some realists and materialists, revolted by what seems to them to be irresponsible "cleverness," aim, like the Stoics, to secure agreement on a set of basic truths that should provide a foundation for common agreement and mutual respect. Most of those who engage in philosophical thought have some such fundamental aims. Their thinking is associated with their meditations on life and death and with their conception of how men ought to conduct themselves. In their philosophizing they often approach near to prophecy or poetry. Philosophers who today talk of philosophical "puzzles" minimize these aspects of philosophical thought, whereas those who talk of "problems" or "predicaments" tend to stress them. But whether minimized or stressed, they are there.

Now it looks very strange when Lenin, in a book where the views of Berkeley, Mach, and Poincaré are under discussion, calls upon his comrades to close the ranks. It is important first to see what justification there could be for these methods. If someone asserts as true something he knows to be false, it is idle to argue with him about the truth of what he is saying, though it may be important to argue with those he might mislead. For he is making the assertion in order to deceive, not in order to add to the sum of knowledge. Again, if someone is carried away by his hopes and interests to enunciate false statements as gestures of faith or defiance, concern with the detail of his falsehoods may lead his opponents to lose sight of the practical reasons for which he uttered them. Such men, in uttering what have the appearance of statements, are chiefly endeavoring to achieve some practical aim. Since intellectual illumination is not their object, argumentative procedures that assumed that it was would be out of place, in the sense that they would not be directed at the main point of what the men were doing. Thus, when Lenin, in *Materialism and Empirio-Criticism,* writes abusively, he is assuming that idealists are conscious or unconscious deceivers, that their arguments are not really concerned with reaching truth, but are a sort of slogan to rally supporters and discourage the enemy. He conceives himself as replying to slogans by slogans, to actions by actions. It is likely that he was all the more ready to behave like this in that he was convinced of the practical bearing of all genuine (Marxist or scientific) thinking. Furthermore, social circumstances or psychological concomitants can be enquired into in the case of *any* sort of view, whether it be true or false. For example, Marxists consider that the methods of the natural sciences, being based on experience and practice, lead toward truth. But although this is so, there is no reason why sociologists should not investigate the social background of physicists and compare it with that of biologists, nor why psychologists should not enquire whether there is a special type of personality that predisposes men to become scientists. Such enquiries, it will be seen, are quite irrelevant to the truth or falsity of the theories that the scientists put forward. Descartes's pride no more discredits his scientific discoveries than Darwin's humility accredits his. Whether a scientific theory is true or false is settled by scientific argument, not by reference to the nature of the propounder's motives. Suppose, then, that a Marxist admits this but asserts that philosophy is in a different case since it is an ideology. But philosophy proceeds by argument, and whether an argument is acceptable or not depends on how well it has been conducted. Philosophical arguments may be a different sort of argument from scientific ones, but in the one case as in the other sociological and psychological questions about the arguers are quite different from and quite irrelevant to the acceptability of the arguments themselves. It is only when an argument is manifestly bad and yet its expounder sticks to it in the face of annihilating criticism that we begin to feel justified in asking *why* he should continue arguing in this curious way. That is to say, the *unmasking* of ideologies, in the sense of showing the class interests that prompt them, is only in place when the belief that is thus unmasked has already been shown to be false. Thus, quite apart from questions of good manners that may differ from place to place and time to time, no controversialist is entitled to refer to his opponent's motives unless the arguments that his opponent has used have been shown by argument to be untenable. If someone refuses to consider an argument on the ground that the man who put it forward has an axe to grind, this refusal is a political act, not a scientific or philosophical one.

This completes what I have to say about the direct relationship of Marxist ethics with the Materialist Conception of History. I shall now pass on to consider some of the details of Marxist ethics, commencing with a brief account of some important arguments from Marx and Engels' *Holy Family*. I have chosen this way of beginning both because the arguments are of considerable intrinsic interest and also because they enable us to see some of the moral considerations that influenced Marx and Engels at the time when their system of ideas had just been formed.

3. Marx and Eugène Sue

In 1842–43 the *Journal des Débats* published in daily installments Eugène Sue's novel *The Mysteries of Paris*. It was then published in book form and widely read throughout Europe. It is an extraordinary mixture of melodrama, moralizing, and social criticism. The main plot concerns the efforts of Rodolphe, Prince of Geroldstein, to rectify by his own efforts some of the wrongs of modern society that were to be found in the life of Paris. Fleur-de-Marie, a pure-hearted young waif (who is subsequently discovered to be Rodolphe's daughter) is rescued from her miserable life among Parisian criminals, becomes conscious of sinfulness, repents, and dies after having been admitted to a convent and made its abbess. Le Chourineur (the Ripper), a simple-minded assassin whose crimes are due to poverty and misfortune rather than to an evil nature, is reclaimed by Rodolphe and gratefully saves his life. Le Maître d'Ecole (the Schoolmaster), a criminal who appears to be quite beyond reclamation, is blinded by the orders of Prince Rodolphe so that he may not be able to injure others any more and will also be forced to meditate on his crimes and perhaps repent of them. In the course of the many loosely knit episodes of which the story is composed, Sue describes the miseries of the poor and the callousness of the rich. He proclaims that much crime is due to poverty, that the poor are much less blameworthy for their crimes than the rich are for theirs, and that it is much more difficult for the uneducated poor to obtain justice than for the educated and well-to-do. Incidents in this and others of his novels are used by Sue to show the need for social reforms. Thus, he considers that the death penalty should be abolished, but that blinding might be the supreme penalty for particularly atrocious crimes. He also advocates the establishment of farms where ex-convicts could work and re-establish themselves in society. Regeneration, however, on his view, could only occur as the result of genuine repentance which, therefore, should be the chief end of punishment. In discussing the social evils of unemployment, he proposes the establishment of a People's Bank to give help to men who are unavoidably out of work. He also sketched a scheme for pawnshops which would lend money without interest to respectable artisans. He holds that women were unjustly treated by the Civil Code, and that they should have the right to keep their own property and to obtain divorce. It should be mentioned that Sue took pains to give an accurate account of life in prisons and among the very poor. He later wrote *The Wandering Jew* and other "social novels," and in 1850 was elected to the National Assembly as a deputy of the extreme left. Although Louis Napoleon, on the ground that he was a distant relation of his, struck Sue's name from the list of his opponents who were to be imprisoned and exiled, Sue refused this privilege and insisted on accepting these penalties along with the rest of the protesting deputies. Under the influence of Sue there was founded in 1843 a periodical called *La Ruche Populaire* ("The People's Beehive"). This was edited by artisans, and had at the head of the first issue the following quotation from the *Mysteries of Paris:* "It is good to give help to honest and unfortunate men who cry out for it. But it is better to find out about those who are carrying on the struggle with honor and energy, to go to their aid, sometimes without their knowing it . . . and to ward off betimes both poverty and the temptations that lead to crime." Sue was accused by some of "disguising communism under entertaining forms," by others he was praised for drawing the attention of the prosperous classes to the misery which they tried to ignore.[14]

Now in 1843 Bruno Bauer, a leading figure among the "Young Hegelians," had founded at Charlottenburg a periodical called *Die Allgemeine Literaturzeitung.* A young man called Szeliga (who later had a reasonably successful career in the Prussian army) discussed in this

---

14. These details are to be found in *Eugène Sue et le Roman-Feuilleton*, by Nora Atkinson (Paris, 1929). The author does not mention Marx.

periodical certain of the social ideas of the *Mysteries of Paris*. He took Sue very seriously, and sought to give his views the sanction of the Hegelian philosophy. Marx and Engels' *Holy Family,* published in 1845, was intended as a general attack on the ideas of Bruno Bauer and his supporters as developed in the *Allgemeine Literaturzeitung.* Two long chapters of the book, written by Marx himself, are given over to criticizing Szeliga for taking Sue so seriously, and to a destructive analysis of the moral and social ideals recommended in the *Mysteries of Paris.* It is thus possible to obtain from these chapters a pretty good idea of Marx's moral outlook at the time when his social theories were being developed. In my view they throw considerable light on some important aspects of Marx's ethics.

Marx considers that the "conversion" of le Chourineur by Prince Rodolphe transforms him into a stool-pigeon and then into a faithful bulldog. "He is no longer even an ordinary bulldog, he is a moral bulldog."[15] Similarly he considers that Rodolphe, in "rescuing" Fleur-de-Marie, has changed her from a girl capable of happiness "first into a repentant sinner, then the repentant sinner into a nun, and then the nun into a corpse."[16] So too, in blinding the Maître d'Ecole, Rodolphe has, according to Marx, acted in the true Christian fashion according to which "it is necessary to kill human nature to cure it of its diseases."[17] Again, Rodolphe deplores the fact that maid-servants may be seduced by their masters and driven by them into crime, but "he does not understand the general condition of women in modern society, he does not regard it as inhuman. Absolutely faithful to his old theory, he merely deplores the absence of a law to punish the seducer and to associate terrible punishments with repentance and expiation."[18] Marx's general comment on the ethics of Rodolphe's conduct is as follows: "The magic means by which Rodolphe works all his rescues and all his marvelous cures, are not his beautiful words, but his money. This is what moralists are like, says Fourier. You must be a millionaire in order to imitate their heroes. Morality is impotence in action. When-

---

15. M.E.G.A., I, 3, p. 342.
16. Ibid., p. 353.
17. Ibid., p. 355.
18. Ibid., p. 373.

ever it attacks a vice, morality is worsted. And Rodolphe does not even rise to the point of view of independent morality, which rests on consciousness of human dignity. On the contrary, his morality rests on consciousness of human frailty. It embodies moral theology."[19] And in conclusion Marx argues that even Rodolphe's morality is a sham, since his activities in Paris, though they have righting the wrong as their ostensible aim, are really a means of gratifying himself by playing the role of Providence. His moral hatred of wrong is a hypocritical cover for his personal hatred of individuals.[20]

Is all this an attack on morality as such, or is it merely an attack on what Marx considers to be false morality? It certainly looks as if Marx is both attacking morality as such and as a whole ("Morality is impotence in action"), and is also attacking false morality. (". . . Rodolphe does not even rise to the point of view of independent morality, which rests on consciousness of human dignity.") If this is what he is doing, then he is inconsistent. For false morality can only be criticized in the light of a morality held to be less false, whereas if *all* morality is rejected, this must be in favor of something that is not morality and that does not allow that the drawing of moral distinctions is a legitimate activity. Marx seems to be saying the following four things: (*a*) that it is bad for criminals to be cowed and rendered less than human by means of punishment, repentance, and remorse; (*b*) that those who advocate punishment and urge repentance do so out of revenge, hypocritically; (*c*) that punishment, repentance, and remorse, even if aided by reforms of the penal laws and by measures enabling the poor to help themselves, can never reach and destroy the roots of crime; (*d*) and that the moral approach to crime is powerless to check it. His comments on Sue's novel show that he thinks there is something in human nature that should be preserved and is in fact destroyed by punishment and repentance. But it is not altogether clear *what* Marx thinks is wrong about them. Le Chourineur, from being a man, though a rough and dangerous one, repents and becomes, in Marx's opinion, a mere "moral bulldog." What, then, is bad about this new condition? Is it that le Chourineur has lost his pride and independence and now wishes

19. Ibid., pp. 379–80.
20. Ibid., p. 386.

only to be an obsequious hanger-on of Prince Rodolphe? If this is so, then perhaps Marx's objection is not to repentance as such, but to false repentance, and not to punishment as such, but to the punishment that breaks a man's spirit. Again, is it Marx's view that all those who support the punishment of criminals are really doing nothing but find outlets for their own resentments or support for their own interests? Is *all* justice hypocritical?

Now Marx clearly has an ideal of what it is to live a truly *human* life. Fawning upon rich benefactors is not a part of this ideal, nor is dwelling on one's personal guilt or renouncing the world in a nunnery. Someone lives a truly human life if he exercises his native abilities, enjoys nature and human society, and maintains a decent independence in relation to other men. In so far as punishment cripples the criminal, takes away his independence, and makes him obsequious, it has, according to Marx, done harm rather than good. It will be objected, however, that the criminal has ignored the rights of other people and can therefore hardly lay claim to remain unharmed by them. In an article he wrote in the *New York Times* in 1853[21] Marx considered this reply in the form given to it by Kant and Hegel, viz., that the criminal, in denying the rights of someone else, calls down upon himself the denial of his own rights by other people, so that his punishment is a fitting retort to his own deed. Marx admits that this view has the merit of regarding the criminal as a being who is worthy of respect, but he argues that the whole conception is dangerously abstract. For it takes account only of the free-will of the criminal and the violation of rights in general, but ignores the fact that the criminal is a concrete human being with particular motives and temptations living in a society organized in a specific manner. The view of Kant and Hegel, he asserts, only dresses up in philosophical language the ancient *lex talionis* of an eye for an eye and a tooth for a tooth. And he concludes: "Punishment, at bottom, is nothing but society's defence of itself against all violations of its conditions of existence. How unhappy is a society that has

---

21. *Gesammelte Schriften von Marx und Engels*, pp. 80 ff. (ed. Riazanov). Translated and quoted in *Pages choisies pour une éthique socialiste*, ed. Maximilien Rubel, Paris, 1948. M. Rubel's collection and arrangement is a most valuable contribution to the understanding of Marx's ethical teaching.

no other means of defending itself except the executioner." But these comments in the *New York Times* do not reveal all of Marx's mind on the subject. For from the passages I have quoted from the *Holy Family* it is clear that Marx thought that punishment was bad because the societies that inflicted it were bad. If a society is so organized that independent and courageous men are driven to crime, or if in the society acts are prohibited that are necessary for the proper development of human nature, then when the society in question "defends itself" by the punishment of criminals, its professions of justice are hypocritical. They are hypocritical, in Marx's view, for two reasons: in the first place, because the criminals are either unusually independent men or helpless victims and therefore are in neither case deserving of punishment; in the second place, because the just course would be to change the society instead of forcing men into crime and then punishing them for what they could not help.

If I have interpreted Marx correctly, it would appear that no one, on his view, would commit a crime unless he was an unusually vigorous man pent in by bad laws, or a feeble man in the grip of bad social circumstances. He does not, in the passages I have referred to, consider the possibility that someone might deliberately violate the rights of another. The only wrongdoing that he appears to admit might be freely willed without excuse is the hypocritical ardor to punish the unfortunate. In so far as his admiration is for vigor and power, it is for something that certainly does command admiration, though the admiration is not for anything moral in it. Power or vigor is admired, as in a tiger, for the beauty or economy of its exercise, but is not a feature of human beings that necessarily commands moral approval. In any case, a man who admires power and vigor to the extent of even commending it in a man who breaks the chains of law, is hardly consistent in excusing these feeble criminals who are the victims of social circumstance. If power is good, then feebleness is bad, and if feebleness is excused, then it may be necessary to condemn power. Furthermore, even though a society is bad, it may nevertheless be better to punish and prevent certain violations of right such as murder that take place within it, than to allow the wrongdoer to go scot-free, however physically admirable or abjectly excusable he may be. The right to life and to personal property may be defended in a society that is in many

other respects a bad one. Many of those in it who defend these rights
may, by these very actions, be defending much else that ought not to
be, such as exploitation of man by man. Is it wrong, then, to protect
the genuine rights because other rights are violated? Ought those who
support law and order in this society always to suffer the pangs of a bad
conscience? Marx can hardly say "Yes," because he has ridiculed the
idea of remorse and expiation. Marx's position, it would seem, ought
to be that in such a bad society those who support the punishment of
wrongdoers ought to work to remove the injustices that lead to wrongdoing—the sincerity of their remorse would be shown by the practical
strength of their reforming zeal. But if remorse and repentance are
rejected, a good deal of the driving force behind the activities of reformers will have been dissipated.

It is clear that, mixed up in Marx's moral indignation—a thing
which he himself has just described as impotent—is the belief that
crime is the outcome of social circumstances, that social circumstances
change in accordance with some *impersonal* impetus, and that in a classless society there would be no crime because there would be no occasions for it. We may see in Marx's judgments some of the confusion
that has beset much of the "progressive" moral thinking of our time.
Morality is regarded as somehow inferior to science, and yet the most
bitter moral criticisms are directed against industrial and scientific society. Or the "progressive" moralist will prefer one sort of morality, a
morality of power and achievement, and will also profess a more than
Christian solicitude for the welfare of those who have failed through
weakness. He will say that it is "uncivilized" to indulge in moral indignation, and will nevertheless vehemently attack the vice of hypocrisy.
But such criticisms as these, however justified they may be, do not take
us to the heart of the morality, or moral substitute, that Marx gave to
the Marxist movement. In the sections that follow I shall try to get a
bit closer to it by considering both the critical and constructive aspects
of it in some detail. The attack on morality may be better described,
I think, as an attack on "moralism," and this will be the theme of the
next section. This will be followed by a section in which is discussed
the Marxist doctrine of how man's lost unity may be restored. In the
section after that I briefly discuss the Marxist theory of the state, since
Marx's condemnation of punishment was at least partly the result of

his view that the state which administers punishment is a means by which the dominating class interests are secured.

4. Marxism and Moralism

The adjective "moralistic" is today used in spoken English to express criticism of exaggerated or misplaced moral judgments. For example, someone may be said to have a moralistic attitude toward crime if he is more concerned with the guilt of the criminals than with ways and means of stopping crimes from being committed. More generally, the noun "moralism" is used for an exaggerated or misplaced zeal for conventional moral rules. In chapter 25 of the *Categorical Imperative* Professor Paton says that his defense of the Kantian moral theory may be criticized by some people as "the product of moralistic prejudice" (p. 264), and it is clear from the context that a moralistic prejudice is one that results from an excessive emphasis on moral considerations. In the *New Yorker* for 26 September 1953 there is a criticism of a play based on the murder for which Edith Thompson and Frederick Bywaters were hanged. The critic mentions the theory that Mrs. Thompson's letters describing her own unsuccessful attempts to murder her husband were romantic imaginations, and writes that this hypothesis was "too much for a literal-minded and moralistic judge and jury." Here the force of the adjective "moralistic" seems to be that the judge's and the jury's moral disapproval of Mrs. Thompson's adultery prejudiced them against recognizing an important possibility. Perhaps there is also the suggestion that the judge and jury overestimated the badness of adultery. Again, in a leading article in the London *Times* of 28 October 1953, it is stated that those who wish for the general recognition of the Chinese government by other governments do not base their contention on the "moralistic conception" that recognition is a "moral benediction." Here too the word "moralistic," and the phrase "moral benediction" are used somewhat pejoratively to disclaim any fanatical concern with the making of moral judgments. The adjective "moralistic" and the noun "moralism" are, then, used to indicate and depreciate the exaggeration of morality itself, or the exaggeration of those parts of morality that are concerned with the reprobation of guilt. It is easy to see, therefore, that when Marx appears to be attacking morality, he may really be intending to attack moralism.

Now in the parts of the *Holy Family* in which he discusses the *Mysteries of Paris* Marx more than once refers approvingly to Fourier's criticisms of capitalist morality, and it is interesting to notice that "moralism" was one of the things that Fourier had attacked. According to Fourier there are four "false and deceptive sciences," and to these he gives the names "moralism," "politics," "economism," and "metaphysics." (The analogy with the theory of ideologies is striking.) Moralism was the term used by Fourier for what he regarded as the pre-scientific repressive methods of controlling the passions of mankind. It was his view that the passions should not be suppressed, but first studied, and then utilized. (A well-known example of this view of his is the scheme by which scavenging, an occupation that disgusts most grown-up people, should be undertaken by children, who enjoy playing with mud and dirt.) An objective study of contemporary society would show, he believed, that it was riddled with falsehood and hypocrisy; that what was thought to be repression of the animal desires was really a diverting of them from real to imaginary satisfactions; that men were cheated by appeals to their patriotism into sacrificing their lives for other men who were in search of commercial gain; that women were robbed of happiness by being educated to ideals of chastity; that reformers who persuaded governments to suppress social evils such as slavery were misled by the "philanthropic illusion" that mere repression was sufficient to stop evils that were rooted in human nature. Fourier thought that moralism was a lazy creed, resulting from an unwillingness to study and understand the workings of the passions. When Marx said that morality was "impotence in action" (he actually used the French phrase *impuissance mise en action*), he was no doubt thinking of Fourier's view that moralists take the lazy, quasi-magical course of forbidding and suppressing crime instead of the patient, scientific course of understanding its motives and redirecting them to the social good ("harmonizing" was one of Fourier's favorite expressions). "Moralism," then, in Fourier's system, was the name given to the complex of practices and attitudes in which (1) the part to be played by scientific understanding in improving the lot of man was ignored, in which (2) the human passions were to be suppressed instead of utilized for the common good, and in which (3) the inevitable failure of suppression and repression was followed by concealments and hypocrisies. The current senses of "moralistic" that I have just mentioned agree well enough with this conception. The critics of Kantian moral philosophy mentioned by Professor Paton think that Kant gave too much weight, in his analysis of morality, to the influence of moral reason as compared with men's passions and self-interest. The writer in the *New Yorker* thought that the judge and jury were insufficiently informed of the realities of human passion, and were therefore hasty in their judgment of Mrs. Thompson. The writer in the *Times* thought that indignation at Chinese intransigence might lead governments to be concerned with punishment when they should be concerned with future good.

It seems to me that a fundamental feature of the attack on moralism is the idea that blaming social evils, or preaching against them, or suppressing them, are inadequate ways of dealing with them, and should at any rate be preceded, if not replaced, by an understanding of them. Marx put this very clearly in a review he wrote for the *Gesellschaftsspiegel* of a French book about suicide. "Man," he wrote, "seems a mystery to man: one knows only how to blame him, there is no knowledge of him."[22] This is a view that is very easily confused with the idea that morality should be abandoned in favor of a science that is at the same time a transformation of the social world. I have already discussed this more general and radical idea, so that it is sufficient now to say something about the somewhat less radical one that I have just described. And in the first place I suppose I need take up very little space in saying how very widespread and important a view it is today. That preaching, moral indignation, and even moral seriousness could be well dispensed with if only the causes of social evils were known and remedies for them thereby became possible, is the conscious creed of some and an unexpressed assumption of many more. It is an important element not only of the Marxist outlook but of much that is regarded as "progressive" in liberalism and in non-Marxist socialism. Nor is it devoid of all foundation. For, as Marx himself pointed out, not all the evils

22. M.E.G.A., I, 3, p. 394 (*Der Mensch scheint ein Geheimnis für den Menschen: man weiss ihn nur zur tadeln und man kennt ihn nicht*).

of society are the result of deliberate wickedness on the part of individual men. Unemployment, for example, is something that is almost as unwelcome to some employers, many of whom may be put out of business in the course of it, as it is to its working-class victims, and it certainly cannot be prevented by telling employers that it is their duty not to dismiss their employees, or by ordering them to provide jobs and wages for them. Analysis of what brings it about, however, has suggested ways in which, in certain circumstances, governments can take measures that prevent it. If these measures are followed by other evils, this does not mean that anyone has aimed at producing these either, and further enquiry and ingenuity may discover new remedies to be applied by governments, by other corporate bodies, or by individuals. In general, many of the social evils from which men suffer are no more the result of human malevolence than are such physical evils as disease or earthquake. Revilings or penalties are, in such cases, as futile as shaking one's fist at a storm. Furthermore, it is possible that some deliberately evil acts, such as looting or rape in wartime, or a cowardly suicide during a financial depression, would not have occurred if the situation within which they arose had been prevented from coming about. Thus, when a soldier is shot for rape or looting it may well occur to those who have to enforce the penalty that such crimes would not take place if war itself could be prevented. It is almost as though *society* were responsible for the crime rather than the men who are punished for it. But tempting as it is to talk in terms that appear to shift moral responsibility from the individual to society as a whole, we should not allow ourselves to be misled by this language, and the following seem to me to be some main considerations to be borne in mind.

(*a*) It is always the case that evil deeds depend upon circumstances in the sense that if the circumstances had been different the deed might not have been committed. If Judas had not met Jesus he would not have betrayed him, but no one would argue that it was the accident of their meeting rather than Judas himself that was responsible for the deed. (Some people, perhaps even Marx, sometimes speak as though circumstances give rise to passions and motives and that these drive men willy-nilly this way and that. But if this were so, there would be no actions at all, and so no responsibility and no morals, and discussion of the sort we are here engaged in would be nonsensical. But most people, and Marx and Marxists most of the time, do not speak in this way except in metaphor.) The idea rather is that there are persistent social circumstances, such as poverty, which offer temptations that a proportion of men may be expected to succumb to, so that the way to reduce wrongdoing is to remove or reduce the temptations to it by producing circumstances in which they can seldom arise. The production of such circumstances, of course, would also remove from some other people the chance of valiantly overcoming these temptations, but this would be justified chiefly on the ground that it is more important to protect those who would be victims of crime than to provide occasions for moral heroism. Marx seems to have thought, and perhaps he was right, that some of the "crimes" that take place in evil societies are not wrong at all, but are justifiable acts of revolt against intolerable restraints. The practical conclusion that may be drawn is that, besides the duties of protecting individuals from lawless acts and helping the victims of war, unemployment, and poverty, there is, somehow, a duty to overcome lawlessness in general, and to prevent war, poverty, unemployment, and other social evils.

(*b*) There is, I have said, "somehow" a duty to attempt these things. But whose duty is it? And how is it to be pursued? It is natural to suppose that the duty rests on those best able to fulfill it, that is, on those whose influence in society is greatest, and thus it came about in the nineteenth century that statesmen and well-to-do people concerned themselves with "the condition of the people," as it was called. This meant that those who were influential in public life were thought to have a duty not only to uphold the law and to help the unfortunate but also to try to change those social conditions in which crime and misfortune accumulated. But on the Marxist view, the moral and social conceptions of the bourgeois ruling class must reflect and support their own interests, which are not the interests of the working classes. From this it is concluded that any benefits that the working classes have received from the bourgeoisie—and it cannot be denied that they have received some—have been unwillingly conceded to them, either as the price of their support against the landowning interest, or in the hope of enticing them away from more radical courses. Marxists, therefore, believe that the only duty that a member of the bourgeoisie can have to help promote the transformation of society must take the form of joining the working-class party that is out to destroy the capitalist order. The working-class Marxist is thus in the happy position of having a duty that is consistent with pride in his class, whereas the bourgeois Marxist must be ashamed of his birth and can only do good when he has renounced it. Thus all reforms promoted by non-Marxists are regarded as hypocritical maneuvers. Not only is moral endeavor diverted from the fulfillment of duties *within* the social order to the duty of transforming it, but it is not admitted to be moral endeavor unless it is under the direction of the Communist Party.

(*c*) It is obvious, therefore, that the Communist creed gives definite guidance about whose duty it is to take action to cure the evils that are held to pervade capitalist society. It is the duty (as well as the interest) of the proletariat to take this action, and particularly of the members of "the party of the proletariat." From this it follows that anyone who seriously desires to cure the evils in question will join the party of the proletariat. The non-Marxist who wishes to see these evils brought to an end has no such definite course open to him. He may lose faith in the efficacy of individual action without knowing what is to replace it. In his perplexity he often turns to the state, for the state is a powerful body capable of drastic action in the public sphere. I do not think it is at all fanciful to say that a result of increased preoccupation with the cure of pervasive social evils has been a transfer of moral concern from individuals and families to state and party. Churches, both because they are conservative in outlook and because they wished to avoid political entanglements, have been more interested in the alleviation of social evils than with their cure. There was a period when industrial concerns like Lever Brothers endeavored to fulfill the newly conceived duties by such means as housing schemes for their employees. But when giant evils are regarded as maladies requiring equally giant cures, men look for giant physicians, therapeutic Leviathans, in the form of governments and mass parties. It may well be that there are other possibilities of remedy not yet apparent to us, but until these are manifest the attack on moralism must tend to a transfer of moral interest. Praising, blaming, and preaching have not been eliminated but have taken on new forms in other places. If the clergyman's sermons no longer inspire many men to action, governments try to persuade traders to lower their prices or to preach workmen into temporary contentment with their wages.

(*d*) Another feature of the attack on moralism is a rejection of *moralizing*. Moralizing is calling people's attention to moral principles which they ought to follow, and those who reject moralizing have the idea that not only is it useless—and this is the point that we have so far been considering—but also that it is insincere. Marxists, and many non-Marxists too, feel that there is something mean and hypocritical about those who preach morality, as though the preaching were incompatible with the practice of it. I think that this attitude has arisen in part because of the social leveling that has been in progress since the French Revolution. People are unwilling to listen to sermons unless they accept the authority of the preacher or of his message, and throughout the nineteenth century the old message and the old preachers commanded less and less respect, so that now, in the mid–twentieth century, many people regard moral preaching as a base substitute for moral action. Just as Shaw held that "those who can, do; those who can't, teach," so the anti-moralist seems to believe that "those who will, do; those who don't, preach." (Well-bred, sheltered people often suppose that the main moral principles are so plain that there is something tedious and ill-mannered in mentioning them. They may be right as regards their own social circle, but there are levels of society in which there is very little, if any, conception of duty.) In Marxist morality moral approval is reserved for deeds only, and neither words nor intentions are allowed to have moral weight. This may be illustrated by a passage from *The German Ideology* in which Marx criticizes the German bourgeoisie for its cowardly acceptance of the morality of "the good will."[23] Marx seems to have believed that Kant taught that a good will was good in abstraction from deeds, but he was quite wrong in believing this, since in the passage in which Kant describes the good will he says that it is not "a mere wish," but "the straining of every means so far as they are in our control."[24] But Marx, in the passage in question, was concerned to draw a contrast between French

23. M.E.G.A., I, 5, pp. 175 ff.
24. *Groundwork of the Metaphysic of Morals*, chap. 1.

liberalism, which was a liberalism of deeds which carried through the French Revolution, and German liberalism, which he thought had been a liberalism of mere intentions that led nowhere; and to draw another contrast between the concrete interests (such as reform of taxation) which gave vigor to French liberalism, and the formalism which, he believed, had rendered German liberalism powerless.

Two associated but distinct theses are involved in this panegyric of action. In the first place Marx is asserting that if someone does not practice his professed moral principles, then they are not his principles at all but mere verbal professions. This is just what Kant holds in his doctrine of "maxims," but in Marxism it becomes associated with the theory of the union of theory and practice and gets a peculiar moral application. It is argued, for example, that people who preach reform but give support only to projects of gradual improvement, show by their deeds that they have found little to quarrel with in the existing social order. Now part, but only part, of this argument is correct. Moral principles are practical principles, and we know what a man's practical principles are from his deeds more than from his words alone, so that if what a man does differs widely and often from what he says he believes he ought to do, we feel justified in concluding that his moral talk was *mere* talk so far as it concerned himself. Involved with this is the view of the *Theses on Feuerbach* that there is no impassable barrier between thoughts (or acts of will) "in the mind" and practice (or deeds) in the natural world. But this truth should not be confused, as Marxists do confuse it, with the falsehood that sincerity in wanting to cure social ills is possessed only by those who work with the Communist Party for the violent overthrow of the capitalist system. If it were perfectly clear that the evils in question would be cured in this way, and would not be cured but would get much worse if this course were not adopted, then there would be some justification for doubting the sincerity of cautious bourgeois reformers. But once it is allowed to be possible that there may be other means of curing the evils in question, or once it is granted that some of them may not be curable at all, this "activism," as the attitude in question is sometimes called, loses its plausibility. "By their fruits ye shall know them" is one thing, and Marxist "activism" is quite another. But this "activism" exerts a powerful spell on people of good will who wish to help in the cure of social evils and are persuaded that there is one way only in which this can be done.

A second point to notice in Marx's attack on the "good will" is that he depreciates the intentions and aims of the agent by comparison with his deeds and their effects. This is different from the point that it is by the deeds of men that we chiefly get to know their intentions. This second point is that the intentions of men matter very little by comparison with what they set in motion by their deeds. I think that this view has colored Marxist thinking ever since Marx's day and accounts, in part, for an aspect of it that puzzles non-Marxists. When some line of Marxist policy fails, the leader responsible for it may be cast aside, vilified, and shot, even though he may have struggled his utmost to bring the policy to success. It is well known that men like Bukharin who appear to have spent their lives in the Communist cause, are reviled as traitors to it because the policy they advocated was abandoned by the Party. The non-Marxist feels that to blame and disgrace a man *merely* because his policy fails is morally indefensible. Now *part* of the Communist objection to such men may be that if they do something that harms the Party they cannot sincerely believe in the Party. That is, *part* of the objection may result from a stupid misapplication of the dictum "By their fruits ye shall know them." But I suggest that there is more in it than this, and that another reason for the Communists' attitude is that they judge a statesman entirely in terms of what he achieves, and that they judge what he achieves entirely in terms of its success in promoting the aims of the Communist Party. I think it is important to notice that when this attitude is adopted the statesman is regarded as a means to the securing of certain aims and as nothing else. The judgment that is passed on him is passed merely in respect of the success or failure of his instrumentality and not in respect of him as a person. His loyalty to the cause as he understands it counts for nothing by comparison with the fact that he miscalculated or was frustrated by events. Thus the Marxists who behave in the way I have described are treating the men they call traitors not as persons, not as beings with some independent moral value, not, as Kant put it, as "ends," but as broken links in some impersonal process. Yet there is something almost compelling about the way in which the Marxist comes to this. We judge men's sincerity, he argues, by their deeds; intentions that are belied by deeds were never there, but are simulated by hypocritical words; men's sincerity is shown by their work for the oppressed, and therefore by their work for the Party that champions the oppressed; men who, from within this Party, pursue policies that endanger its success are the most dangerous enemies of mankind. It is in some such way, it seems to me, that Marxists pass from the condition in which they demand responsible moral commitment to that in which they require only me-chanical, and therefore irresponsible, obedience. They have followed the well-worn path that leads from moral indignation, through revolt and revolutionary administration, to cynicism and ultimate nihilism.

A further element in Marx's criticism of the Kantian "good will" was, it will be remembered, that the German liberals who made pro-fession of it were not pursuing any specific, concrete interests, but merely thought in terms of a formal equality of man that they failed to link with any of the real needs of their time. He accuses them, that is, of being for "equality" but not for any specific equalities. Marx, like Hegel and Fourier, suggests that morality is not an affair of pure prac-tical reason detached from the passions of men. He regards Kant as holding that there is a pure moral reason, distinct from the passions, that ought to bring them into subjection to itself but is frequently un-able to do so. We may develop Marx's view on this matter somewhat as follows. Those who suppose that there is reason on the one hand and passion and interests on the other go on to maintain that morality requires the suppression of the latter by the former. They look upon man as split in two and hope for unity to be established by one half dominating the other. Yet in fact, the argument proceeds, the half that is to play the role of master is not a reality at all, but an abstraction, the shadow of a shade. The shade, on Marx's view, is the soul as the central feature of religious belief, and the pure moral reason is the shadow of this. Marx thought that the morality of repression was bound up with belief in this soul, and that a morality of development would discard it. In the Christian morality, he held, man was divided against himself, whereas the rejection of supernatural beliefs and of their philosophi-cal counterparts was implicit in any system that looked forward to the development of integrated human beings. In the next section, there-fore, we must consider the Marxist ideal of man's lost unity restored.

5. Man's Lost Unity Restored

In recent years, particularly in France, a good deal has been written about Marx's so-called *Paris Manuscripts* or *Economic-Philosophical Manuscripts*, an unpublished and uncompleted work in which Hegelian notions are associated with economic theory. It used to be held that the obscure arguments contained in this work find no place in the Materialist Conception of History that Marx developed soon after, but more careful study has made it clear that, although Marx gave up the terminology of these manuscripts, the ideas themselves had a lasting effect on his system of thought. They play no obvious part in the writings of Lenin and Stalin, but we are justified in giving some attention to them because of the part they have played in forming the Marxist moral ideal. What I shall have to say about them is, of course, only a very brief outline of what would need saying if our main concern had been with the development of Marx's own views rather than with the Marxist outlook that has grown from them.[25]

Now there are two key words in Marx's *Paris Manuscripts*, the word *Entäusserung*, generally translated "alienation," which in German has the meaning of giving up, parting with, renouncing, and the stronger word *Entfremdung*, which means "estrangement." Marx took these words from Hegel's *Phenomenology of Mind*, and we must therefore first see what they were there used to express. The fundamental idea of Hegel's *Phenomenology* is that mind is not a simple, self-contained substance distinct from and independent of the external world, but a complex being that develops from mere sense awareness through a series of phases in which more and more of its potentialities are unfolded to an ultimate self-consciousness which contains in itself all the earlier

25. The reader is referred to: Hyppolite, "La structure du 'Capital' et de quelques présuppositions philosophiques dans l'oeuvre de Marx," *Etudes sur Marx et Hegel*, Paris, 1955, pp. 142–68. Rubel, *Pages choisies pour une éthique socialiste* (Paris, 1948). (This excellent anthology is almost indispensable for the student of Marx's ethical ideas.) H. Popitz, *Der Entfremdete Mensch* (Basel, 1953). (A detailed, documented analysis.) Pierre Bigo, *Introduction à l'oeuvre economique de Karl Marx* (Paris, 1953). Abram L. Harris, "Utopian Elements in Marx's Thought," *Ethics*, vol. 60, no. 2, Jan. 1950 (Chicago).

phases. Mind is activity, and since there can be no activity without an object on which it is exercised, Hegel considered that mind could only become conscious of itself by becoming aware of the objects that its activity brought to being. We may get an idea of what Hegel means if we consider that an artist or man of science can only come to realize what he is capable of by producing works of art or by framing theories and then considering them as objective achievements—he will certainly learn more about himself in this way than by trying to catch himself thinking as Bouvard and Pécuchet tried unsuccessfully to do in Flaubert's novel. There is no mind, according to Hegel, without distinction and opposition, and in the Preface to the *Phenomenology* he writes of "the earnestness, the pain, the patience, the *labour* of the negative." This is no mere metaphor, and at various stages of the *Phenomenology* Hegel shows how mind's consciousness of itself is improved by such means as the manual labor of the slave who comes to learn about *himself* in carrying out the plans of his master, or in the subtleties of speech and architecture, or in the worship given to the gods. "The labouring consciousness," he says in connection with the slave, "thus comes to apprehend the independent being *as itself.*" It is Hegel's view that mind could not develop by staying at home; it must work for its living, and this means that it grows by consuming itself, by putting itself into what, to begin with, appeared opposed and alien. (We may see here a development of Locke's defense of property as something into which *a man has put himself*.) This going outside itself by which mind develops its powers is called by Hegel *Entäusserung* or alienation. Without it man would have remained at the level of mere animal life and there would have been no civilization. It follows that there could be no progress or civilization without opposition and division. And this division must be in the minds of men. On the one hand there is mind as externalized in its works, and on the other hand there is the mind that confronts them. Hegel mentions various occasions when this opposition between mind and its products was particularly acute. One was when the ancient city-state had collapsed and the individual, feeling oppressed and deserted under the Roman despotism, retreated into himself or fled to God, and thus opposed his religious life that was dedicated to God to his everyday life in which he was subject to Caesar.

Whereas the Athenian of the age of Pericles had felt at home in the city, the Christian of the Imperial period felt a stranger in the pagan world. Again, with the coming of the Enlightenment in the eighteenth century, men lost their earlier assurance of their place in the scheme of things and were torn between their faith and their intelligence. (We may think here of the portentous conflict within the mind of Rousseau, and of the later "romantic agony.") Hegel uses the word *Entfremdung* for these unhappy divisions in the mind of man as, through conflict, he moves on to new achievements. Briefly, the theme of the *Phenomenology* is the mind's progress from mere unreflective living through opposition, labor, alienation, and estrangement, to the ultimate harmonious self-consciousness. This, fundamentally, is the theme of the Marxist philosophy of history in which mankind passes from classless primitive communism through class struggle to the ultimate communism in which, freed from class divisions, men take conscious control of their destiny.

I do not propose to discuss the details of Marx's criticisms of Hegel's *Phenomenology*—it is sufficiently obvious that, like Feuerbach, he considered that Hegel concerned himself with abstract categories instead of with concrete realities. But whereas Feuerbach had given to Hegel's metaphysical language a *psychological* interpretation, Marx made use of it for *social* criticism. The main point of Marx's translation of economic language into Hegelian language is that he draws an analogy between the condition of the proletarian in capitalist society and the condition of the estranged, divided mind that has not yet achieved harmonious self-consciousness. According to Hegel the estranged mind is lost in a world that seems alien to it, although it is a world that it has labored to construct. According to Marx men living in capitalist society are faced by a social order that, although it results from what they do, exerts a senseless constraint over them as if it were something purely physical presented to their senses. Again, according to Hegel the acute points of estrangement come after periods of relative harmony, and according to Marx the estrangement of man in capitalism has reached a degree not touched before. A savage living in a cave, he says, does not feel a stranger there, since he has discovered that by so living he can improve his life. But a proletarian living in a cellar is not at home there since it belongs to another who can eject him if he does not pay his rent.[26] The contrast is between a man who by his labor transforms the alien world into something that he recognizes as his, and a man whose labor helps to construct a system that takes control of him. The one man's labor is an enhancement and extension of himself, the other man's labor is his own impoverishment. And it is not only the results of his labor that have this effect, but the labor itself is an activity quite foreign to his nature. "The worker feels himself only when he is not working and when he is at work he feels outside himself."[27] Under capitalism, then, the human labor which could, if consciously employed, extend the power of man, is blindly spent in subjecting him to his own unconsciously formed creations.

Before we comment on this let us see how, in the same work, Marx develops the idea by showing the part played by money. Money, he argues, leads to the substitution of an unnatural, distorted society for the natural society in which human powers come to their fruition. It does this by becoming the necessary intermediary between a desire and its satisfaction. For the possession of money enables a man to satisfy the most exorbitant desires, and the lack of it prevents him from satisfying the most elementary ones. Someone with no money cannot effectively desire to travel and study however much these activities might contribute to his development as a human being, whereas someone with money may realize these desires even though he is quite incapable of profiting from them. Thus money has the power of turning idea into reality, and of making a reality (i.e., a genuine human power) remain a mere idea.[28] It is natural and human, he argues, for love to be responded to by love, trust by trust, for the man of taste to enjoy pictures, for forceful and eloquent men to influence others. But money distorts all this by enabling the man who is devoid of love to purchase it, the vulgar man to buy pictures, the coward to buy influence. Marx illustrates this by the famous passage in Shakespeare's *Timon of Athens* in which Timon says that "Gold! Yellow, glittering, precious gold" will "make black, white; foul, fair; wrong, right; base, noble; old, young;

26. M.E.G.A., I, 3, pp. 135–36.
27. Ibid., p. 85.
28. Ibid., p. 148.

coward, valiant;" etc. This was a favorite passage of Marx's throughout his life, and he quoted it twenty years later in *Capital*, volume 1, to illustrate his argument that it is not only commodities that may be turned into money but also "more delicate things, sacrosanct things which are outside the commercial traffic of men." "Modern society," he goes on, "which, when still in its infancy, pulled Pluto by the hair of his head out of the bowels of the earth, acclaims gold its Holy Grail, as the glittering incarnation of its inmost vital principle." [29] In *Capital*, volume 1, commodities are defined by Marx as goods produced for exchange, [30] and it is money that makes such exchange possible on a large scale. In capitalist society almost all goods are produced for sale and are therefore commodities, and this, according to Marx, prevents most of the members of that society from seeing that the exchange value of these goods results from the labor put into their production. This is not concealed in feudal society where direct domination prevails, since a man who has to do forced labor or to pay tithes cannot fail to notice that, fundamentally, it is his labor, that is, *himself*, that he gives, and that it is to the lord or the priest that he gives himself. But in capitalist society the goods that are produced for sale take on a fetishistic character, as if their exchange value were something inherent in them, like the god that is supposed to inhabit the stone. Men are kept at it producing goods for money as if money or commodities were the end of life. First gold, and then capital, became the Fetish that commanded men's lives just as some stone idol controls the lives of African barbarians.

Marx's religious comparison here shows the continuing influence of Feuerbach. In *Capital*, volume 1, Marx underlines the comparison. He argues that primitive people believe in nature-gods because they do not know how to arrange their affairs with one another and with nature. "Such religious reflexions of the real world," he writes, "will not disappear until the relations between human beings in their practical everyday life have assumed the aspect of perfectly intelligible and reasonable relations between man and man, and as between man and nature." So too, he holds, with the commodity fetish. "The life process of society, this meaning the material process of production, will not lose

29. *Capital* (Everyman edition), p. 113.
30. Ibid., p. 9.

its veil of mystery until it becomes a process carried on by a free association of producers, under their conscious and purposive control."[31]
"Mystery" is one of Feuerbach's key words, and "conscious and purposive control" is Feuerbach's and Marx's substitute for the Hegelian
self-consciousness. The equation of "life process of society" with "the
material process of production" is, however, a departure from his earliest views which obviously diminishes their moral impact.

In the first place, then, let us consider Marx's view that when, as in
capitalist society, goods are produced for sale, i.e., for money, most
people's lives are as pointless as are the lives of those who worship
non-existent gods. The reference, it will be remembered, is to Feuerbach's argument that it is because of their disappointments in this life
that men have imagined a world of gods who provide merely substitute
satisfactions for their real needs. Now it seems to me that Feuerbach
and Marx were much too ready to suppose that the world can be so
ordered that substitute satisfactions will not be necessary. Some of the
chief evils that beset mankind seem to be inseparable from the condition of being human. Death is the source of many of our main griefs
and the source, too, of many of our religious hopes, and as long as men
die and want to live, and as long as some die when others remain alive,
the need for religious consolation will continue. There is no need for
me to dwell on other griefs such as personal ugliness or insignificance
often cause which, though not universal as death is, nevertheless give
rise to the same need for a spirit world. It is those who are lucky, sheltered, hard, or unusually intelligent, who may expect to escape this
need, but it must remain, I should suppose, a feature of any human
society that we are justified in thinking about. If this is so, no amount
of social remodeling is likely to extinguish the propensity of human
beings to split themselves and the world into something material and
something spiritual.

But on the face of it money is not as closely linked with the condition of being human as belief in another world is, for men have lived
without money and might conceivably do so again. Marx is on stronger
ground, therefore, in looking forward to the dispelling of the money
illusion. His view appears to be that money diverts men's minds from

31. Ibid., pp. 53–54.

their real concerns to illusory ones just as, on his view, the worship of the gods diverts them from their primary earthly concerns. Now I do not think that this matter is nearly as simple as Marx thought it was. He assumes that he knows what men's "real concerns" are, or, as he puts it in the *Paris Manuscripts,* what a "human" life is and must be. In this work men's real concern is to develop their powers free from illusion, but in *Capital* the reality of human society is, as the passage quoted in the last paragraph shows, "the material process of production." This is one of the points at which confusion enters into the whole Marxist scheme of things. When we talk about men's real concerns we are talking in moral terms about what they *ought* to concern themselves with, but when Marx talks about "social reality" he means society as it really is in contrast with society as it falsely appears to people who do not understand its workings. In the *Paris Manuscripts* he was still a moralist, whereas in *Capital* he claims to be a man of science saying what *must be.* Nowhere, it seems to me, is he clear whether he is thinking of moral illusions or of material illusions, of mistakes about what we ought to do or of mistakes about what is. This may be seen even in his use of the passage from *Timon of Athens.* It seems to me that Timon's mistake was to have believed that money could buy friendship. He found when his money had gone that the men he had been giving it to were not his friends at all, and he ought to have concluded that you get friends by giving yourself rather than by giving money. Marx does not draw the conclusion that money cannot buy love or taste, but he rather concludes that it can buy these things and that therefore people without it cannot get them. The story of Timon shows that money is *not* all-powerful, not that everything can be done with it. In *Capital* Marx says that money is a "radical leveller, effaces all distinctions," and there is a sense in which this is true. In an aristocratic society only members of the aristocracy may be allowed to live in manor-houses or to wear certain styles of dress, but once the society is sufficiently permeated by commerce anyone with the money to buy one may live in a manor-house and the style of clothes one wears will depend on what one is able and willing to buy. But it does not follow from this that money will buy even prestige, since this is something that *nouveaux riches* often fail to obtain with it.

This brings me to a further aspect of this point. Marx is arguing that in a money economy people mistake the shadow for the substance, the symbol for the reality. Money is a symbol enabling goods to be equated with one another, but people live on food not on money. Now this is true if we take "live" in the sense of "keep alive," for coins and banknotes have no intrinsic power of nourishing. But money may also be regarded as a sign of success, and in this sense the possession of money, although it may not chiefly concern the buying of goods and services, is by no means empty or pointless, for the prestige it brings is real enough. Here again the Marxist tendency is to regard such things as prestige as illusory and to confuse this with the judgment that they are bad. Again, an individual whose life is spent in the pursuit of money may, if those psychologists are right who say so, be endeavoring to hoard it as a substitute for excrement, but he does get satisfaction of a sort from his strange behavior. People may obtain money (1) in order to buy goods or services with which to keep alive and develop their powers; or they may obtain it (2) in order to get social prestige—and this course is reasonable only in a society where money does give social prestige; or they may obtain it (3) to satisfy some unconscious desire. Now (1) and (2) are not quite as different as they may at first seem, for people tend to spend their money in ways that at least will not bring social disapproval. But (3) is quite different from (1) and (2), since the pathological miser hoards with a passion that is not much affected by social disapproval.[32] Thus his obsession may bring pleasure in one way and pain in another, in so far as he meets social disapproval. It is also different from (1) and (2) in that the miser does not know what is leading him along the course he is following, would probably wish to do something else if he did know, and is generally unhappy except when he is adding to his hoard or counting it over. On the other hand, people may admit to themselves that they want "to get on," and not want to do anything else when this is pointed out to them. At any rate their pursuit of money is not empty or mistaken *merely* because money is a symbol. If it is mistaken, it is because there are other things more worthy of pursuit than the prestige that money brings. It is not mistaken because money is a symbol for eating and drinking and other so-called "material" activities. It is worth noticing that religious belief

32. I rather think that Timon was a pathological *giver*.

cannot be regarded as significantly like the behavior of the pathological miser, since in any single community it is widespread, if not universal, and brings men together in activities that are esteemed, whereas the miser is at odds with his fellow men and therefore with himself.

The second point I should like to make about Marx's early account of "estrangement" is that it is linked with his later view that it is through the division of labor that man is divided and repressed. Indeed, one of his criticisms of money is that it facilitates the division of labor. Now Marx distinguished different sorts of division of labor. In the first place there is what in *Capital*, volume 1, he calls "the social division of labour in society at large." This includes the natural division of labor between men and women, young and old, strong and feeble, as well as that between the various crafts and professions.[33] It is his view that in all societies except primitive communism it is inseparable from private property and classes. This he contrasts with what he calls "the manufacturing division of labour" in which capitalist employers assign to their workmen particular tasks determined by the organization of their industry. Men engaged in the manufacturing division of labor Marx calls "detail workers"; these are men who, for example, do not make a watch but only one part of a watch, and, Marx says, "a worker who carries out one and the same simple operation for a lifetime, converts his whole body into the automatic specialized instrument of that of that operation."[34] But even this is not the most specialized type of division, for the extreme of specialization arises when machinery has been invented and the individual worker's job is determined by the structure and working of the machine. Marx calls this "machinofacture." He says that machinofacture requires the "technical subordination of the worker to the uniform working of the instrument of labour"[35] and leads to child labor, long working hours, and unhealthy working conditions. Now Marx holds that *all* types of the division of labor limit the activities of individuals and divide them. In *The German Ideology* he writes: ". . . As long as man remains in natural society . . . as long therefore as activity is not voluntarily, but naturally divided,

33. *Capital*, pp. 369ff.
34. Ibid., p. 356.
35. Ibid., p. 452.

man's own deed becomes an alien power opposed to him, which en-
slaves him instead of being controlled by him. For as soon as labour
is distributed, each man has a particular, exclusive sphere of activity,
which is forced upon him and from which he cannot escape. He is a
hunter, a fisherman, a shepherd, or a critical critic, and must remain
so if he does not want to lose his means of livelihood; while in communist society, where nobody has one exclusive sphere of activity, but
each can become accomplished in any branch he wishes, society regu-
lates the general production and thus makes it possible for me to do
one thing today and another tomorrow, to hunt in the morning, fish
in the afternoon, rear cattle in the evening, criticize after dinner, just
as I have a mind, without ever becoming hunter, fisherman, shepherd,
or critic."[36] And in *Capital* he writes: "Even the division of labour in society at large entails some crippling both of mind and body."[37] But of
course in the latter work his chief concern is to show the much greater
evils that follow from the subdivision of labor that is characteristic of
machine industry. The question therefore arises of what communism
is a remedy for, and of what sort of remedy it is. Is it a remedy for the
evils of *all* division of labor? If so, then under communism there would
be *no* division of labor. Or is it a remedy for the extremes of the division of labor such as occur in machine industry? If so, a division of
labor that accorded with natural aptitudes might still exist in communist society. It will be seen from the passage I have quoted from *The
German Ideology* that when that book was written Marx looked forward
to the end of the division of labor, in the sense that no one would be
confined to one sort of job. A few years later Engels wrote a little essay
in the form of a series of questions entitled "Grundsätze des Kommu-
nismus." Question 20 is: "What will be the results of the eventual abolition of private property?" and in the course of answering it Engels
says that industry will be managed according to a plan, that this will
require men whose capacities are developed "on all sides," and that
in such a society children will be trained to pass easily from job to
job. In this way, he continues, classes will vanish.[38] Marx did not in-

36. P. 22.
37. I, p. 384.
38. M.E.G.A., VI, 1, pp. 516–19.

corporate this idea into the *Communist Manifesto* where the communist society is vaguely described as "an association in which the free development of each is the condition for the free development of all." But in 1875, in his *Critique of the Gotha Programme,* Marx returned to this idea when, in describing the second phase of the communist society of the future, he says that "the servile subjection of individuals to the division of labour" will disappear, and with it the opposition between intellectual and bodily work. It is not clear whether this means that the division of labor will disappear or whether it will continue but that men will no longer be enslaved by it, but as communist industry is to be highly productive we may suppose that Marx meant that the jobs could be divided without the men who carry them out being divided.

The root of the matter, as with so much else in Marxist theory, is contained in *The German Ideology.* The paragraph following that which I quoted on pages 219–20 commences as follows: "This crystallization of social activity, this consolidation of what we ourselves produce into an objective power above us, growing out of our control, thwarting our expectations, bringing to nought our calculations, is one of the chief factors in historical development up till now."[39] What is here being said is that human inventiveness has led to an organization of society that no one has planned, and that this organization, with its division of labor, is something which each individual, and each generation of individuals, must accept as a social fact to which they must adjust themselves. The argument is that men have to fit themselves to the results of their efforts instead of producing by their efforts something that they want. Thus, when there is a division of labor individuals are drawn into some limited mode of work (which is therefore a limited mode of life) which directs their activities in a direction that they have not chosen. If people are to live complete lives instead of merely partial ones, they must, in a highly developed society, be able to choose and perform lots of jobs. (We need not pursue here Engels' secondary point that in communist society a more generalized type of ability will be called for.) The communist ideal is one in which nothing happens that has not been planned and in which everyone can live the sort of life he wants to. Now quite apart from the obvious objection that such a state

39. Pp. 22–23.

of affairs is most unlikely to be achieved, I think we may make the more radical objection that it could not conceivably be achieved. For if plans are to be carried out, things will be done that some people have objected to, or if nothing is done that anyone objects to plans cannot be carried out. Furthermore, as I argued on pages 176–77, to assume that a society is completely under human control is to assume that no one ever makes a mistake or miscalculation. Marxists are so anxious to free men from unwilled social forces that they propose to subject them to an infallible and unavoidable social plan, the organization and operation of which they have never explained.

I have already shown how very similar to the views of Fourier on "moralism" Marx's views are, and now, in conclusion, I should like to show how closely Marx's objection to the evils of the division of labor resembles another part of Fourier's ethical theory. Fourier believed that the social order of his time ran counter to three of the most important and fundamental human passions, the Cabalist passion or passion for intrigue, the Butterfly passion or passion for variety, and the Composite passion or passion for mingling the pleasures of the senses and of the soul. The Cabalist passion we need not now discuss, although it is important enough since, according to Fourier, it involves the confounding of ranks so that superiors and inferiors come closer together, and thus is incompatible with rigid class distinctions. The other two, however, are regarded by Fourier as justifying two of his most characteristic proposals, the passage in the course of each working day from one job to another, and the mingling of bodily and mental elements in all work and all enjoyment. According to him the subdivision of labor in industrial society with the long hours at monotonous tasks that it then involved was quite incompatible with human happiness. In one of his accounts of what he called "attractive labour" he describes a day in the life of a member of the future society as consisting of "attendance at the hunting group," "attendance at the fishing group," "attendance at the agricultural group under cover," and attendance at four or five other groups as well as work in the library, visits to the "court of the arts, ball, theatre, receptions," etc. There is no need to underline the similarity between this and the account in *The German Ideology* of the member of communist society who hunts in the morning, fishes in the afternoon, rears cattle in the evening, and criticizes after dinner.

In discussing the Composite passion Fourier argues that the attempt to enjoy intellectual pursuits without mingling them with the pleasures of eating, drinking, pleasant company, etc., leads to a thin and bored state of mind, whereas the attempt to enjoy the pleasures of the senses without any intellectual admixture leads to an unsatisfactorily brutish condition. He extends this idea in ingenious ways so as to maintain, for example, that an ambition that has no element of interest about it is inferior to one in which more is at stake than mere glory or reputation. If we consider Marx's condemnation of the division of intellectual from bodily labor, his criticism of German liberalism for its detachment from real social interests, and his general requirement that social arrangements should satisfy the whole of human nature and not lead to its division into mutilated parts, we can see how much of the moral stimulus of Marxism came from Fourier. In Fourier this positive moral impetus is as strong as the criticism of moralism. Marx, however, more sophisticated but less clear-headed than Fourier, spent so much effort in criticizing the existing social order that he had none left for the task of describing the one that was to replace it.

6. The Supersession of the State

It will be remembered that Marx, in his discussion of Sue's *Mysteries of Paris,* and in a later newspaper article, criticized the institution of punishment on the ground that it was better to cure social evils than merely to repress their consequences. But another reason why Marx was hostile to punishment was that, in so far as it is a means of upholding rights, it is carried out by a state or government, and states or governments are organizations for protecting the interests of a ruling class. Because he believed that this is what the state essentially is, Marx held that all its activities, even those that might on the face of it appear innocent enough, must in some way express its nature as an instrument of class domination. "Political power," he wrote in the *Communist Manifesto,* "properly so called, is merely the organized power of one class for oppressing another." We have already seen enough of the Marxist theory to realize that law and politics are held to be superstructural by comparison with the basic productive forces. Hence the nature and exercise of state (political) power can only be understood in terms of underlying technological or industrial conditions. The view is that as the various technological epochs succeed one another, different sets of interests proceed to organize their supremacy. In the Ancient World it was slave-owners who saw to it that the laws were formulated and enforced in ways favorable to them; in feudal society it was the landowners, and in capitalist society it is the bourgeoisie, who rule by methods that ensure the supremacy of the social arrangements that their interests require. The proletariat is destined to dispossess the bourgeoisie and to inaugurate a society without classes and without domination.

This is the general view, but we must now elaborate some of the details. Why is it, we may ask, that a government is needed to promote the interests of a ruling class, when the *real* power of this class consists in its control of the productive forces? The Marxist answer is that where classes exist, opposed interests exist, so that it becomes necessary for those whose position in the scheme of production is unfavorable to be kept from rebelling against those whose position is favorable, whether these dissidents are the adherents of an outmoded or the pioneers of a new system. Threats of force, and also the use of it, are therefore employed to prevent the social order from collapsing in continuous civil war. Now the state just is an organization which, within a given territory, makes and upholds by force and threat of force the rules of conduct that foster the interests of a ruling class. As Lenin put it in his literal way: "It consists of special bodies of armed men who have at their disposal prisons, etc."[40] Police, armies, judges, officials, punishment, prisons—these, according to Marxists, make up the state. Of course, a ruling class maintains itself in power by other means besides coercion. For example, there will be men who frame and advocate the view of the world, the ideology, that expresses the outlook and interests of the ruling class. Such ideologies will spread from the ruling class to the subject classes and bind the latter to the former by bonds of speculation. But on the Marxist view the essence of the state is coercion.

It is also an important Marxist view that in primitive communist society there was no state. The idea that state and society are not the same thing is familiar enough. Locke's "state of nature," for example, was a

---

40. *State and Revolution*, p. 10.

social condition in which there was no "political superior," and many writers since have pointed out that in many of the simpler societies there is no distinct organization for dealing by force with breaches of custom. No doubt the distinction between society and state came into Marxism from the writings of Saint-Simon (which Marx and Engels both quote) and from the Saint-Simonian ideas that were discussed in Marx's family and in the University of Berlin when Marx was a student there. Indeed, Saint-Simonianism was a very active movement in Europe at the time when Feuerbach, Marx, and Engels were forming their views, and Comte (who in his early years was Saint-Simon's secretary) on the one hand, and Marx and Engels on the other, may be regarded as developing in rather different ways certain doctrines laid down by Saint-Simon. Saint-Simon, then, regarded the state as a relic of the military and theological era that was being replaced by the industrial era; hence in the state order was secured by means of authority and force, whereas industrial and scientific society, the spontaneous outcome of labor and inventiveness, needed no theological authority or military caste to foster its development. According to Saint-Simon the priests, kings, soldiers, and lawyers who support the state have no real functions to perform in industrial society and will soon find themselves out of work there.[41] The Marxist theory is, then, that the state arises when an exploiting class organizes force in its interests. But if this is so, it will have no *raison d'être* when classes have been abolished and class conflicts have ceased to rage. The form of organization that primitive communism knew nothing of will, under the communism of the future, be superfluous. Marxists write of the following sequence of future events: (1) the proletarian attack on the bourgeois state; (2) the "smashing" (*zerbrechen*) of the bourgeois state by the party of the proletarian class (Marx's letter to Kugelmann of 12 April 1872); (3) the establishment of a proletarian state which will act, as by their very nature all states *must* act, in the interests of a class, but this time of the proletarian class; (4) the overcoming of all opposition from other classes, and in particular from the bourgeoisie, by vesting all the means of production in the proletarian state—the so-called "dictatorship of the proletariat," a phrase used by Marx him-

41. See G. D. Gurvich, *Vocation actuelle de la sociologie* (Paris, 1950), pp. 572–80.

self more than once, and notably in his *Critique of the Gotha Programme;* (5) a period of "withering away" of the proletarian state which is completed when there is no more class opposition and when production has reached a point enormously higher than was possible in capitalist society—the "withering away" is indicated in Engels' *Anti-Dühring;* (6) the transition from capitalism to communism is to proceed via "socialism," a system under which private property has been abolished without yet removing all scarcity; under socialism it is not yet possible for each individual to receive all that he wants, and the principle of distribution is that each individual's reward is proportionate to the amount of work he has done, deductions being made for depreciation of plant, new capital projects, sickness, and old age benefits, etc.; (7) under communism itself the individual, his work no longer "alien" to him, works according to his capacity and receives in accordance with his need. (I do not know of any explanation of the word "need" in this context. It seems to mean just "desire.") (8) If a proletarian revolution takes place in one state while capitalism continues in others, then the proletarian state must continue in order that the transition to communism may not be interfered with from outside. This is the reason given by Stalin in his *Report to the Eighteenth Congress of the Communist Party of the U.S.S.R., 1935,* for the fact that the Soviet state has not yet "withered away," and is showing signs of becoming stronger.

I feel pretty sure that the account of the matter given in Lenin's *State and Revolution* is a reasonable interpretation of the views of Marx and Engels and a reasonable application of them to later circumstances. Perhaps there is some doubt about the meaning of "smash" in Marx's letter to Kugelmann, since the qualification "on the Continent" might leave open the possibility of a revolution in England or the U.S.A. without this dismal act of destruction. However, Marx's and Engels' preface to the 1872 German edition of the *Communist Manifesto* seems to imply that the proletariat could not secure its ends by means of "the ready-made state machinery" anywhere. So far as the authority of dead writers can be used in such circumstances, it appears to tell against "reformist" interpretations of them in this regard. Nor is it unreasonable for Stalin to argue that internal social changes brought about in Soviet Russia need to be protected against possible attacks from without. The dubious element in his argument is that leading Communists such as Trotsky and Bukharin "were in the services of foreign espionage organizations and carried on conspiratorial activities from the very first days of the October Revolution." The question to consider, therefore, is not whether the Marxist-Leninist theory of the state is a consistent development of the tradition—in the main it obviously is; nor whether Marx and Engels would have approved of present-day Communist Party interpretations of it—this we can never know; but whether, as it stands, it is a tenable account of the state and of what politics is, and whether the prophecies involved in it are credible.

Let us consider it first, then, as an account of the state and of politics. And let us agree straight away that the distinction between society and state is both valid and important. The word "state," of course, is ambiguous, and can mean either a society governed through laws, police, judges, etc., or the governmental organization itself as a *part* of the state in the first sense of the word. But the Marxist theory does not run into any difficulties because of this ambiguity. The main difficulty in the theory, it seems to me, arises from the association in it between politics and the state. As with so many Marxist doctrines there is a good deal of vagueness here, but it seems pretty clear that Marxists, like many others, use the term "politics" in a sense that links it indissolubly with the state and hence with government and force. People are entitled to attach meanings and to develop them so long as they make their intentions clear. But social theorists have suggested, rightly, in my opinion, that there are disadvantages in associating "politics" exclusively with the state, with government, and with force, because the effect of this is to *dissociate* the term "politics" from other forms of organization where it is normally and usefully employed. This dissociation, of course, is intended by Marxists, but I think that their view of what is possible falls into error because of it, for if force and politics and domination are not merely aspects of the state but spread more widely than the state does, then the abolition of the state may not be the abolition of force and politics and domination. Now suppose we interpret "politics" widely to indicate the means used to influence people, to get them to do what one wants them to do. (This is the idea of Professor Harold Lasswell, but I am not developing it in his way.) Then politics will form a part or aspect of almost all social activity, whether within a family where children try to influence parents and parents children, or a church where differences of policy lead to party maneuvers. But influence is exerted in different ways for different ends. What is called "force" or "coercion" is influence by means of threat with some physical penalty as a pain in the event of non-compliance. Marxists rightly point out that influence is obtained or exerted by what they call economic means—by the threat of dismissal from a job or of lower wages, for example. And their theory is probably intended to mean that economic influence is more fundamental than, and the cause of, influence by means of laws and penalties, that the latter sort of influence is always sought for as a means of consolidating the former. This would amount to saying that state laws are always made and enforced in order to get people to work for purposes they would otherwise reject. (The idea that laws may develop from custom and, in some cases, *protect* some people from exploitation, is just completely ignored.) If it is objected that, say, the refusal to employ them could bring them to heel through fear of starvation much more readily than legal threats, the answer is that they might then use violence against their employers and the law has been made just to prevent this.

This, I think, is the sort of consideration that the Marxist theory is designed to emphasize. And the objection to it surely is that it is absurdly incomplete. In the first place, coercion, i.e., influencing by violence or the threat of violence, is more widespread than government is. It is a feature of what Locke called "the state of nature," as in the "Bad Lands" beyond the United States frontier in the nineteenth century, or on the high seas before piracy was suppressed, as well as, sporadically, within organized societies. In the second place, the users of what might be called "naked force" in some circumstances prove more powerful than the wielders of economic power. Engels objected to this "force" theory, which Dühring had sponsored, that if it comes to fighting those win who have the best fighting equipment and therefore the most advanced industrial development. Now of course, other things being equal, a more industrially advanced people will win a war against an industrially inferior nation. But there are other things which may not be equal, particularly the will and energy to struggle valiantly. A notable example of this is the defeat of the highly armed forces of Chiang Kai-shek by the Chinese Communists who obtained many of their arms by capturing them. Indeed, an indifference to industrial advance can, in some circumstances, prove a strong lever to upset the plans of highly industrialized groups, as happened in the conflict between Dr. Moussadek and the Anglo-Iranian Oil Company. The weak can often gain an end by blackmail, as when a beggar exposes his sores. This brings me to a third difficulty in the Marxist view. The Marxist theory of the state is based on the assumption that there is one basic type of exploitation, and that this is economic in the sense of being bound up with the productive forces and productive relations. Although it has not, as far as I know, been worked out in detail, the idea is that certain groups of people are in a favorable position in relation to others, in that through their ownership and control of certain means of production—slaves, land, factories, and raw materials—they can gain advantages for themselves at the expense of the rest of the community. Now I have already made the objection, on pages 155–57, that technological, political, and moral factors are all so intimately concatenated that to say that the first determines the other two is to move about abstractions, and it is now easy to see that questions of ownership and control are legal and political functions involved in the very processes of production. But even if (though baselessly) we grant that there are solely economic actions, these are not the only ones by which individuals can gain advantage for themselves at the expense of others. Clever people, for example, have natural advantages which they often use to their own benefit in pursuit of pre-eminence and power. It is true that clever people generally wish to exploit their abilities in the economic sphere, but this is as much because economic predominance is a sign of success as because it brings success. I suggest that Marxists are quite wrong in supposing that there is one fundamental type of favorable position in society, that of owning and controlling the means of production, and that all other types of favorable position are derivative from this and unimportant by comparison with it. In some circumstances, as the cases of the beggar and of Dr. Moussadek show, weakness can be a favorable position from which exploitation may be exercised. Granted that if people are in favorable positions then some of them will utilize them to exploit others, then the only way to abolish exploitation is to prevent there being *any* favorable positions. This is the point at which the optimism of the Marxist theory is so deceptive, for it is only if economic exploitation is the source of all exploitation that abolition of it can free everyone from all exploitation.

The term "exploitation," of course, when it is used of the relations of men toward one another, is a moral term that suggests that the exploiters (*a*) get the exploited to do what the exploiters want them to do, (*b*) do this to the advantage of the exploiters, and (*c*) do it to the disadvantage of the exploited. Or we may say that exploitation is taking undue advantage of a favorable social position. It is clear, therefore, that use of the word "exploitation" normally implies a view about what taking undue advantage of a favorable social position is, or implies something about the morality of (*a*), (*b*), and (*c*) above. Is it always wrong to get someone to do what you want him to do? Is it always wrong to do this to your own advantage? Is it always wrong to do this to someone else's disadvantage? An affirmative answer is more readily given to the third question than to the other two, but we need to consider them all if we want some idea of what constitutes undue influence of one person over others. Marxists leave these questions undiscussed but appear, from their criticisms and proposals, to argue somewhat as follows. Economic exploitation is the source of all exploitation and is essentially the exploitation of class by class. It is therefore of the first importance that this type of exploitation should be got rid of and that steps are taken to do what will lead to this. It is the dictatorship of the proletariat that will lead to this, so that anything that brings that dictatorship nearer is good. The argument loses all its force if economic exploitation is not the source of all exploitation, and it loses most of its force if there is any doubt about ending economic exploitation by means of a proletarian revolution.

Now most people would say that there must be quite a lot of doubt about this. For, they would argue, we cannot tell in advance how honorable or how clever or how energetic the proletarian leaders will be. Furthermore, large social upheavals are apt to raise problems that no one had foreseen, so that their ultimate outcome is something that we cannot reasonably regard as certain when we make our present decisions. Such considerations appear obvious to anyone who has had any contact with public affairs or who has any knowledge of history, but Marxists seem to regard them as unimportant. How has this come about? It is at this point of the argument that we must make brief mention of the notion of surplus value. According to the Marxist theory of surplus value there is nothing that a capitalist, whether an individual or a company, can possibly do that could put an end to his exploitation of his workpeople short of his ceasing to be a capitalist, since the extortion of surplus value is a necessary element in the process of employing men to make goods for sale in a market at a price that keeps the employer in business. Anything, therefore, that puts an end to profits puts an end to surplus value and puts an end to exploitation in this sense. Since the proletarian dictatorship *is* the dispossession and the suppression of the capitalists, it *is* also the end of exploitation, in this sense. We might almost say that exploitation is *defined* out of the social order through the dictatorship of the proletariat. Now in Marx's *Capital* the capitalist system is indicted for the way in which workers are kept working long hours in unhealthy conditions that barely enable them to keep alive. Suppose that, as appears to be the case in this country now, workers under what is still predominantly a capitalist system—for that is what Marxists say it is—do not work long hours and are able to live fairly comfortable lives. Is anyone going to say that they are still exploited because, *however* comfortable they may be, surplus value is being filched from them so long as their labor contributes to the profits of any employer? This would surely be a most metaphysical sort of exploitation that could exist when no one was aware of it. It might be argued that what is wrong is that the employer usually obtains a much larger proportion of the proceeds than the employee does and that this inequality is unjust. According to Engels, however, as we saw on pages 181–82, it is absurd to demand any equality that goes beyond the abolition of classes. So we still seem to be left with the view that what is wrong about capitalist exploitation is neither misery nor inequality but something that can only be discovered by reading Marx's *Capital*—or rather those parts of it that do not refer to the miseries of work in early Victorian England. This is so obviously unsatisfactory that Marxists have had to seek for other palpable evils to attribute to capitalism now that the old ones have largely disappeared from the areas in which capitalism prevails. These new evils are imperialism and war, and they are alleged to result from the capitalists' search for profits. I cannot here discuss the Marxist theories about these phenomena, but it is obvious that they pursue their general plan of "economic" interpretations when they regard the pride, frustration, and miscalculation that seem to play such a large part in causing wars as merely phenomenal by comparison with such factors, which they dignify with the adjective "real," as industrial expansion and the struggle for markets.

There is a great deal more that might be said about this view, but I shall confine myself to two points only. The first concerns Engels' argument—for what he says may be taken as an argument—that since there was no state and no exploitation under primitive communism, there need (and will) be no state and no exploitation under the communism of the future. There is an element of truth here, viz., the claim that the state is not an essential feature of human society. But those societies in which there is no state, in which, that is to say, there is no specific organization for the making and maintenance of law by force if need be, are small and simple ones, and, I should have thought, necessarily so. For people can work and live together without ever clashing only when they share a common and fairly simple outlook and are all, so to say, under one another's eyes. But industrial societies, as we know them, are large and complex, and offer all sorts of opportunity for idiosyncrasy and evasion. It is unbelievable that the members of such vast and complicated societies should work together with as little need for a law-making and law-enforcing body as the members of a small community. However, this is just what Marxists do believe. What is established first by the proletarian dictatorship, and is then upheld by force spontaneously exerted against lawbreakers by "the armed workers" (who are "men of practical life, not sentimental intellectuals, and they will scarcely allow anyone to trifle with them"), will, according to Lenin, become under communism a matter of habit.[42]

My second and last point concerns the Marxist objection to Utopianism. Lenin, in *State and Revolution*, recognized that the Marxist views about the future communist society might be criticized as Utopian. In rebutting this charge he says that "the great Socialists" did not *promise* that communism would come but *foresaw* its arrival; and in foreseeing communism, he goes on, they "presupposed both a produc-

---

42. *State and Revolution*, p. 79.

tivity of labour unlike the present and a person unlike the present man in the street. . . ."[43] Marxists, then, according to Lenin, do not say that they will inaugurate a communist society of abundance and freedom, but, like astronomers predicting the planetary movements, say that it will and must come. To promise to do something is Utopian, to foresee that it must come is not. And I think that he is arguing that "the great Socialists" also foresaw a greatly increased productivity and a new type of human being, whereas Utopians merely hoped for these things and called upon people to bring them about. Lenin's objections are based on the discussion of Utopian socialism in Engels' *Anti-Dühring*. According to Engels, Saint-Simon, Fourier, and Owen, the Utopian socialists whose views paved the way for Marx's *scientific* socialism, regarded socialism as "the expression of absolute truth, reason, and justice," thought that it was a mere accident that it had not been discovered earlier, and assumed that it needed only to be discovered "to conquer the world by virtue of its own power."[44] "What was required," they held, "was to discover a new and more perfect social order and to impose this on society from without, by propaganda and where possible by the example of model experiments."[45] They imagined the outlines of a new society "out of their own heads, because within the old society the elements of the new were not yet generally apparent; for the basic plan of the new edifice they could only appeal to reason, just because they could not as yet appeal to contemporary history."[46] Hence they produced "phantasies of the future, painted in romantic detail."[47] Their inadequacy in this regard was due, according to Engels, to the fact that they lived at a time when capitalism was still immature and did not yet allow the lineaments of the new society to be discerned within it.[48]

Utopians, then, make promises rather than predictions. (It is not relevant to our present point, but surely promising is a guarantee that the promissee may make a prediction about the future behavior of the

43. P. 75.
44. *Anti-Dühring*, p. 25.
45. Ibid., p. 285.
46. Ibid., p. 292.
47. Ibid., p. 291.
48. Ibid., p. 285.

promissor.) They appeal to reason and justice, and imagine reasonable and just societies "out of their own heads," instead of observing the first beginnings of a new society within the existing one. They think it is sufficient to advocate a new society of the sort they have imagined, or to try to bring it into being on a small scale, for the world to be convinced by their scheme.

Now this last point is important. It is a defect of Utopias of most sorts that they leave vague the means of transition from the existing state of affairs to the future ideal. This means that two things are left vague, viz., *who* are to bring the changes about, and *how* they are to proceed in doing it. Marxists claim that there is no vagueness in their view on these particulars. It is the proletariat, under suitable leadership, who will bring the changes about, and they will do so by a revolutionary dictatorship under which the bourgeoisie are expropriated and suppressed. But of course this very precision (such as it is) may turn many influential people against Marxist scientific socialism. But according to the Marxists this does not matter in the long run, because the already existing proletariat is the first beginning of the new society. When a party has been formed to lead it, socialism is no longer an aspiration but an actual movement. But although Marxists are right in pointing out that Utopians often fail to show how the transition from the actual to the ideal is to be effected, and although Marxists do have a theory and policy about this, this is not enough to show that their view is at all adequate. The first difficulty in it is this. Marxists claim that *their* view of the future society is not invented out of their heads, but is based on the first beginnings of the new society already apparent within capitalism. These first beginnings must be the proletarian class beginning to be organized by and in a party. But what is there here that certainly foreshadows a condition in which there is no force and no domination? Nothing, it seems to me, except the fact that Communists, if they get the chance, are going to put an end to private property, unless it be the increase in productivity that *capitalism* has brought with it—that other forms of organization will increase it still further is mere aspiration. Lenin, in the passage I have just quoted, says that men in communist society will not be like the present man in the street. Let us see what Engels says about this. We may look forward, he says, following Saint-Simon, to "the transformation of political government over men into the administration of things and the direction of productive processes."[49] "The seizure of the means of production by society," he goes on, "puts an end to commodity production, and therewith to the domination of the product over the producer. Anarchy in social production is replaced by conscious organization on a planned basis. The struggle for individual existence comes to an end. And at this point, in a certain sense, man finally cuts himself off from the animal world, leaves the condition of animal existence behind him and enters conditions which are really human. . . . Men's own social organization which has hitherto stood in opposition to them as if arbitrarily decreed by Nature and history, will then become the voluntary act of men themselves. . . . It is humanity's leap from the realm of necessity into the realm of freedom."[50] Anarchy, then, is replaced by plan, politics by "administration" (whatever this may be), the struggle for existence by peace, the animal by something "really human," divided mankind by unified mankind, specialization by universal adaptability.

I feel sure that anyone who reflects on these contrasts must conclude that, for all that Marxists *say* about their views being based on observed facts in the capitalist world, in fact their future communism is even more out of touch with human realities than are the speculations of the Utopians whom they criticize. Furthermore, the future they depict is extremely vague, and they refuse to make it more precise on the ground that such *precision* is Utopian, that detailed specification of not yet developed societies are romantic fantasies. (We may compare this with the exponents of Negative Theology who can only say what God is *not*, but never what he is.) But if they are right in this last contention, then surely they are wrong in claiming that their view differs from Utopianism in being predictive in any important sense. Very vague predictions are of even less practical value than are detailed wishes. I do not think that the "predictions" about communist society have much more content in them than the more baffling among the utterances of the Delphic Oracle. What is this "administration" that is so different from "government," and this "planning" and "direction" that are consistent with the full development of each individual

49. Ibid., p. 285 and p. 309.
50. Ibid., pp. 311–12.

and can be made effective without the use of force? They are so different from anything that we have had experience of in developed societies, where administrators (generally) have the law behind them, where planning and direction meet with opposition, and where all must reconcile themselves to some limited and specialized career, that it is hard to attach any definite meaning to them at all. And what scientific prediction can it be that says we shall leave the condition of animal existence behind us? This is something that even Fourier might have repudiated, and that Owen would have taken seriously only during that period of his life when he was in communication with departed spirits. It is difficult to see how any attentive reader of their works could have taken at their face value the Marxists' profession of being scientific socialists rather than Utopians. They do in some manner fill in the gap between present conditions and the future society they look forward to—they insert between the two a real and active movement, but this has the function, not of making their system a scientific one, but of being a seat of authority which can give unquestioned guidance to any doubter within it. Marxism is Utopianism with the Communist Party as a visible and authoritative interpreter of the doctrine striving to obtain supreme power. The scientific part of Marxist politics concerns the methods by which the Communist Party maintains itself and aims to spread its power, and here Marxism and *Realpolitik* go hand in hand. But the alleged goal of the Marxist activities is a society in which there is administration without law, planning without miscalculation, direction without domination, high productivity without property or toil, and, it would seem, unrepressed men who nevertheless have left the condition of animal existence behind them.

Conclusion

A Reader. You have joined issue with Marxism on so many different topics that I am in danger of losing sight of the main issues—if, that is
to say, there are any. So I should like to ask you whether you think
there is any fundamental flaw in the Marxist philosophy that is the
source of all the particular errors you claim to have noticed.

The Author. There is, in my view, a pretty fundamental incoherence in
it, but I should hesitate to say that it is the source of *all* the errors.
Marxism, it seems to me, is a mixture of two philosophies which
cannot consistently go along together, positivism on the one hand
and Hegelianism on the other.

Reader. Can you explain this briefly and in less technical terms?

Author. It is not easy to do *both* of the things you ask, but what I mean is
that on the one hand Marxists reject speculative philosophy in favor
of the scientific methods, and on the other hand they import into
their philosophy features from the philosophy of Hegel, a speculative philosopher who allowed only a limited value to the scientific
methods.

Reader. I am not yet convinced, for might it not be argued that the
Marxists have transformed what they have borrowed from Hegel so
as to make it consistent with the positivistic part of their theory?

Author. Marxists do claim to have transformed what they have borrowed from Hegel, and they don't like being called positivists. Nevertheless I think the inconsistency is there. Marxists *both* claim to
rest their views on what can be observed and handled, *and* maintain such theories as that the material world has contradictions in
it because nothing can move without being and not being at the
same place at the same time. To accept Zeno's argument at its face
value is to argue contradiction into the material world where cer-

tainly it is not perceived, and this is the very thing that speculative philosophers are criticized for doing.

Reader. Isn't this a minor slip rather than a fundamental error?

Author. It is surely a most important thesis of the Marxist philosophy that matter develops into new forms by means of the contradictions in it. This, indeed, is the feature of dialectical materialism that distinguishes it from mechanical materialism, and my argument is that, rightly or wrongly, it is established speculatively and not by the methods of the sciences or by observation.

Reader. I now see that your objection is more than a mere debating point, but I wonder whether you have not made too much of the Marxist opposition to speculative philosophy. The quotations you gave from Marx's early writings show that in the eighteen-forties he, like Feuerbach, was much occupied in refuting the claims of speculative philosophers and in showing that speculative philosophy was a sort of disguised theology or rationalized religion. But must we suppose that this had any considerable effect on his later views?

Author. The effect can hardly be exaggerated. Feuerbach had thought he could show that religious beliefs were the illusory outcome of human failure, and that speculative philosophy was, so to say, the educated man's substitute for religious belief. Marx extended this idea so as to maintain that moral and political beliefs are disguises for economic interests. The whole theory of ideologies, therefore, is a development of Feuerbach's theory of religion, and assumes, like that theory, that the way to know the real world is to look and see and manipulate and move around in it. Speculative philosophy, according to Marx, is an ideology, that is to say, a set of unfounded views of the world manufactured at the prompting of wish or interest.

Reader. When, therefore, at the beginning of our discussion you said that Marxists inconsistently combine positivism and Hegelianism, by "positivism" you meant the rejection of speculative philosophy, or of metaphysics, as it is generally called today, in favor of the methods of the sciences?

Author. Yes, I was using the word to cover just those two things, the rejection of metaphysics and the acceptance of science. But it is commonly used to cover something else as well, a view about what science itself really is. According to this view, it is impossible to obtain any knowledge of what is the cause or source of our experiences, and science, therefore, must consist in ascertaining how our experiences are correlated *with one another.* Those who hold this view say that when physicists talk about such things as electrons, which, of course, are not entities that are directly seen or touched, what they are *really* talking about is what they do see or touch when they set up the appropriate apparatus and see, for example, the photograph that results from using it. On this view the electron *is* the experiments, the photograph, and, for all I know, the clarification that ensues. This view is akin to phenomenalism, the view that physical objects are permanent possibilities of sensation, and, like phenomenalism, is rejected by Marxists because they regard it as a form of Idealism. It is this theory that Marxists have chiefly in mind when they attack positivism. They themselves combine their rejection of metaphysics with a sort of scientific realism much as d'Alembert and other Encyclopedists did, and much as did Comte, their nineteenth-century successor.

Reader. Marxists seem to think that this realism of theirs gives due weight to the importance of *practice* in human knowledge. Indeed, the notion of practice seems to play a very important part in the Marxist philosophy as a whole. Would you say that Marxism is a sort of pragmatism?

Author. I don't think it is very profitable to compare such an ambiguously formulated philosophy as Marxism with such a vague one as William James's pragmatism or with such an obscure one as Dewey's instrumentalism—three impalpables, we might say, that can never touch. But by considering the various things that are meant by the expression "union of theory and practice" in Marxism, we can make our way toward some of its most characteristic teachings. You may remember that when we considered the Marxist theory of science we came to the conclusion that by "practice" Marxists mean the verification of theories by observation and experiment, experimentation itself, and the *making* of the things that the theories are about. Bacon was one of the intellectual heroes of the Encyclopedists and he had said a lot about the practical possibilities of science, which he regarded as a sort of rational alchemy. His idea was that if only we could discover the natures that make the different sorts of thing the sorts of thing they are, we should be able to engender them ourselves, and, by adding, removing, and mixing, to transform one sort of thing into another as the alchemists had hoped to do with the Philosopher's Stone. I dare say that these ideas came to Marx and Engels through Feuerbach, but however that may be, they believed that science and industry were fundamentally the same thing. Like Bacon, they were fascinated by the myth of Prometheus, and felt that the idea of mankind becoming lord and master of nature was an exalting one.

Reader. I cannot see that you have done much in this book to dispel that idea—if indeed you think it ought to be dispelled.

Author. I do think it is a confused sort of idea in which ethics and science are mixed up together. On the face of it, it is one thing to say that knowledge ought to be used for the improvement of man's lot and quite another thing to say that knowledge just *is* the practical effort to achieve this. And again, it is one thing to say that men ought to develop their native powers, and quite another to say that they ought to subject the physical world to themselves. No doubt the conception that knowledge is human power mingled in Marx's mind with Hegel's idea that men's consciousness of themselves develops as they put themselves into their scientific and artistic and other achievements—but it was not a purely physical world that Hegel had in mind. Now on page 31 I suggested that thinking activity (what Marx calls contemplation) itself only changes the thinking agent, and is therefore distinct from practice which is an activity that brings about changes beyond the thought of the agent. This distinction is not upset by the fact that theoretical activity is often, perhaps always, aided by the performance of practical acts which help in imagining an hypothesis or in verifying it. Science, one might suggest, is contemplation aided by practice, whereas industry is practice aided by contemplation.

Reader. Perhaps this is just what Marxists mean when they talk about the union of theory and practice in scientific enquiry.

Author. I think they must mean more than that. From what Marx says in the *Theses on Feuerbach* it would seem that he thought that practical activity was the genus of which theoretical activity was a species.

Reader. But if that is so, there should be other co-ordinate species of practical activity besides theoretical activity or thinking. I mean that if practice is the genus and thought is one species of it, we should expect to find other species, just as there are other species of color besides red and other species of triangle besides the scalene. Do Marxists say what these other species are?

Author. I can't remember that they do, and I fear that their view has not been properly developed in this regard. It would be rather odd, wouldn't it, to say that walking and breathing and lifting and thinking are various types of practical activity?

Reader. Yes, the first three of these activities appear to be like one another in a way in which they differ from the fourth. But then, the first two don't seem to be quite the same type of activity as the third.

Author. There is clearly a lot that needs enquiry here. But a Marxist who had these points brought before him would argue that if we say that activity is the genus and that thinking and practice are the two species or specifications of it, then we have surreptitiously smuggled an incorporeal soul into the human being.

Reader. Can't we say that a human being can act by way of thought as well as by way of practice without committing ourselves to the view that he has an incorporeal soul? And anyway, why should incorporeal souls be taboo?

Author. I don't think there ought to be any taboos in philosophy, but incorporeal souls are taboo to Marxists, and not only to them. The reason why Marxists suppose that the existence of incorporeal souls would be entailed by the existence of acts of thought or contemplation is that the manifestly practical acts of walking or breathing or lifting are performed by means of bodily members such as legs, lungs, and arms, whereas there seem to be no parts of the body with which we think. Assuming, therefore, that all activities are carried out with or by means of something, thinking, if it is not done by means of any bodily organ, must be done by means of something incorporeal, a soul or spirit. This, I think, is the line of argument that Marxists try to avoid by their rather vague talk about there being no mere contemplation.

Reader. But do we not see with our bodily eyes and hear with our bodily ears, and are not seeing and hearing activities which do not change or even affect their objects in the way that touching and manipulating necessarily do theirs?

Author. I am not sure that we see *with* our eyes in the same sense of "with" as that in which we walk with our legs and lift with our arms. For whereas legs (natural or artificial) are part of what is *meant* by walking, and whereas limbs and holding are part of what is *meant* by lifting, some people have denied that eyes and ears are part of what is *meant* by seeing and hearing. They deny this because, they say, we can conceive of people having the experiences called "seeing" and "hearing" even if they had no eyes and no ears, as blind and deaf men might see and hear in their dreams—and they need no artificial eyes or artificial ears to do this with.

Reader. Need we go into all this? Is it not sufficient to say that thinking is a human activity that is analogous to seeing and hearing rather than to touching and manipulating?

Author. If we do go further into it we shall be starting another book instead of concluding this one. Let us merely suggest, then, that thinking may be better understood in terms of seeing and hearing than in terms of manipulating, and that the Marxist notion of practice is based on manipulating. When one comes to think of it, Engels, in the *Dialectics of Nature,* argued that it is the hand that distinguishes the human being from his non-human ancestors. "No simian hand," he says, "has ever fashioned even the crudest stone knife." Perhaps it is that materialists are unusually impressed with the importance of touching and grasping, and that Marxists have exaggerated this tendency with their view that men first manipulate things with their hands, then improve their manipulations by means of instruments, and thus change the world by their labor—labor being fundamentally *manual.*

Reader. I seem to remember that Veblen said that modern science results from combining the practical matter-of-factness of our everyday tasks and skills with idle, disinterested curiosity. On his view, the practical matter-of-factness, if left to itself, results in a limited, uncurious technology, and curiosity, if left to itself, leads to nothing but amusing myths, but when the two are combined modern science arises and speculative daring is used to explain what is. Do you think that Marxists mean anything like this?

Author. Perhaps they do, though I think that all the time they hanker to belittle speculation and to exalt practical matter-of-factness. An example of this is their scorn for Utopianism—which, as Max Weber pointed out, plays an important part in science in so far as ideal or isolated cases help us to make sense of what is very complicated. Engels, you may remember, considered that Utopians got the scheme of an ideal society out of their own heads, whereas *scientific* socialists *saw* the future society in the beginnings of it actually to be found in the present. He criticizes Utopians as a sort of speculator, but himself regards scientific socialists as a sort of copyist. Yet predictions do more than copy, and science, he holds, is essentially predictive.

Reader. But Marxist social science is only a *sort* of copying, for the *first beginnings* of the future society are not the same thing as the future society itself. On Engels' view, as you reported it, surely a scientific socialist may be compared with a man who can reconstruct the skeleton of some prehistoric animal from some of its bones.

Author. Your example brings even more confusion into the Marxist theory. What Marxists claim principally to be able to do is not to reconstruct a particular prehistoric social form but to predict a universal future one. And they claim that their view is scientific because it is firmly based on what is. They would seem to be suggesting that their predictions of what will be are really nothing but descriptions of what is, or at any rate only a little more than descriptions of it.

Reader. Isn't this the sort of thing that scientists call extrapolation? And don't they mean by this the process of discovering a trend, or direction of change, in some contemporary sequence of events, so that we may have at any rate a reasonable expectation about its immediate future course?

Author. Your last few questions have raised so many problems that I hardly know which one to start with. You are quite right in saying that Marxists regard prediction as a fundamental feature of science. This is shown rather amusingly in Lenin's assertion that Marxists are scientific because they foresee a society free from want and strife, and that Utopians are not scientific because they merely promise such a society. This, it seems to me, is to add clairvoyance to alchemy. The emphasis on prediction can easily foster the notion of the scientist as a sort of magician whose formulae are of interest only because of the material transformations and predictions that they enable him to make. But what differentiates a scientist from a magician is that the scientist is interested in the transformations and predictions because of their bearing on his formulae rather than in his formulae because of the transformations and predictions they may in fact lead up to. Ability to predict does not always go with theoretical understanding. Now you asked whether Marxist social predictions could be regarded as extrapolations from the present state of society. A society with no classes, no social conflicts, no state, and no domination does not seem to be a development of any trend that is at all apparent in the society we now inhabit where conflicts are acute and governments are extending their influence over the lives of their subjects. The only Marxist extrapolations that appear to have any basis are those that indicate coming revolutions, and after all these are events that Marxists are trying their utmost to bring about and may, therefore, succeed in making true. The only predictions that are of scientific interest are those that arise from a correct analysis of the subject-matter.

Reader. But isn't that the very thing that Marxists claim—that by means of the Materialist Conception of History they have provided a scientific analysis of social institutions and development which *explains* both the sequence of past epochs and the necessity of the future communist society?

Author. That is, indeed, the Marxist claim, but I hope I have shown that it is pitched much too high. I hope, too, that you don't want me to go through my criticisms of the Materialist Conception of History again. But in case you do, let me forestall you by saying that in my opinion, for which I have given reasons, the basis-superstructure distinction is untenable, and that, if we provisionally allow the distinction to be made, the Marxist thesis, if it is to amount to anything at all, is that the only way in which important changes can occur in the superstructure is as a result of changes in the basis. Marxists confuse this, I believe, with such truisms as that there can be no superstructure without a basis (politicians and priests must eat if they are to do their jobs), and that changes in the basis lead to changes in the superstructure (inventions set legal and political problems). If I am right in this, then the Materialist Conception of History has received more credit than it deserves, and this from non-Marxists as well as Marxists. If every historian who looks for the influence of industrial and commercial changes on government policy is to be called a Marxist, or even held to be under Marxist influence, then the term "Marxism" has lost all precision. The modern growth of economic and industrial history is not a tribute to Marxist theory but a testimony to the extension of historical curiosity.

Reader. You need have no fear that I shall try to drag you through the whole miserable business again, but you did say that your technological interpretation of the Materialist Conception of History was not the only possible interpretation of it, and I am wondering whether the confusions you have criticized might be avoided in some other version of the theory.

Author. Although my chapter on the Materialist Conception of History is a long one, it is only one chapter in a book that goes into many other topics, and I did not spend time in it discussing the other possible interpretations of Marx's and Engels' vague and sometimes contradictory utterances. If I had, it would have been time wasted, since Professor Bober has done this job in the second edition of his *Karl Marx's Interpretation of History.* His careful treatment of them makes it quite clear that nothing very coherent can be derived from them.

Reader. In your account of the Materialist Conception of History you didn't mention Stalin's discussion *Concerning Marxism in Linguistics*,[1] and I have heard that this modifies in important ways the theory as hitherto accepted. Are there any signs in Stalin's answers to the questions put to him about the linguistic theories of J. Y. Marr of any radical change in the Materialist Conception of History?

Author. Marr, the philologist whose views Stalin criticized, had held that language was a part of the superstructure of society, and was therefore determined by the economic basis and must vary with it. Stalin objected that the Russian language remains substantially the same as it was at the time of Pushkin although the economic basis of Russian society had changed from feudalism to capitalism and from

1. Supplement to *New Times*, No. 26, June 28, 1950.

capitalism to socialism since then. A language, he argued, must be the same for a whole society, for proletarians as well as for bourgeoisie, if communication is to be possible and the society is to hold together. Whereas the changes from feudalism to capitalism and from capitalism to socialism involved sudden breaks or leaps, language develops gradually and in independence of such changes in the economic basis, although, of course, the vocabulary is affected by them. Incidentally, Stalin said: "It should be said in general for the benefit of comrades who have an infatuation for explosions that the law of transition from an old quality to a new by means of an explosion is inapplicable not only to the history of the development of languages: it is not always applicable to the other social phenomena of a basis or superstructural character. It applies of necessity to a society divided into hostile classes. But it does not necessarily apply to a society which has no hostile classes."

Reader. I don't see what is meant by qualifying "apply" with "necessarily" and "classes" with "hostile" in the last sentence, for these qualifications might suggest that "explosions" are *possible* in the society in question, and that not all classes need be hostile. But in spite of such obscurities, the passage is surely very important in so far as it limits the extension of the leap-across-nodal-lines type of change even in non-socialist societies. After all, language is a most important and pervasive social institution. I suppose, then, that since language is not now regarded as a part of the superstructure it must belong to the basis.

Author. I don't think we can draw that conclusion with any confidence. Stalin has distinguished, in the pamphlet we are discussing, between what he calls "production, man's productive activity," which he seems to equate with "the productive forces"; "the economy," which he labels "the basis," and which, I suppose, is what Marx called "productive relationships"; and the superstructure. The productive forces are, so to say, a sub-basis below the economic basis. He goes on to say that "production, man's productive activity" does not have direct access to the superstructure, but can only influence it via the basis, that is, via the economy. He argues that a reason for holding that language is not superstructural is that it is *directly* affected by "man's productive activity" and does not have to wait upon changes in the economy. I suppose he means that language is necessary to and changes its vocabulary in our working relationships. He certainly compares language with "the implements of production," saying it is like them in that it may "equally serve a capitalist system and a socialist system." We might suppose, then, that he intended to place it in what I have called the sub-basis as one of "the productive forces." But he also says that language "is connected with man's productive activity directly, and not only with man's productive activity, but with all his other activity in all his spheres of work, from production to the basis, and from the basis to the superstructure." Some people have therefore suggested that Stalin intended his readers to conclude that language is a third social category additional to the categories of basis and superstructure.[2] However this may be, it seems pretty clear that the basis-superstructure classification has proved inadequate. I hope I may regard this as an indirect confirmation of my thesis that it is impossible to isolate them in fact or even in thought.

Reader. If we do talk about language as a third category, are we not making it into a sort of *thing* with gas-like properties, distinct from the more solid things that make up the basis and superstructure?

Author. It is very difficult to talk about institutions without creating this sort of impression. Stalin actually says in the pamphlet we are discussing that the superstructure "becomes an exceedingly active force, actively assisting its basis to take shape and consolidate itself. . . ."

Reader. Most considerate of it, I'm sure. But may we now return to the topic of the union of theory and practice? We have so far considered this alleged union as a feature of science in general, but it is obviously most important in the sphere of social science, or, as Marxists call it, "scientific socialism." Would it be correct to say that the Marxist argument, in outline, is that social science is the activity of controlling and regenerating society just as natural science is the activity of controlling nature and putting it at the service of man?

Author. That is how I have interpreted the matter.

2. "Marx, Stalin and the Theory of Language," by M. Miller, *Soviet Studies,* vol. 2, no. 4, April 1951.

Reader. I suppose it might be said that someone who rejected Marx's Baconian theory that *natural* science is control over nature might nevertheless argue that *social* science is necessarily a practical affair. Don't you think that although there may be people whose interest in the physical world is idle and detached, no one could possibly take a merely detached interest in human society?

Author. Of course a passion to reform society brings more people to the study of the social sciences than a passion to change the surface of the earth brings to the study of physics and chemistry. But this does not mean that social science is social reform—or "scientific socialism"—any more than physics is factory-building.

Reader. I can't have made my point clear. I meant that what social scientists say in their capacity of social scientists *affects* the social world in a way in which what physicists say in their capacity of physicists does not affect the physical world.

Author. I suppose that all the atoms in the universe are unconscious of what is said about them, whereas it is only most of the people in the world who are unconscious of what social scientists say about them.

Reader. But what social scientists say does influence some people sometimes.

Author. What physicists say influences some atoms sometimes. Perhaps the point is that physical theories are of practical importance only when they are utilized in some human project—they influence the physical world through the aims of people. But it seems to me that this is just what social theories do—people who are aware of them, or, more often, of some simplified version of them, use them in the course of furthering some aim of theirs or to influence other people's aims.

Reader. Perhaps you are right. But at any rate I think that Marxists must have a more radical view of the practical bearing of social science.

Author. I am sure they have. When they talk of "scientific socialism" they mean that social predictions can be *made* true by human action. Predictions that were not based on good grounds when they were first made may nevertheless help to bring about their own fulfillment by becoming the *aims* of a well-organized and determined group of men. Not all predictions that have been transformed into aims can realize themselves in this way, but predictions about the *destruction* of an institution may well do so when the institution in question is in any case difficult to maintain or demands a great deal of self-restraint or intelligence from the men who uphold it.

Reader. Are you not yourself now putting forward the sort of useless truism that you have criticized in Marxism? A fragile institution is one that is unlikely to withstand attacks, and therefore the prediction that it would break down was correct even when it was made, although attacks on it inspired by the prediction may hasten its end.

Author. What you have said might have been true if you had been speaking of a *weak* institution, although when we say that someone is weak we don't always mean that he hasn't long for this world. But the word "fragile" was properly chosen, and it is one thing to say that something is fragile, another thing to predict that it will break, and still another thing to set about breaking it. But if someone says it will be broken and tries to break it, it is more likely to be broken before, although how much more likely will depend upon what efforts are made to protect it. Imagine a very fragile vase in a room where everyone is anxious that it should be preserved. It may be that it is impervious to destructive agents in the atmosphere, so that the only occasion on which it is in any danger of being broken is when someone cleans it. If it nevertheless breaks it will be through an accident. Now suppose that one man in the room changes his mind and wants to break it. Even if all the rest still want to preserve it they now have to be very wary to see that he doesn't get near enough to carry out his design. If he uses force to try to get near it, it may get broken in the ensuing confusion. In such circumstances, and especially if the iconoclast, as we may call him, persuades others to join with him, it is the easiest thing in the world for the vase to be broken, and very difficult for it to be preserved. Now whether any human institutions are immune to violence I do not know, but I think that the introduction of violence into a society which has institutions which need peace if they are to flourish will almost certainly destroy these institutions. And the benefits of exchanging goods produced for sale can only be secured in a fairly peaceful and settled society.

Reader. This is a most depressing aspect of the thesis about the union of theory and practice. Have we now dealt with all of its repercussions in the Marxist philosophy?

Author. No. It has some quite interesting moral aspects. I don't think it is fanciful to suppose that when Marxists deplore the separation of mental from physical labor they are not only concerned with the class antagonisms involved in it but also with the narrowing of the individual's life which they think it entails. There is a very long tradition in European thought which makes the cultivation of the mind the chief aim of human endeavor. This tradition has even affected moralists who might have been expected to oppose it, such as the materialist Epicurus, who talked of the powers of the mind to increase pleasures by means of memory and anticipation. Fourier broke with this tradition to the extent of arguing that in the highest good both sorts of pleasure must co-operate, since neither is at its best without the other. I should guess that this idea impressed Marx and Engels at a very early stage of their careers.

Reader. But surely the distinction between mind and body isn't the same as the distinction between theory and practice?

Author. They are not precisely the same, but there can be no practice, that is to say, no action in or on the material world, without the body. Marx considered that it was not consistent with materialism to admit a purely mental activity in which the body was not committed.

Reader. Now we seem to be in danger of muddling two quite different things—the factual distinction between mind and body and the ethical distinction between the value of mental activity and the value of bodily activity. If Marxist materialism is true, and if there can't be any purely mental activity, then there is no point in talking about purely mental pleasures or purely mental values.

Author. I agree. You may remember that this issue of the mingling (or muddling) of fact and value arose when, on pages 179–80, I discussed a passage from Mr. Berlin's *Karl Marx.* I there said that on the Marxist view moral valuations are a sort of "false consciousness," so that it is when we are thinking "in the manner of the natural sciences" that we are free from illusions. But questions of fact and value so often mingle in Marx's writings that he may well have wished to deny the distinction, as Mr. Berlin says he did. Sometimes we have to forget the theory of ideologies if we are to make anything of Marxist ethics.

Reader. Is there anything more to be said about the union of mental and physical labor?

Author. It is of some interest to know that Stalin has said that there is no longer any antagonism between mental and physical labor in the U.S.S.R. "Today," he says, "the physical workers and the managerial personnel are not enemies but comrades and friends, members of a single collective body of producers who are vitally interested in the progress and improvement of production. Not a trace remains of the former enmity between them."[3] He goes on to distinguish between the antagonism between mental and physical labor, the distinction between them, and the *essential* distinction between them. The *essential* distinction between mental and physical labor, he says, "will certainly disappear," but some distinction, though inessential, must always remain, "if only because the conditions of labour of the managerial staffs and those of the workers are not identical." Stalin explains that by "essential distinction" he means "the difference in their cultural and technical levels." You will notice that when Stalin talks of "mental labour" he has industrial managers in mind, not mathematicians or literary critics. He appears to accept a pretty fundamental division of labor, as, of course, any reasonable person must.

Reader. Are there any other moral aspects of the union of theory and practice?

Author. Perhaps there is a trace of it in the scorn that Marx and his followers have for moral intentions, for what Marx called "the good will," by comparison with deeds and consequences. But we saw that his view is very confused here because no one would ever say that a *mere* intention was good apart from any efforts to realize it. Marx, as a materialist, is very touchy about anything that is supposed to be locked up in an incorporeal mind. I also wonder whether his attack on moralism was not associated with some such idea—that guilt and repression are not practical, though what he really meant was that they pervert practice.

3. *Economic Problems of Socialism in the U.S.S.R.* (Foreign Languages Publishing House, Moscow, 1952), p. 31. The other quotations are from p. 34.

Reader. The "union of theory and practice" formula does seem to cover quite a lot—the verifying of hypotheses, the making of experiments, using scientific knowledge and testing it in the processes of manufacture, social science as inseparable from social revolution, Fourier's morality of Composite passions, and, if you are right, Marx's morality of deeds.

Author. Before we finish I should like to emphasize once more the way in which the aim of achieving self-consciousness appears to dominate the Marxist philosophy. The philosophers of the Enlightenment had attacked *traditional* ways of living as fit only for children who unquestioningly accept their parents' guidance. Hegel's Absolute was full self-consciousness where nothing was vague, where, as he put it, there was no "immediacy." Feuerbach transformed this speculative view into the psychological one that a heightened knowledge of ourselves would dispel religious illusions. Marx thought that Hegel's "self-consciousness" and Feuerbach's "self-disillusionment" were too theoretical and abstract, and therefore sought to make them practical and concrete in terms of the self-conscious revolutionary deed that will hasten society's passage to communism. Or let us look at the sequence of ideas in relation to freedom. Philosophers of the Enlightenment had said that men would be free when, abandoning traditions that they were not responsible for, they themselves chose the rules they would live by, but they assumed that all men would choose the same *fundamental* rules though within these they would pursue different policies. Marx thought that as long as there was private property, as long as individuals entered into a social order that had developed unplanned from the clash of individual policies, individuals were not free because their society was not under their control. Liberals attacked tradition in order that individuals might choose their own ends, but they believed in an economic harmony that was as uncontrived as tradition—the *individual* was to be self-conscious, but the social harmony was maintained by a *hidden* hand. For the Marxists no hands were to be hidden, no faces were to be masked, no mysteries to be unrevealed. As Marx put it in *Capital,* the relations between man and man and man and nature were to be "perfectly intel-

ligible and reasonable," and society was to be "under their conscious
and purposive control."

Reader. You said that the philosophers of the Enlightenment assumed
that if people consciously and rationally chose their principles of
conduct they would all choose the same fundamental ones. I take
it that you mean that they still assumed the existence of a natural
moral law revealed by candid and intelligent reflection.

Author. Or if not natural law, then rules for the attainment of happiness
that were equally though differently authoritative.

Reader. The liberal view was, then, that people should be free to make
"experiments in living" within these fundamental rules. But this is
bound to lead to a lot of variety and to set people at odds with one
another. Marxists, it seems to me, want to calm the liberal turbu-
lence, but I'm not at all clear what sort of calm it is that they look
forward to.

Author. I have not been able to find much about the "purposive control" and "perfectly intelligible and reasonable" relationships that
I just mentioned. The liberal idea was that each individual should
have "purposive control," while the whole, in the main, was left to
adjust itself. But the Marxist wants there to be "purposive control"
of the whole society, and thinks that once economic exploitation—
which so far as we are concerned means privately owned industry—
is abolished, this will be compatible with individual freedom from
coercive control. If a conscious plan is to be pursued by the whole
society and no one is to oppose it, there must be unanimity of aim
among the members of the society. Either there is a *natural* unanimity of aim which was only kept from expressing itself earlier by
private industry, or else an *artificial* unanimity of aim will be somehow secured during the interim period of proletarian dictatorship.
Lenin's reference to habit, which I called attention to on page 232,
suggests the latter, and seems therefore to adumbrate the restora-
tion of a traditional form of society, for habitual behavior, though it
may result from past choices, is not itself chosen or self-conscious.

Reader. I think you are exaggerating, for surely individuals can acquire
habits in a society that is not predominantly traditional. Lenin was
not talking about traditions at all, he was talking about habits.

Author. I believe I have a point here, although I may have exaggerated it. If Lenin means that self-seeking or recalcitrant individuals are to be forced into conformity during the period of proletarian dictatorship when there is still a coercive state, then in the subsequent social order where there is no state there must be non-coercive means of securing universal co-operation. What could these be? I don't suppose that Lenin thought that nonconformity would be *bred* out of men. If he had thought that the social order would have become so attractive that everyone would immediately see that to co-operate in it was the rational thing to do, then he need not have talked of habit since it would have become unnecessary even though it in fact arose. Surely he must have meant that new generations would be inducted into a non-coercive social order which they would not dream of questioning, and this, I suggest, is a traditional order. We should not be surprised at this. Saint-Simon, with his "New Christianity," and Comte, with his "Religion of Humanity," had looked forward to a future in which the volatile liberal anarchy was replaced by something more akin to the Catholic society that had preceded it. Marx despised the Saint-Simonians and positivists for engaging in ritual performances when they might have been destroying capitalism, but I think he shared with them the ideal of a smoothly running, organized society.

Reader. Your reference to Saint-Simon and Comte reminds me that Marxism has sometimes been called a secular religion. Do you think there is any advantage in talking about it in such terms?

Author. I don't think that much is to be gained by it. There is some similarity between the Communist Party and the Roman Catholic Church in the way in which authority is organized, since both are continuously existing societies which accept the decisions of a supreme body on matters of doctrine and policy. But after all, Protestant churches are quite differently constituted and are none the less religious. If we take "religion" in the sense in which it involves belief in a supernatural world and a *mysterium tremendum,* Marxism, with its stress on material nature and its opposition to mysteries, is profoundly anti-religious. Indeed, Marx's philosophy took its rise from Feuerbach's attempt to dissolve religion by exposing its psychological basis. In this connection I should like to call your attention to an *ad hominem* criticism that can be brought against Marx and Marxism. Marx agreed with Feuerbach that belief in God and Heaven divided the believer's mind and prevented him from dealing adequately with the realities of this world here below. But, we may ask, does not the constant striving for a vaguely conceived communist society of the future divert the Communist's energies from the realities of the world here *now*? There are more ways than one in which the shadow can be sought instead of the substance.

Reader. I rather think that some Marxists, if ever they read this book, will say that your analysis of Marxism leaves out the dialectical features of it altogether.

Author. It is easy to make that sort of accusation because the term "dialectical," on Marxist lips and pens, is not only very vague, but also a term of esteem.

Reader. Still, I don't think you should run away from the charge by suggesting that "undialectical" is just a term of abuse.

Author. I tried to explain in Part One, Chapter II, that when Marxists talk about the dialectics of nature they conceive of the physical world as in constant change, of the coming of emergent qualities, and of contradictions in the nature of things. When they talk about dialectics in social affairs they think of social oppositions, of revolutionary "leaps," of progress through destruction—of *mors immortalis,* immortal death, as Marx put it. In spite of all these doctrines, Marxists, in my opinion, have argued undialectically in one important sense of the word. A dialectical change, it will be remembered, is one in which the process is not by repetition, not "in a circle," as Stalin put it, but "onward and upward," "from the lower to the higher." Stalin was obviously trying to contrast something he believed was genuine progress with repetition and re-arrangement of what already is, and I think he was right. But progress of this sort cannot be predicted except in a most general and uninformative way. No doubt it is a submerged awareness of this that makes Marxists so emphatic in their refusal to predict the details of communist society. Yet the assertion that social science is prediction and control is an essential feature of Marxism. (The attempt to do without prediction led to syndicalism.) Progress can be reported but not predicted.

Reader. This is an unexpected reversal of roles. Are there any other aspects of Marxism that are open to this strange accusation?

Author. Another sense of "dialectical" is that in which it is opposed to the "metaphysical" procedure of considering things in isolation from one another instead of in their real and intimate connections. Now it seems to me that the basis-superstructure distinction suffers from this very defect, for all that Marxists say about the superstructure influencing the basis. The Marxist error is to regard as parts what are really aspects. There is no behavior that is just political behavior, no behavior that is just economic behavior, and so on. The political man, the economic man, the poet, indeed, and the priest, are abstractions, not interacting forces.

Reader. The objection might be made that you misrepresented the case when at the beginning of our discussion you said that Marxists inconsistently combine a belief in the adequacy of scientific method with Hegelianism. For, it might be said, Marxists hold that science is itself dialectical so that there is not the opposition that you have claimed.

Author. When Marxists say that science is dialectical they are using Hegelian terminology but are not thinking Hegelian thoughts. When they are not meditating on nodal lines, they are asserting that no scientific theory should be regarded as beyond criticism, that the various sciences should not be isolated from one another, and that laws of change should be sought for as well as laws of equilibrium. These are things that non-Marxists say in other words.

Reader. Marxists often speak approvingly of the dialectical method in politics. Lenin, I believe, is praised as a leading practitioner of it.

Author. When the word is used in such contexts it connotes approval of the ability to deal effectively with the singularities of events. The dialectical political strategist never allows his ultimate principles of action to divert his eyes from concrete details or to prevent him from adapting himself rapidly to changes in the situation. There is no philosophical profundity here, but rather a peculiar, though not altogether unsuitable, choice of a word. The dialectical statesman also knows how to deal with *unexpected* changes in the situation—though their unexpectedness must be due to his lack of social science. It is curious that these political uses of the term "dialectical" are not unlike the eulogistic use of the word "empirical" now common in this country, the use, namely, in which the adaptable, flexible approach to political events is contrasted with the rationalistic, rigid approach.

Reader. Before we part I should like to ask whether you could sum up your criticisms of Marxism in a phrase or two.

Author. Let me be briefer still and say that Marxism is a philosophical farrago.

Reading List

The following has no claim to be a bibliography, but is an annotated list of books and articles that I have found of particular value for the understanding of the philosophy of Marxism.

Adams, H. P., *Karl Marx in His Earlier Writings* (London, 1940).
　Contains summaries of all the early writings (including the Doctoral Dissertation) and is therefore particularly useful for those who do not read German.
Barth, Hans, *Wahrheit und Ideologie* (Zurich, 1945).
　This learned and skillfully constructed book deals especially with the origins of the idea of an "ideology," and stresses the importance of this notion in Marx's thought. It is a notable contribution to the history of ideas.
Berlin, Isaiah, *Karl Marx* (London, 2nd edition, 1948).
　Especially chapters 3, 4, and 6 for a clear and perceptive introductory treatment.
Bober, M. M., *Karl Marx's Interpretation of History* (2nd edition, revised, Cambridge, Harvard University Press, 1950).
　It is essential to read the greatly revised second edition, which is a masterly exposition and criticism of Marxism by an economist. The most detailed and important criticism of the Materialist Conception of History that I know of.
Bochenski, I. M., *Der Sowjetrussische Dialektische Materialismus (Diamat)* (Berne, 1950, 2nd revised edition, 1956).
　A short and clear exposition of current philosophical views in the Soviet Union, with a useful bibliography of about five hundred items.
Hook, Sidney, *From Hegel to Marx*. Studies in the Intellectual Development of Karl Marx (London, 1936).
　Contains expositions of the views of those who chiefly influenced Marx's early thought (Hegel, Feuerbach, Stirner, etc.). There is an Appendix with translations of important philosophical passages from Marx's early writings.
Hyppolite, Jean, "La Structure du 'Capital' et de quelques

présuppositions philosophiques dans l'oeuvre de Marx." *Bulletin de la Société Française de Philosophie,* 42e année, No. 6, Oct.–Dec. 1948 (Paris).

The leading French Hegelian scholar uses his knowledge of Hegel to illuminate Marx's thought. This valuable article is discussed by Aron, Bréhier, Madame Prenant, Rubel, and others. It is reprinted, without the discussion, in Hyppolite's *Etudes sur Marx et Hegel,* pp. 142–68.

Popitz, Heinrich, *Der Entfremdete Mensch: Zeitkritik und Geschichts-philosophie des jungen Marx* (Basel, 1953).

A detailed exposition of Marx's earliest writings showing their connections with the philosophy of Hegel.

Popper, Karl, *The Open Society and Its Enemies.* Vol. 2, *The High Tide of Prophecy: Hegel and Marx* (London, 1945).

This book is too well known to need comment from me, except to say that the detailed discussion of Marx's social theories contained in it relates especially to methodological matters that I have not myself dealt with. The criticism is all the more telling by virtue of the sympathy shown toward some of Marx's aspirations.

Rotenstreich, Nathan, *Marx' Thesen über Feuerbach.* Archiv für Rechts- und Sozialphilosophie, XXXIX/3 and XXXIX/4 (Berne, 1951).

A commentary on the much-quoted "theses" in which the preeminence of "practice" in the Marxist outlook is demonstrated.

Rubel, Maximilien, *Pages choisies pour une éthique socialiste.* Textes réunis, traduits, et annotés, précédés d'une introduction à l'éthique Marxienne (Paris, 1948).

The form taken by this anthology makes it an important contribution to the interpretation of Marx. See the same author's *Karl Marx: Essai de biographie intellectuelle* (Paris, 1957).

Venable, Vernon, *Human Nature, The Marxian View* (London, 1946).

A painstaking analysis and rather uncritical defense of the social theory of Marx and Engels.

Wetter, Gustav A., S.J., *Der Dialektische Materialismus: Seine Geschichte und sein System in der Sowjetunion* (Freiburg, 1952). Translated into English from the 4th revised German edition by Peter Heath with the title *Dialectical Materialism* (London, 1958).

A comprehensive (647 pp.) account of philosophy in the Soviet Union, containing detailed summaries and criticisms of leading books and articles published there. Indispensable for the student of Marxist-Leninist philosophy. There is a bibliography of 266 items, most of them in Russian or by Russians. The same author has a work in Italian, *Il materialismo dialettico sovietico* (Giulio Einaudi Editore, 1948), in which more space is given to "the classics" such as Lenin.

Index

The typeface used for this book is ITC New Baskerville, which was created for the International Typeface Corporation and is based on the types of the English type founder and printer John Baskerville (1706–75). Baskerville is the quintessential transitional face: it retains the bracketed and oblique serifs of old-style faces such as Caslon and Garamond, but in its increased lowercase height, lighter color, and enhanced contrast between thick and thin strokes, it presages modern faces.

The display type is set in Didot.

This book is printed on paper that is acid-free and meets the requirements of the American National Standard for Permanence of Paper for Printed Library Materials, z39.48-1992. ♾

Book design by Rich Hendel, Chapel Hill, North Carolina
Typography by Tseng Information Systems, Durham, North Carolina
Printed by Edwards Brothers, Inc., Ann Arbor, Michigan, and bound by Dekker Bookbinding, Grand Rapids, Michigan